The Ottoman Balkans, 1750–1830

The Ottoman Balkans, 1750–1830

Edited by

Frederick F. Anscombe

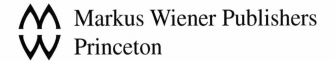 Markus Wiener Publishers
Princeton

Reprinted from *Princeton Papers: Interdisciplinary Journal of Middle Eastern Studies*, volume XIII.

For information write to: Markus Wiener Publishers
231 Nassau Street, Princeton, NJ 08542
www.markuswiener.com

Cover illustration: "Halt of Caravaniers at a Serai, Bulgaria." From Thomas Allom (1804–1872), *Constantinople and the scenery of the seven churches of Asia Minor, illustrated* (London, Paris, Fisher, son, & co. [1838]), vol. 2.

Book design by Dhiraj Aggarwal, e-BookServices.com

Library of Congress Cataloging-in-Publication Data

The Ottoman Balkans, 1750-1830 / edited by Frederick F. Anscombe.
 p. cm.
 Includes bibliographical references.
 ISBN 1-55876-382-1 (hardcover : alk. paper) -- ISBN 1-55876-383-X (pbk. : alk. paper)
 1. Balkan Peninsula--History. 2. Balkan Peninsula--History--19th century. 3. Turkey--History. 4. Turkey--History--19th century. I. Anscombe, Frederick F.
DR36.O88 2005
949.6--dc22

                                                          2005026945

Contents

Introduction

FREDERICK F. ANSCOMBE

The papers presented in this volume operate in the widening gap between the recent trajectory of Ottoman studies and a continuing path of Balkan historical studies. Over the past two decades a number of Ottomanists have published studies which challenge, with varying degrees of success, the assumptions and conclusions crafted by previous generations of noted scholars. One of the shibboleths to come under concerted attack is the old notion of a long Ottoman "decline" beginning in 1566, the year of Süleyman the Magnificent's death.[1] While some Ottomanists continue to debate a more appropriate date to mark the onset of "decline," it now seems acceptable among others to question the very notion of decline at any point in the empire's history. Such developments in the field of Ottoman history seem to have had less impact upon Balkan studies than might be expected, however. Although there are now very promising junior scholars in several countries of southeastern Europe who approach the Ottoman period with open minds, and some admirable work of high quality and nuance has been published since the end of the Cold War,[2] much of what has been produced concerning the Ottoman period still seems restricted by the conventions of "national" history and too often ignores Ottoman sources, let alone recent work in the wider field of Ottoman studies. It is significant that perhaps the most noted work of Ottoman Balkan history to appear in recent years was a reissue of L. S. Stavrianos's monumental *The Balkans Since 1453*, originally published in 1958, a book meticulous in tracing national histories of certain (generally Christian) groups but less so with Muslims, particularly any who could fall into the broad category of "Turks."[3] They are the eternal interlopers, regardless of how many generations of them were born, lived, and died in southeastern Europe, the dead wood obscuring the view of the (national) forest.

The tenacity of the "Ottoman period as *x* centuries of darkness for nation *y*" paradigm is reflected also in recent works which have attempted to explain southeastern Europe to a wide audience, drawn to the region by the recent wars of Yugoslavia's disintegration. Robert Kaplan's *Balkan Ghosts* is the best-known of these. In a sense, the history recounted in *Balkan Ghosts* is rubbish (dangerously so, since the author writes compellingly—suspicion remains strong that President Bill Clinton long delayed American intervention in the Yugoslav wars because Kaplan's book taught him that oppression, murder, rape, and pillage were just Balkan traditions from time immemorial). Yet, in another sense, *Balkan Ghosts* is quite illuminating, because Kaplan talked to people in the region and simply parrots the popular beliefs drummed into them from an early age by aggressively nation-building school curricula, literature, and folklore.[4] Misha Glenny, another journalist, performs a similar service in his book *The Balkans, 1804–1999* by retelling the grisly tales drawn from published works on the history of southeastern Europe.[5] Works by academics are not necessarily any more rigorous in their search for evidence and interpretation. Andre Gerolymatos recently published a study of the roots of that supposedly endemic Balkan tendency to war in which he proved himself just as ready to revel in bloodthirsty (but often apocryphal) stories of the Turkish yoke as did Kaplan and Glenny. While Gerolymatos does occasionally acknowledge the existence of recent scholarship challenging the old Balkan paradigm of the Ottomans, he does not use any of it to challenge the myths he prefers. "[Nationalist] folklore so often distorts the historical reality. But that doesn't mean that myths and legends offer no insights into the past."[6] Yet unsubtle folklore more clearly offers insights into present beliefs rather than past "reality," and Gerolymatos's implication that the Yugoslav wars of disintegration can be blamed upon the Ottoman yoke seems, itself, both simplistic and ahistorical.

Those readers afraid of drowning in my personal pool of pessimism will no doubt welcome a lifeline. As stated before, there are scholars in southeastern Europe who, having been freed of the old Marxist straitjacket, are now more than ready to test assumptions of this remaining pillar of history under the old regimes, nationalism. They face daunting challenges, including the financial and other problems besetting the educational systems in most of these countries. Even in North America, where a dissertation on the Ottoman Balkans all too often serves as a one-way ticket out of academia,[7] at least a few researchers have been open to new ideas about the Ottoman period. At the same time as the Gerolymatos book appeared, Dennis Hupchick published a survey of Balkan history. It included the following assessment of "decline."

> Historians traditionally characterize the period beginning with the death of Suleyman I in 1566 and extending through the eighteenth century as one of Ottoman decline. The word "decline" implies that factors inherent to the Ottomans' society led to its gradual deterioration, with deleterious effects on the empire's internal administration, its international position, and the condition of its assorted subjects. Ottoman society's institutions, [which functioned so well for 250 years] . . . did slowly begin to unravel following the mid-sixteenth century. Little evidence exists, however, to suggest that they did so on their own account and of their own accord. Compounding forces exerted by the Ottomans' Western European antagonists primarily were responsible for that development. Rather than "decline", it is more accurate to speak of Ottoman internal "destabilization", a result of consistent external, Western European economic and military-technological pressures. Either way, the period left a lasting negative legacy on the empire's Balkan subjects.[8]

Just as Hupchick has considered recent additions to Ottoman historiography, it behooves Ottomanists to think carefully about the quotation above. While the old long-decline paradigm needed revision, it would be just as misguided to overlook the fact that many parts of the empire endured extended periods of turmoil in the second half of the eighteenth and the first decades of the nineteenth centuries. This era saw large-scale Christian uprisings (the first not prompted by the approach of foreign armies since the fifteenth century), of Serbs in 1804 and of Greeks in 1821. It also witnessed the violent overthrow and deaths of two sultans, Selim III and Mustafa IV in 1807–8. This extended turmoil ushered in and legitimated the age of rapid, far-reaching reforms, begun symbolically by the destruction of the Janissary corps in 1826. Difficult times afflicted many Ottoman provinces, and several excellent studies of conditions in Arab lands in the eighteenth century have appeared over the past fifteen years.[9] Much less has been published about southeastern Europe, in spite of the importance of the Balkan provinces as the leading area of enduring concern for the sultan's government and as the staging ground for the most unsettling developments of the period.

The studies collected in this volume are intended to improve Ottomanists' knowledge of conditions in a crucial part of the empire in crisis, and to add detailed pictures to the often sketchy information available to Balkanists interested in pre-nation-state history. The authors have picked issues which arose in different areas of the Balkans during this period, analyzed the roots of the problems and, where possible, assessed Ottoman authorities' attempts to resolve them. Several articles presuppose some background knowledge on the part of the reader, but others should be readily comprehensible to undergraduate students and educated general readers. For all, it is hoped that these studies will lead to a greater appreciation of the complexities of the Ottoman empire in the eighteenth century, of "decline," and of the exhaustive reform efforts of the nineteenth century.

Several common points of interest arise in the papers, suggesting the types of issues that should have concerned the Ottoman authorities the most. As in most pre-modern states, the Ottoman government of the eighteenth century had only a few basic purposes, beyond boosting the status and wealth of its principle figures: to deliver justice and peace within the realm, to wage war against foreign enemies (by this period more often wars of defense, fought on Ottoman territory, rather than wars of offense), and to raise the revenue necessary to carry out these tasks effectively. It is thus no surprise to see that the issues of concern generally fall into these categories. Not a surprise, perhaps, but distinctly alarming, since problems in these areas would affect major pillars of Ottoman legitimacy.

Two papers concern principally questions of justice and the application of law. Michael Hickok's exploration of issues involved in the investigation of murders in Bosnia makes clear that Ottoman central and provincial authorities had multiple avenues by which they could approach the crime of murder, following sharia, *kanun*, and customary law. Judge and governor could choose the approach which best met the state's interest in each case. In his analysis of several incidents of murder in Karaferye (Greece), Antonis Anastasopoulos echoes Hickok on this point and stresses that the state did retain its longstanding interest in seeing justice done, even in the chaotic years of this period, and that the subjects of the sultan had enough faith in this state interest to continue to apply to Istanbul for justice. The old system still functioned.

Yet in all of the papers of this volume there are at least hints of problems in the legal system. Hickok, Virginia Aksan, and Rossitsa Gradeva all refer to the intrusion of foreign policy into the arena of administration of justice, adding to the avenues of legal approach identified by Hickok. A lengthening menu of such approaches offered flexibility to Ottoman authorities, but it also offered opportunities to clever transgressors, of whom killers seeking to avoid blood retribution (expected under customary law) by moving to areas more clearly ruled by sharia in Bosnia offer but one example. The rise of foreign influence and international legal principles could well complicate further legal questions in the empire, as it was to do in extreme form in the nineteenth century, when many non-Muslim Ottoman subjects came to enjoy legal immunities under the capitulations regime.[10] The use of differing legal principles even in this earlier period increased the likelihood of conflict between officers of the government, who could well disagree over the choice of legal approach. Since *kadı*s had only limited resources at their disposal to impose justice, such conflict and division could be very damaging. Indeed, Hickok notes that orders from Istanbul seemed to mandate much less active cooperation between *kadı* and *vali* by the end of the eighteenth century, in comparison to the 1750s.

When local and central authorities proved unable to craft a strong, unified response to legal challenges, the administration of justice could crumble quickly. Gradeva's and my papers focus upon well-armed groups of varying sizes that were able to defy divided local authorities. Distracted by external threats and weakened by losses in the wars of the late eighteenth and early nineteenth centuries, Istanbul could muster neither the will nor the material means necessary to ensure the maintenance of justice and the application of law in the provinces. At best, the government could only hope to restrict "banditry" to its most hospitable bases, the frontier areas of the Danube and rough terrain such as Albania. While the justice system still offered hope to individuals in relatively well controlled areas such as Karaferye and central Bosnia, truly ambitious criminals could thrive in the mountains and in the borderlands.

Questions of taxation and the related issue of land tenure complicated Ottoman efforts to reimpose peace and justice in the Balkans. Ottoman records contain many complaints about excessive taxation, but in a sense such grievances were normal and could be managed. The avaricious tax collector is a well-known figure worldwide. Where the justice system continued to function, such wrongs could be redressed (as in the case of Ali Rüşdi Efendi cited by Anastasopoulos). A more serious problem emerges in this period, however, because more taxes were deemed illegal *per se*. In the case of Osman Pazvantoğlu, whose virtually impregnable position in Vidin is analyzed at length by Gradeva, it is clear that this rebellious officer of the sultan attracted widespread support from both Muslims and Christians due to his attitude toward new taxes, introduced by Sultan Selim III to pay for military reforms. The introduction of an array of taxes and other innovations unsanctioned by religious law undercut the moral authority of the sultan among Muslims, further weakening his loyal representatives' ability to promote justice among an unsettled population.

That much of the population lived in uncertain circumstances is reflected in the high incidence of land disputes. In some areas peasants fled or were pushed off the land *en masse*, as armies and brigand gangs criss-crossed the Balkans. Few parts of the peninsula escaped these phenomena, although some areas recovered from the disruptions relatively quickly.[11] Other territories, especially border regions such as Vidin, Little Wallachia, and Serbia, were lastingly affected, as Aksan and Gradeva show. The majority of peasants involved there were Christians, and those who most often took advantage of the chaos to seize lands were Muslim military men. In these areas the Janissaries themselves were often recent migrants, driven out of lost border fortresses, very badly paid, and in all likelihood inclined to a feeling of entitlement *vis-à-vis* the distrusted Orthodox peasantry. They perhaps foreshadow the later refugees from Black Sea territories conquered by Russia, who are generally blamed for the excessive ferocity with which the relatively minor Bulgarian uprising of 1876 was crushed. As in issues of taxation, during times of peace the central and provincial authorities were able to keep extralegal land seizures by Janissaries and *ayan* under some degree of control, as Aksan and I show, but the pressures of war and its aftermath loosened that restraint. In these periods relations between Muslims and *zimmi*s, which never really recovered from the shocks of the long war of 1683–99, were probably at their tensest. Christians dreaded lawlessness and scapegoating, while Muslims feared the appearance of Christian *haydud* bands in their midst, even though they rarely posed a serious threat to state or regional, rather than local, stability. It is instructive to consider the actions of both Christians and Muslims in the Serbian "rebellion" of 1804: it started out as a campaign to assist in the reimposition of the sultan's justice and law over the local Janissary bands and became an open revolt only when Istanbul's troops turned on their erstwhile Christian allies following the defeat of the Janissaries. Christian military bands stirred deep unease.

In all of the issues mentioned so far, it is clear that war added enormously to the strains upon the Ottoman system in the Balkans. This was always the case, but in this period the frequency and duration of conflict (1768–74, 1787–92, 1799–1802, 1804–12, 1821–30) was exceptional, with the stresses compounded by Ottoman defeat in all of these wars. The reasons for that string of defeats—military "decline," or something more complex?—is worthy of a volume of papers in its own right, but the bad effect of those losses on Ottoman provincial life is undeniable. Is Hupchick thus right to attribute Ottoman "destabilization" to "consistent external, Western European economic and military-technological pressures?" It is certainly a defensible assertion. As it had in previous centuries, the empire held doggedly to a handful of cardinal principles, as in the field of law and justice, but showed flexibility in the means used to achieve desired results. To speak of "decline" in a system which was never truly static or "mature" is indeed misleading. Given time, the empire presumably still could have repaired weaknesses which grew apparent in key areas such as the military and taxation. Yet time was a luxury of bygone years. The formerly leisurely adoption and adaptation of methods practiced by earlier regimes had to give way to a regimented quick-march—in short, to "reform" as finally introduced by Sultan Mahmud II and carried on through the rest of the existence of the empire. It needs to be borne in mind, however, that every regime in Europe was facing similar pressures to improve its military and boost the strength of the state. In this period practically every part of mainland Europe, from the Iberian peninsula to France to Italy to Russia, faced the threat or reality of revolts and revolutions, and many thought the Habsburg empire just as destined for demise as the Ottoman. Hupchick traces the period of crisis in the Ottoman Balkans to pressure from western Europe, but it is also reasonable to say that the Ottoman position on the periphery of the continent delayed by several decades each step of its inevitable confrontation with the European revolution in state and military power.[12]

Comparison with developments elsewhere in Europe is but one area in which there remains much scope for research.[13] None of the contributors to this volume chose to study a topic drawn from the period between the fall of Selim III and the formal recognition of an independent Greece. The background and course of the Serbian and Greek revolts, for example, would be well worth researching in Ottoman records but generally have been left oddly untouched. It is hoped that the studies presented here will not only help to bridge the gap between Ottomanist/Middle Eastern and Balkanist historiographies but also encourage more historians from both traditions to fill in these and the many other remaining lacunae.

Notes

1. To cite but a few of the more notable examples: Cornell Fleischer, *Bureaucrat and Intellectual in the Ottoman Empire: The Historian Mustafa Ali (1541– 1600)* (Princeton: Princeton University Press, 1986); Rifaat Ali Abou-el-Haj, *Formation of the Modern State: The Ottoman Empire Sixteenth to Eighteenth Centuries* (Binghamton: SUNY Press, 1992); Jane Hathaway, *Politics of Households in Ottoman Egypt: The Rise of the Qazdağlıs* (New York: Cambridge University Press, 1997); Rhoads Murphey, *Ottoman Warfare, 1500–1700* (New Brunswick: Rutgers University Press, 1999); Ariel Salzmann, "The Ancien Régime Revisited: 'Privatization' and Political Economy in the Eighteenth-Century Ottoman Empire," *Politics and Society* 21 (1993): 393–423.
2. Catherine W. Bracewell, *The Uskoks of Senj: Piracy, Banditry, and Holy War in the Sixteenth-Century Adriatic* (Ithaca, N.Y.: Cornell University Press, 1992) is an outstanding example.
3. Leften S. Stavrianos, *The Balkans Since 1453* (New York: New York University Press, 2000). Maria Todorova, *Imagining the Balkans* (New York: Oxford University Press, 1997) is more noted (and noteworthy) but is a work more directly concerned with the intellectual history of western Europe over the past two centuries than with the Ottoman Balkans *per se*.
4. Those interested in the underappreciated role of literature in nation-building should read Andrew Wachtel, *Making a Nation, Breaking a Nation* (Stanford: Stanford University Press, 2000).
5. Misha Glenny, *The Balkans, 1804–1999: Nationalism, War and the Great Powers* (London: Granta Books, 1999).
6. Andre Gerolymatos, *The Balkan Wars: Conquest, Revolution, and Retribution from the Ottoman Era to the Twentieth Century and Beyond* (New York: Basic Books, 2002), 79. Gerolymatos lists even fewer works by Ottomanists in his bibliography than does Glenny, all at least thirty years old.
7. It may well be coincidence that none of this volume's contributors works at a university in the U.S. Leaving aside those native to the region, however, most historians who have made significant contributions to the study of the Ottoman Balkans work in western Europe.

8. Dennis Hupchick, *The Balkans: From Constantinople to Communism* (New York: Palgrave, 2002), 164. Mark Mazower also shows a mind very open to reconsideration of the Ottoman period in the Balkans. See his *The Balkans* (London: Weidenfeld and Nicolson, 2000).

9. Abraham Marcus, *The Middle East on the Eve of Modernity* (New York: Columbia University Press, 1989) for Aleppo, and Hathaway, *Politics*, for Egypt.

10. The capitulations, which governed the status of Europeans in Ottoman lands, originally granted limited legal privileges and protections to visiting Christians, who otherwise would have been practically defenseless unless they paid the *cizye* head tax. By the era of reform of the nineteenth century, the capitulations had expanded to confer an extensive degree of legal immunity through extraterritoriality. The damage arose from the extension of those extraterritorial immunities to many (overwhelmingly Christian) Ottoman subjects through the granting of a form of "honorary citizenship"—the *"beratlı/barataire"* mentioned in Gradeva's paper.

11. Archeological evidence can belie national traditions of desertion of the land to escape "Turkish oppression." See, for example, John Bennet, Jack Davis, and Fariba Zarinebaf-Shahr, "Sir William Gell's Itinerary in the Pylia and Regional Landscapes in the Morea in the Second Ottoman Period," *Hesperia* 69 (July–September 2000). Archeology is perhaps the richest barely-tapped resource for Ottoman history.

12. For the international history of Europe in this era, see Paul Schroeder, *The Transformation of European Politics, 1763–1848* (New York: Oxford University Press, 1996). For analysis of the economic challenges facing the states of Europe in their efforts to modernize, see Paul Kennedy, *The Rise and Fall of the Great Powers: Economic Change and Military Conflict from 1500 to 2000* (New York: Random House, 1988).

13. Such comparison has been done most forcefully by Salzmann in "Ancien Régime." In this volume Hickok has drawn explicit comparisons, while several other contributors have done so more fleetingly or implicitly.

Crisis and State Intervention in Late Eighteenth-century Karaferye (mod. Veroia)[1]

ANTONIS ANASTASOPOULOS

Modern historiography has invariably considered the eighteenth century a period of reduced central control over the Ottoman provinces. The state was giving ground, while the provincial elites (*ayans*) were expanding their power, since their cooperation and good will had become essential for administering smoothly the affairs of the realm. This phenomenon has traditionally been viewed as an aspect of and a factor that accelerated the general "decline" of the Ottoman Empire.[2] In more recent years, it has been singled out as the trademark of a whole era: the period of "decentralization"[3] or "the age of the *ayans*."[4] The wars against Russia in the second half of the eighteenth century enhanced the self-confidence of the *ayans*, because the state depended extensively on their services for the recruitment of troops as well as for the collection and dispatch of provisions; besides, governors who were ordered to participate in campaigns often entrusted the administration and security of their districts to *ayans* for the duration of their absence.[5] As a result, central authorities were faced with serious challenges from their provinces in the closing decades of the century.[6]

A study of state involvement in instances of local crisis in the provinces can contribute some evidence as to whether the central authorities maintained overall control of the empire or had been reduced to overlords with only nominal authority.[7] When faced with a serious problem, the inhabitants of a region presumably turned to that person or authority that was thought to be best equipped for coping with it successfully.[8] In fact, reports about local crises kept reaching the central authorities quite often even in the last decades of the eighteenth century, that is, when their control over the provinces is considered to have been at a low. The persistence of that practice over the centuries is connected with the role of the Porte as redresser of wrongs and guarantor of the welfare of its subjects.

Public order was indispensable for the proper functioning of the Ottoman system of administration, and its preservation was projected as one of the basic duties of the state and its officials. According to the Islamic tradition of government that the Ottomans had adopted, the subjects of the state were entitled to conditions of order and justice, so as to be able to produce wealth, part of which the state would then collect in the form of taxation for the needs of the army, the administration, and the palace. Consequently, official Ottoman ideology put particular emphasis on justice and the protection of the subjects from oppression and the excesses of corrupt officials and roaming outlaws.[9] It is obvious that such a policy in the long run promoted the state's own interests, as it secured the loyalty of its subjects and guaranteed its continuing existence. Regardless, however, of whether the state's concern for its subjects was indeed genuine or not, the population of the empire benefited from this ideological stance, since it entailed Istanbul's obligation to intervene in the provinces and restore order whenever it received a petition that reported a breach of law.[10]

In the light of late-eighteenth-century developments, though, it is an issue whether people of that time were petitioning the Porte because its intervention was known to be effective or just because it was a natural last step to take when everything else had failed. There were also occasions when the Porte intervened in the name of the people, but really following reports that it had received from its own provincial officials and not from members of the local society. A second issue is whether the government had developed consistent operable mechanisms of dealing with local crises that were challenging—in reality or theoretically/ideologically—the proper functioning of Ottoman institutions. That would include a mechanism of checking, either at the center or locally, the truth of claims submitted to it. In fact, it seems that the Porte took all claims to be true in principle and expected provincial authorities eventually to establish if they were justified or not.[11] It is, therefore, important to investigate carefully the role played in such cases by state officials, such as governors, deputy governors, and judges, because they represented the interests of the state but exercised their authority in the local setting. Such systematic investigation could lead to an attempt to determine whether there were one or several patterns of state intervention in crises in the provinces, as well as their evolution over time. Here we will focus on one particular case from Karaferye in the southern Balkans in 1782; we will also try to draw parallels with and point out differences from other occasions of state intervention in the region and elsewhere, so as to place that particular incident in a wider context.

In the second half of the eighteenth century, the town of Karaferye was the center of a *kaza*, which belonged to the *sancak* of Selânik (Salonica). The judge (*kadı*) of the Islamic court was the immediate representative of the Ottoman state in the region,[12] but the affairs of the *kaza* were also under the jurisdiction of the *sancak* authorities. Those were the pasha-governor (*mutasarrıf*) or his deputy (*mütesellim*), who was usually selected from among the local notables. Karaferye and a large section of the *kaza* were part of the imperial estates (*havass-i hümayun*), and their fiscal revenue was farmed out on life-term contracts (*ber vech-i malikâne*). The tax farmer then subleased the district's income to a third party who held the title of *voyvoda*; strictly speaking, the *voyvoda*'s authority was fiscal, as defined by his contract with the *malikâne* holder,[13] but he certainly played an important political role in the affairs of the *kaza*. Karaferye had a mixed population of Muslims and Christians (as well as some Jews).[14] The Muslim and Christian community leaders, usually described as *ayan*s and *kocabaşı*s respectively, were another significant factor in local politics. Military authority was entrusted basically to the commander (*serdar*) of the janissaries,[15] but also to the mercenary troops (*sekban*s) charged with fighting brigandage and securing the passages of the region.

The single most important source about Ottoman Karaferye is the registers of the town's Islamic court of law (*kadı sicilleri*). The surviving registers of the latter half of the eighteenth century mostly contain incoming orders either from Istanbul or Salonica, a fair proportion of which were issued in response to petitions of individuals or groups of people or to reports by local officials. Overall, the court registers demonstrate both that the sultan's subjects made quite extensive use of their right to appeal to him, and that correspondence among various authorities—including Istanbul—was frequent.[16] As valuable a source as they are, Ottoman decrees and court registers were compiled for the needs of Ottoman administration and therefore usually do not supply detailed accounts of how cases developed from beginning to end.[17] Given that there are not any supplementary sources that could fill the narrative gaps of the court registers of Karaferye or counter the version of events found in them, the surviving material usually gives hints rather than definite answers to the questions and hypotheses of the modern historian.

Information about the 1782 incident comes from one decree (*buyruldu*) issued by the deputy governor of Salonica and two imperial decrees (*ferman*), which have been copied in the judicial registers of Karaferye. According to them, the *serdar* of Karaferye was murdered a few days after his appointment to the post. A group of more than twenty men stormed his residence and killed him with a bullet from a firearm, while also wounding one of his men in the course of the battle. The intruders had a casualty too, as they lost one of their men in the exchange of fire. The motive for the attack was not specified. At first, it was said that the murder was completely unjustified; later, it was stated that it was related to local antagonisms and grudges that the inhabitants of Karaferye held against one another. Such problems were not unusual in the town[18] and frequently were intrinsically linked to the wider struggle for local domination, which was in turn closely connected with financial interests and the control of the fiscal and military resources of the region.

Four inhabitants of Karaferye were identified as leaders of the group of men who carried out the attack. Those four were Elhacmehmedağazade Seyyid Osman Bey, Hafız Ali and Abdullah Agha, the sons of Mustafa Agha, and Osman Agha.[19] The dead intruder was said to be a man of Osman Bey. Initially, the incident was reported to the *mütesellim* of Salonica, but soon the Porte, too, was informed about it. The state appointed an agent of its own to the case and ordered the Islamic court of Karaferye to hold a public trial and determine the identity of the culprits of the attack; those found guilty should be imprisoned.[20] There was also a financial aspect in the case, but it was not explained very well in the documents. According to the imperial decrees, the court of law was expected to establish the debts of the accused, collect them and return them to their rightful owners (*zimmetlerinde sabit olan hukuk-i ibad şerᶜle tahsil ve istirdad; şerᶜan sabit olan hukuk-i ibad marifet-i şerᶜle tahsil ve ashabına istirdad*).[21] On the whole, the state put particular emphasis on the judicial resolution of the crisis. All parties involved were summoned to appear in court and present their arguments; the judge would then decide who was guilty of what and who was innocent. However, things did not develop as smoothly as planned, since the state agent, who had been appointed in order to assist the court of law, was accused of misconduct. The eventual outcome of the case is sadly not known, because no further entries about this incident can be found in the surviving registers of the Islamic court of Karaferye. We do not have any minutes of the investigation that was carried out or private correspondence or diaries of those involved in the affair either.

We can discuss the case in some detail, however, on the basis of the three decrees issued by the authorities of Salonica and Istanbul. The *buyruldu* was issued by Abdurrahman, the *mütesellim* of the *sancak* of Salonica, on 12 June 1782, and was addressed to the *kadı* of Karaferye as well as to the district's elite and petty functionaries (*ayan-i vilayet ve zabitan ve iş erleri*).[22] Abdurrahman did not state in his decree whether he had been informed about the incident through official channels or from a private petition, nor did he give any concrete instructions. The case had not yet been reported to Istanbul, since the *mütesellim* warned that if the culprits of the murder were not tracked down, arrested, and eliminated, news of the attack would reach the Porte and then more people would be implicated in and criticized for what had happened. The higher a case reached, the more burdensome and costly it became for the local population, since more officials were involved in restoring order and the people of the region in question were obliged to cover their expenses and fees as well as to cope with their illegal demands.

It has been argued that the eighteenth-century *kadı*'s power was severely compromised by the rise of the *ayans*,[23] but this and other cases suggest that, as far as official rhetoric was concerned, he was the undisputable heart of the Ottoman system of administration and also a vital link between the state and the locality in crisis management. In fact, the only Karaferye authority to which the *buyruldu* actually referred was the *kadı*,[24] even though the arrest of the culprits required by all means the use of force, and the *mütesellim* did not dispatch troops or even an agent to oversee the operation. He entrusted the local elements in Karaferye with the arrest but did not specify them, which is a sign either of indifference or of confidence in local institutions and notables, with the *kadı* occupying a special place among them. The *mütesellim* only asked to be notified of the progress of the investigation.

It seems as if he did not treat the particular incident as very serious, and he also apparently thought that it could be dealt with locally.

The formulation of the *mütesellim*'s decree offers itself to remarks on official ideology as expressed by a state official who probably was of local origin.[25] The *mütesellim* called the culprits of the attack *eşkiya* (outlaws, bandits) and classified the incident as *fitne* (sedition, disorder).[26] Both words form part of the standard terminology used by the state and its representatives when referring to the disruption of the daily routine of provincial life. To initiate action, the *mütesellim* pointed out that *fitne* was not to God's liking, but he also had recourse to a much more immediate threat, namely the possible intervention of the central authorities. Besides, he insisted on two motifs connected with the ideal of order. First, he indicated in the opening phrase of his decree that it was a holy duty of the elite and those in power to guarantee the welfare of the poor subjects of the sultan and to maintain order in the realm; actually, the *serdar* had been appointed so as to fulfill these duties for the benefit of the local populace. Second, he stressed the danger of disorder spreading to other regions if tolerated; such an eventuality was obviously an unwelcome menace to the stability of the Ottoman system.

Things did not turn out the way Abdurrahman had hoped that they would. On the contrary, the culprits of the attack were not arrested and the central authorities did get informed of and involved in the affair. The first *ferman* was issued one month after the *buyruldu*, in mid-July 1782.[27] It was addressed to Hasan, the new *mütesellim* of Salonica, and to the Islamic judge of Karaferye (called *naib*, i.e. deputy judge, this time), who remained the only local recipient of decrees about the incident. In the light of their ascendancy in the Balkans in the second half of the eighteenth century, it is important to note the absence of the *ayans* of Karaferye from among the addressees of this and most *fermans* of that period.[28] The Porte was informed about the incident from dispatches that the new *mütesellim* had sent to it. Hasan actually held the title of imperial head doorkeeper (*dergâh-i muallam kapıcıbaşılarından*), and did (or was forced by circumstances to do) what his predecessor had chosen not to, namely inform the government of what had happened in Karaferye. Probably the new *mütesellim* was an outsider, because it was noted in the *ferman* that the incident had taken place prior to his arrival in the region. If Abdurrahman was indeed a local *ayan*, one may assume that he was bound by a notion of local interest, which Hasan did not share; instead, his own loyalty was to the sultan—even though it is not known if his title still bore with it a special link to or a sense of duty toward the Palace in the closing decades of the eighteenth century—and the governor who had appointed him. However, Hasan was not the only informant of the central government. An *ilam* of the *naib* of Karaferye had also reached Istanbul in the meantime.[29] Thus, the local judge performed his role as channel of communication between the center and the periphery.

On the ideological level, the formulation of the decree of the central authorities strongly resembles that of the former *mütesellim*. The culprits of the attack were again branded *eşkiya*, only that this time it was specified that the group behind the four leading figures were brigands (*zümre-i eşkiyadan mâlumülesami şekavetkârları tahrik . . .*). The incident was not called *fitne*, but was given another usual characterization of situations that the state viewed as instances of disorder: *ihtilal-i belde* (disturbance of the public order of the town). Furthermore, the decree stated that it had been reported that following the incident, the poor subjects of the sultan (*fukara*) had been left feeling insecure, and that if the situation was not remedied, they would be increasingly oppressed and tormented by the day, while the region would experience chaotic conditions. That was sufficient cause for alarm and necessitated the state's intervention with a view to restoring order (*kaza-i mezkûr gereği gibi taht-i nizama* [sic] *ve rabıtaya idhal*). Thus, the incident was coated with an ideological garb, which presented it as something more dangerous than a mere criminal act, namely a threat to the stability of Ottoman society. Nevertheless, the state did not step in by virtue of its authority alone, but, as always, because it had been asked to issue a decree that would give a solution to the problem. In other words, the state invoked society and its torment as a means of legitimizing its intervention.

On this particular occasion, the state went one step further and clarified that it was the *valis'* and *mütesellims'* duty to restore order in their regions and to make sure that people prosper. Consequently, the *mütesellim* was charged with bringing to justice those accused of the attack and the murder of the *serdar*. However, he was not alone in the case any more, as the state appointed its own agent. His appointment was a sign par excellence of the state's immediate concern for the case, as he was expected to play a central part in the resolution of the crisis.[30] İsmail, the agent, was an imperial head doorkeeper, like Hasan. Apart from the title, the two men also largely shared jurisdictional area, since İsmail was *mubayaacı* (supervisor of the compulsory sale of grain to the state) of Salonica. It is not known if he was a local figure or not, nor on what grounds he was selected as the state's agent. Due to lack of evidence, one can only speculate that somehow he may have been thought of as a specialist in handling the financial aspect of the case, or that he was the nearest available *kapıcıbaşı*, or maybe that he had mediated for the case to reach Istanbul.[31]

İsmail was instructed to assist not only the *mütesellim* but also the court of law during the trial which was expected to take place. The state believed that that trial would restore order in the town and, thus, gave a solution, which did not deviate from its usual legalistic/judicial approach to disturbances in the provinces.[32] Those accused in the *serdar* case were to be tried in public in the presence of their opponents. The Islamic court of law was ordered to establish, collect, and return what was due by the accused, and also keep in jail those proved—in accordance with the provisions of the law (*şer'an*)—to have committed the murder. Thus, the court of law was once again confirmed as the center of provincial administration. Before closing the decree, the state did not fail to exhibit its traditional distrust of its officials, as it warned them against extracting amounts of money from innocent and decent people, who had nothing to do with the case.[33] Otherwise, the state was content to expect to receive a report about the speedy settlement of the affair and return to the everyday routine. However, for the case to close, the *mütesellim* and the *mubayaacı* had to manage to arrest the culprits first. They also needed to be men of integrity.

Indeed, the *mubayaacı* did not make proper use of his appointment, or so he was accused in a second *ferman* issued between 29 September and 7 October 1782, that is, two and a half months after the first one.[34] It was addressed again to Hasan, *mütesellim* of Salonica, and to the *kadı* of Karaferye.[35] According to the *ferman*, the *mubayaacı* sent a report to the Porte and explained that the *eşkiya* had fled before the arrival of the first *ferman* and had not been found.[36] He and the sharia court then proceeded to confiscate the properties of the accused (*emlak, çiftlikân, mahsulat*). They compiled an inventory and sent it to Istanbul, indicating that if farmed out, the confiscated property would generate an annual income of 5,000 *kuruş*.

However, the case did not end there, as Seyyid Osman Bey, Abdullah Agha, and Hafız Ali exercised their right to send a petition (*arzuhal*) to the Porte and present their version of the facts. Even though one would have imagined that it was in the Porte's interest to accept its agent's version as the truth and close the case as fast as possible, the account of those who had been named as the culprits of the attack and the murder was not rejected, but taken very seriously. This attitude stemmed either from the state's utter respect for the principle of justice or from its realization that it could not ignore the three men, who presumably were persons with influence on local society.[37] In either case, the state acted in a way that eventually was in conformity with the principle of protecting its subjects from the abuses of those in power. Of course, it has to be admitted that there is a third, more prosaic explanation, namely that the three men had good connections that enabled their voice to reach the Porte.

Osman, Abdullah, and Ali complained that they were not related to the murder of the *serdar* and that they had been wrongfully accused by spiteful local enemies despite the absence of legally acceptable evidence against them. They also claimed that their enemies had obtained *ilam*s against them through bribery. Furthermore, they alleged that the *mubayaacı* had concealed that the sultan had ordered that a public trial be held in Karaferye; instead, he had claimed that the *ferman* simply referred to their sentences and arrangements concerning their detention (*kalebend*). He asked them to pay a service fee (*on kese akçe hizmet-i mübaşiriyye*), and when it became obvious that they did not possess the money that he had asked, he confiscated their properties.

To make their case stronger, the three men presented a group petition (*mahzar*) by the people of Karaferye, who confirmed that the accused were not connected with the murder and that the *serdar* had orally named his murderers before he died. The state's agent was accused of misconduct and it was asked that he be removed from the case. Indeed, the Porte confirmed that it was illegal to confiscate the properties without trial, and replaced İsmail with Ali, one of its *gedikli*s (holder of a privilege), who became its new agent to the case. Otherwise, orders remained the same. A trial still had to be held and its outcome had to be reported to the Porte. This time, the local court of law and the new agent were explicitly warned to strictly follow the orders and to avoid siding with one or the other party.[38] It is not entirely clear how the authorities reached this decision. The claims of the three men were sanctioned by the *başdefterdar* who reported that the confiscation had not been carried out in the prescribed way and asked for the replacement of the agent. The *şeyhülislam* was also involved in the affair, but the relevant section of the *ferman* does not allow us to understand exactly how. Most likely, two inhabitants of Salonica informed him about the situation and the illegal actions of the *mubayaacı*, and asked for justice for the three men. On the side of the copy of the *ferman* in the judicial register of Karaferye, the scribe noted that a letter of the grand vizier and a decree of the *mütesellim* of Salonica had also been received about the same case. The arrival of three decrees indicates that by then the affair was taken quite seriously. Considering that originally the *mütesellim* had thought that issuing a *buyruldu* was enough, one is justified in asking whether it had been unrealistic on the part of that official to expect such a case to be resolved at the level of the *sancak* or whether the case reached Istanbul due to bad handling and as a result of the connections of those involved.

What emerges clearly from the authorities' response to the *serdar* incident is that law and order were at all times in the heart of Ottoman official ideology and rhetoric at all levels of administration. The incident was not treated as a simple murder case or as a private affair.[39] It was not seen as a direct challenge to Ottoman authority either. In the eyes of Ottoman administrators it was the subjects' feeling of safety and presumably their trust in the Ottoman system of government at large that was at stake. In case the murder of the *serdar* went unpunished, respect for order could collapse, and that would eventually have a serious impact on a cash-strapped administration that was in need for social and fiscal stability.[40] Besides, Karaferye may not have been an important town, but there were good reasons for the state to dislike unrest in the region. First of all, the routes connecting Macedonia with southern Greece passed through the district. Then, Russia posed in the last third of the eighteenth century a very real threat to the territorial integrity of the Ottoman Empire, and Karaferye was a predominantly Christian region. Finally, the central authorities were struggling for a number of years to restrain the Albanians, who had managed to dominate much of the institutional framework and economic life of southwestern Macedonia. Appearing weak was obviously not an option for the Ottoman state in the face of such internal and external challenges to its authority.[41]

A situation that was somewhat similar to that of 1782 had arisen in the region 162 years earlier. In 1620, Mirza, the *subaşı* of Karaferye, was found dead in a river near the town.[42] Certain aspects of this incident serve as food for thought, both on how crisis situations were dealt with and on the limitations set on the historian by the sources. What is interesting for our purposes is that the early-seventeenth-century incident was handled as a private affair: the relatives of the dead man went to the local court of law, asked for an investigation to be carried out, and accused someone of the murder. That person was arrested, tried in the Islamic court of Salonica, and executed. Even though the victim was an official,[43] like the *serdar* in 1782, there was no mention of applying to higher administrative authorities or of their involvement in the investigation about the murder. Four possibilities open up, when trying to explain why this affair was handled differently from the one in 1782. The first possibility is that the affair of 1620 was indeed considered to be private/personal with no further consequences for the life of the district or for public order as perceived by Ottoman official ideology. The culprit was discovered rather quickly and was found to be a lowly individual (a slave of the *voyvoda*, but still a slave) who posed no threat to the Ottoman system.[44] His motive was not cited in the surviving sources, but he apparently did not express the feelings or serve the purposes of a larger interest group.

This is the likeliest explanation for the different handling, but one should also consider the time distance between the two cases. On the one hand, conditions in the Balkan provinces of the empire were very different in 1620 and in 1782, and the state may have been much more sensitive to responding to what was perceived as a challenge to stability on the latter than on the former occasion. On the other hand, procedures may have been different in the early seventeenth century, so that such crimes were not reported to higher authorities, but were handled locally. Nevertheless, given the tenacity of traditional forms in the Ottoman polity, this explanation is rather unlikely.

Another possibility is that the difference between the two cases is an illusion that stems from the nature of the source material. That is, gaps may exist in the court registers of either 1620 or 1782, or different principles of keeping records may have applied to the two eras. As the 1782 case becomes known to us through incoming orders of the provincial and central administration and not through local registrations, even though a trial must have taken place at some point, so could there have been an appeal to the Salonica or Istanbul authorities in 1620, but without keeping record of it. It was not necessary that such a decree should be mentioned in the surviving entries.

The fourth possibility touches on a methodological problem. Quite simply, it may be a vain anachronism to try to establish strict procedures. Even nowadays, when fixed principles apply (or supposedly apply) to the handling of criminal affairs and crises, not all cases are dealt with identically. It is not unlikely that appealing to Salonica or Istanbul depended on whim and the particular circumstances. In other words, it is possible that there was not a standard procedure. If a case was considered threatening or if it had not been settled locally after a certain period of time, and someone, whether in an official capacity or not, decided to report it to a higher authority, then the situation got out of local control and entered the regional or imperial setting.

From then on, steps and the relevant rhetoric were more or less standardized and the steps of action taken depended both on the urgency of the situation as well as on the efficiency of those involved in resolving the problem.

Still, the main question is why the 1782 incident was not treated as a private affair—as the murder of an individual who happened to hold an office—by his enemies. Was it that the victim was the *serdar*, an official with law-enforcement authority? Was it the number of intruders and the violence of the incident? Was it the identity of the intruders? Or was it the general conditions and balance of power in late-eighteenth-century Karaferye, of which we know very little due to lack of contemporaneous narrative sources that deal with the town's microhistory? It is reasonable to assume that it was local circumstances and people who decided whether a murder would be considered a private matter that could be dealt with locally or whether they would take it to higher authorities and thus transform it into a crisis situation connected with the issue of stability in the region.[45] If circumstances were not taken into consideration, the 1620 and 1782 cases would paradoxically suggest that Istanbul was more readily invited to interfere in local life in the period of decentralization than in the early seventeenth century, when its control over the provinces was supposedly tighter and those involved in the murder had been the deputy and the slave of its appointee.

This would mean that the role of the state was to determine what steps should be taken each time for the restoration of order; it was, though, the local society that decided in the first place what was a crisis and what was not. According to Islamic law, the *kadı* court could investigate homicide only after the victim's next of kin had brought action; there was no prosecution ex officio. Thus, in theory the murder of the *serdar* could have been investigated only if his relatives had applied to the *kadı* and asked for retaliation or blood money; in theory again, it was a decision of the victim's relatives to bring such issues to the public sphere. However, there was no mention of the relatives of the deceased in 1782, and the whole case certainly surpassed the limits of a mere murder. Since Ottoman legal theory had brought matters relating to public order under the jurisdiction of the *ehl-i örf*,[46] a crime with repercussions on local politics lay in a gray zone between sharia and *kanun*, and its handling was determined by local conditions.

As far as state intervention in the provinces is concerned, a comparison with other cases from the near or distant past reveals certain constants. For instance, respect for formal procedures was a very important aspect of Ottoman ideology; it actually was an idea that cut through social groups and geographic regions. Suraiya Faroqhi has pointed out that a *kadı* in late-sixteenth-century Anatolia did not simply try to exert influence on his colleague in Çorum so as to have his robber enemy convicted, but "used his contacts to push his complaint against Canfedaoğlu and his men through the appropriate offices, and . . . secured a rescript which ordered the *kadı* of Çorum to hear the case. On another occasion, probably somewhat later, he secured a rescript that Canfedaoğlu was to be executed if he had killed anyone."[47] In other words, the *kadı* felt that he had to apply to the central authorities, even though contacting the local judge could have sufficed. When compared with the case of 1782 from Karaferye, Faroqhi's study suggests that little had changed over time in the official response of the state authorities to crisis situations in the provinces. At first, a provincial governor, namely the governor-general of Rum, reported the case to the Porte. The imperial council then ordered that the case should be tried by the *kadı*s of Sivas and Gelmugad with the assistance of the governor-general, who apparently acted as state agent. As in 1782, the state did not convict the accused; instead, it entrusted two provincial *kadı*s with establishing the guilt of Canfedaoğlu, and only instructed that he should be sentenced to death in case he was found guilty, as indeed happened.[48] Almost two hundred years later, the procedure was still the same, despite the difference in the geographical setting and the general conditions of the empire. Of course, there is an issue as to whether state officials were equally powerful and efficient in 1595 and in 1782. Apart from that, it becomes apparent that it was not due to weakness or detachment from the provinces that the state only contributed two decrees and an agent to the Karaferye incident. Giving judicial solutions to local problems was an immutable principle of Ottoman administration; in that sense, the state acted predictably in 1782. If a situation was thought to be more critical or urgent, then the authorities could decide to send in troops and restore order.

That happened in Karaferye in 1758–59. There was a conflict between two rival groups of *ayan*s, whose actions had created conditions of *ihtilal-i nizam* and *fitne*, and rendered them *eşkiya* in the eyes of the state. Following petitions by the population of the district, the Porte intervened in order to defend its subjects and its sense of order. At first, the state tried to settle the issue through decrees that were ordering the incarceration and banishment of those involved in the troubles. When it was realized that one of them had a force of four hundred armed Albanians and could not be arrested, the state dispatched troops under the command of the governor of Köstendil and appointed an agent, who was charged with informing the Porte about developments in the case as well as with confiscating the property of the rebel. When troops failed in their mission to arrest him, the state put to use another of its administrative methods by making the local people sign declarations that were holding them collectively responsible against the return of the undesired members of the two groups to the *kaza*. In the meantime, the state filled all vacancies in the administrative framework of the *kaza* so as to facilitate return to normality. The *kadı* of Karaferye was involved in the handling of the affair in his roles as a channel of communication between Istanbul and Karaferye, a notary and a judge, and all relevant documents were copied in his register.[49]

The centrality of the role of the *kadı* also becomes apparent in two cases of expulsion of governors by the janissaries and population of Aleppo in 1775 and 1784. The *kadı* did not take the initiative, but the rebels sought his sanction before taking action, while, on one occasion, he actually met with the governor before his removal. Furthermore, the rebels explained the reasons for their revolt in reports that they sent to the Porte via the Islamic court.[50] Even though the Porte's and the governors' control was certainly weakened and the *kadı* might have been forcibly dragged into action, it is interesting to note that the Ottoman state and its institutions remained stable points of reference. Such cases confirm that the subjects of the sultan could only imagine themselves in the Ottoman context, and that usually they rejected the representatives of the system without contesting the essence of that system.

The murder case of 1782 can also be juxtaposed with another case of the same year which lies midway between that one and the 1758–59 disturbances, and shows that sometimes a warning could precede action through the sharia court, a governor, or an agent. Ali Rüşdi Efendi, former *kadı* of Siroz (Serres) and *ayan* of Karaferye,[51] was accused of oppressing the population of the *mukataa* of Karaferye, which was held as *malikâne* by a certain İsmail, an imperial sword-bearer (*cenab-i hilafetmeabım silahdarı olan mir İsmail*). More specifically, he was accused of meddling in the affairs of the region and in the appointment of armed guards (*pandor*) as well as of charging the population amounts of money disguised as taxes and interfering with the apportionment of taxes. It is not clarified who notified the Porte of his behavior, but it may have been either the *kadı* or the *voyvoda* via the *malikâne* holder, because these two were the addressees of the *ferman* that was issued. Besides, these two officials, *kadı* and *voyvoda*, were the only ones who were entitled to handle the affairs of the inhabitants of the region, as was explained in the *ferman*. The issue was again disturbance of the public order of the region (*ihtilal-i nizam*) that resulted in impoverishment and flight of the *reaya* and subsequently led to reduction of the tax revenue (*mal-i miri*). However, this time it was admitted that the welfare of the subjects was not the sultan's only concern, as it was stated that the revenue that accrued from the Karaferye *mukataa* was large, and obviously, therefore, Ali Rüşdi Efendi's attitude could not be tolerated. As far as ideology is concerned, it is also interesting to note that the *ihtilal* category was used to bring together dissimilar situations, such as fiscal abuses and the murder of a *serdar*. Ali Rüşdi had been exiled in the past for the same sort of behavior, and this time he was given notice that if the Porte heard more of him, he would be immediately sentenced to life banishment to "distant places."[52] The *kadı* was once again heavily involved in the affair. He was held responsible for reporting to the Porte about Ali Rüşdi's behavior, for taking action against him, as well as for protecting the subjects and preventing any similar abuses (he shared this last responsibility with the *voyvoda*).[53]

It is not known why the state refrained from immediately banishing Ali Rüşdi Efendi and contented itself with mere warnings. Maybe it was hoping to exchange leniency for the local notable's compliance, since the use of force caused tension in local life without always having the desired effects. In any case, negotiation was a long-standing governmental practice by the end of the eighteenth century.[54] The individuals who petitioned or were reported to the Porte were in fact bargaining their social and economic status. The Porte was also negotiating its prestige and power. Even though it was not prepared to formally cede portions of its authority to provincial magnates or non-governmental agents, still it was willing to change a decision or a course of action when presented with new evidence, or to display leniency when it appeared that it served its purposes better than decisiveness did.[55]

One lesson to be learnt from state involvement in the local crises of Karaferye in 1782 is that the Porte was after all still the center of the empire and the authority that was providing the institutional framework for dealing with crises and local antagonisms. Its control over the provinces may have been much weaker than in past centuries, but when an affair failed to be settled informally or at the *kaza* or *sancak* levels, appealing to Istanbul was the natural next step despite the danger of exposing oneself to rapacious officials and high costs. On the other hand, the state was happy to fulfill its traditional role as guarantor of order, because the petitions of its subjects and the reports of its officials were offering it an opportunity to reconfirm its authority in the context of the minor or major challenges of the late eighteenth century. In other words, access to local offices and tax farms did bring provincial elites and their interests closer to the state, as has been argued convincingly,[56] but the principles of justice and intervention in the name of the *reaya* enabled the state constantly to reconfirm its ties not only with a small proportion but with all of its subjects and to have a sense of control over its provinces in the adverse circumstances of that time.[57] Of course, the basic question is whether the state maintained real power over the provinces or whether it had been reduced to a mere overlord by default until Mahmud II decisively challenged the authority of the *ayans*.

As far as response to local crises is concerned, the overall picture is that central and provincial officials appointed to a case were given a certain degree of freedom of action, but that Istanbul maintained the prerogative of the final check of their acts through their reports as well as through petitions received from any party involved. Besides, it was unrealistic for the state center to expect to be able to check speedily and accurately the truth of every single claim that came from whatever locality in the Balkans or elsewhere, unless that concerned an issue that had been entered in the registers of the central bureaucracy. If not, the central authorities simply lent their prestige to the petitioners by repeating their version of events in a decree. It was eventually the court of justice or the governor who decided the outcome locally. If a party felt that they had been wronged, they maintained the right to appeal anew to the Porte. Depending on the case's weight, the central authorities might decide to appoint a special imperial agent or to dispatch troops. Such a decision stressed the Porte's concern for the case and obviously made local authorities more careful in their handling of it. On the whole, though, the state appears to be putting trust in the existing administrative procedures, which were definitely decentralized in that the decision was not made in the center of the empire. That characteristic of Ottoman administration is of crucial importance, because institutions and procedures had not changed much since the sixteenth century, but the more powerful the local elites, the more active the role they had to play in crisis management and the stronger the pressure they could apply on state officials and representatives. Since the Islamic court of law played a major part in most cases (even when the state had merely issued a warning to someone), it was obviously susceptible to such pressure. Nevertheless, the state kept entrusting it with bringing an end even to crises which obviously concealed deeper enmities and antagonisms.

This (admittedly sometimes excessive) trust in provincial judges arouses some suspicion, which can lead to the opposite argument, namely that the state's attitude should be interpreted as total paralysis of its mechanisms. A weakened central state whose main predicament was the preservation of the privileges of its elite may have been content to issue decrees and devolve authority to officials lower in the hierarchy rather than to spend its energies in resolving local crises, which were not that threatening to the Ottoman way. The higher the number of *ferman*s issued for a single case, the stronger the suspicion that the state was unable or indifferent to act effectively and close the case. However, only further research can give more safe indications as to the relationship of the Ottoman state with its provinces in the late eighteenth century and its attitude toward anomalous situations that arose in the periphery and were reported to it. This is particularly true of Ottoman Karaferye, whose systematic study is still in its infancy.[58]

Notes

1. Veroia is Karaferye's Greek name. The town of Veroia is situated some 60 kilometers west of Salonica in present-day Greece.
2. For a classic account of Ottoman "decline," see Bernard Lewis, "Some Reflections on the Decline of the Ottoman Empire," *Studia Islamica* 9 (1958): 111–27.
3. Halil İnalcık, "Centralization and Decentralization in Ottoman Administration" in *Studies in Eighteenth-Century Islamic History*, ed. Thomas Naff and Roger Owen (Carbondale: Southern Illinois University Press, 1977), 27–52.
4. Bruce McGowan, "The Age of the *Ayan*s, 1699–1812," in *An Economic and Social History of the Ottoman Empire, 1300–1914*, ed. Halil İnalcık with Donald Quataert (Cambridge: Cambridge University Press, 1994), 637–758.
5. Yuzo Nagata, *Muhsin-zâde Mehmed Paşa ve Âyânlık Müessesesi* [Muhsin-zâde Mehmed Pasha and the Institution of *Ayan*ship] (Izmir: Akademi Kitabevi, 1999), 105ff. On the *ayan*s, a broad term used to designate the members of the provincial elites of the Ottoman state, see Yücel Özkaya, *Osmanlı İmparatorluğu'nda Âyânlık* [The *Ayan*ship in the Ottoman Empire] (Ankara: Türk Tarih Kurumu, 1994); idem, "Rumeli'de Âyânlık İle İlgili Bazı Bilgiler" [Some Information Concerning the *Ayan*ship in Rumeli], in *VIII. Türk Tarih Kongresi (Ankara 11–15 Ekim 1976). Kongreye Sunulan Bildiriler*, vol. 2 (Ankara: Türk Tarih Kurumu, 1981), 1407–16; Yuzo Nagata, *Muhsin-zâde Mehmed Paşa*; idem, *Tarihte Âyânlar. Karaosmanoğulları Üzerinde Bir İnceleme* [The *Ayan*s in History. An Investigation About the Karaosmanoğulları] (Ankara: Türk Tarih Kurumu, 1997); Deena R. Sadat, "Rumeli Ayanlari: The Eighteenth Century," *Journal*

of Modern History 44 (1972): 346–63; Gilles Veinstein, "'Âyân' de la région d'Izmir et commerce du Levant (deuxième moitié du XVIIIᵉ siècle)," *Revue de l'Occident Musulman et de la Méditerranée* 20 (1975): 131–47.

6. Tepedelenli Ali Pasha and Osman Pasvanoğlu are the best known among those who challenged the authority of the Porte in the Balkans. On the former see Katherine Fleming, *The Muslim Bonaparte: Diplomacy and Orientalism in Ali Pasha's Greece* (Princeton: Princeton University Press, 1999) and the extensive bibliography that the author cites; on the latter, see Deena R. Sadat, "Âyân and Ağa: The Transformation of the Bektashi Corps in the 18th Century," *Muslim World* 63 (1973): 206–19 and Robert Zens, "Pasvanoğlu Osman Paşa and the Paşalık of Belgrade, 1791–1807," *International Journal of Turkish Studies* 8 (2002): 89-104.

7. According to Abraham Marcus' view, the state remained the center of political power and a stable point of reference for all societal groups in eighteenth-century Aleppo despite the serious challenges to its authority (Abraham Marcus, *The Middle East on the Eve of Modernity: Aleppo in the Eighteenth Century* [New York: Columbia University Press, 1989], 74). However, from the 1770s onward, the state "steadily lost its control, and the local leaders and power groups increasingly decided the course of events" (ibid., 87).

8. For instance, an *imam* of Karaferye, who was challenged locally, applied to Tepedelenli Ali Pasha and not to Istanbul in 1812. Ali then issued a decree that resembled those of the sultan so much in style, formulation, and rigor that it did not leave much room for disobedience. Displaying, however, respect for procedures and an awareness of his limits, Ali did not address the decree to the *kadı*, but to a local notable, the *voyvoda* and the *serdar* (KS volume 103/page 14/entry 2 [27 May 1812]). "KS" stands for "Karaferye Sicilleri," the registers of the Islamic court of Karaferye, kept in the Veroia branch of the General State Archives of Greece.

9. See Halil İnalcık, "Adâletnâmeler" [Rescripts of Justice], *Belgeler* 2 (1965): 49–52; Uriel Heyd, *Studies in Old Ottoman Criminal Law*, ed. V. L. Ménage (Oxford: Oxford University Press, 1973), 176–77, 227–28. See also Boğaç A. Ergene, "On Ottoman Justice: Interpretations in Conflict (1600–1800)," *Islamic Law and Society* 8:1 (2001): 52–87, on variant definitions of justice by the Ottoman state and seventeenth-century challengers of its authority and on how both sides used their versions of the notion of justice in order to legitimize the perpetuation of a status quo that favored them and promoted their interests.

10. It is difficult to see to what extent the society's view of order and the law concurred with that of the state. Marcus has argued that, for the society of Aleppo, order emanated from government authority and the rule of law (Marcus, *The Middle East on the Eve of Modernity*, 73).

11. Gerber has noted that the *kadı* court and the central government may have developed closer ties in the eighteenth century than before, but that the state

still refrained from interfering with the legal procedure as such (Haim Gerber, *State, Society, and Law in Islam: Ottoman Law in Comparative Perspective* [Albany: State University of New York Press, 1994], 43–46). Cf. Ronald C. Jennings, "Limitations of the Judicial Powers of the Kadi in 17th c. Ottoman Kayseri," *Studia Islamica* 50 (1979): 151–54.

12. On the centrality of the role of the *kadı* in provincial administration and local life, see Gerber, *State, Society, and Law*, 16, 55–57, 181.

13. For an example of a contract from 1759, see KS 81/232/1.

14. There are no reliable demographic data for late-eighteenth-century Karaferye. According to Felix Beaujour, the French consul in Salonica and a careful observer, the town was inhabited by 8,000 people, while Salonica, the *sancak* center, had 60,000 inhabitants (Louis-Auguste-Félix de Beaujour, *Tableau du commerce de la Grèce, formé d'après une année moyenne, depuis 1787 jusqu'en 1797*, vol. 1 [Paris: Ant.-Aug. Renouard, 1800], 128). William Leake, a British agent, estimated that around 2,000 families lived in Karaferye in the beginning of the nineteenth century, and noted that 1,200 of them were Greek (William Martin Leake, *Travels in Northern Greece*, vol. 3 [London: J. Rodwell, 1835], 291). Indications from archival sources also suggest that the urban Muslim and Christian communities were of roughly equal sizes; on the other hand, the countryside was inhabited almost exclusively by Christians. The land was the main source of wealth, but crafts (especially the production of towels and bath sets) and commerce were also quite developed.

15. According to a letter of appointment issued by the *ağa* of the janissaries, the *serdar* was the head of the local janissaries, *cebecis*, *topçus*, and *top arabacıs* of the district, but was also responsible for maintaining public order (KS 82/589/2 [28 February–8 March 1760]).

16. Both remarks are corroborated by petitions, reports, and registers of the central bureaucracy (mainly the *Rumeli Ahkâm Defterleri* series) kept at the *Başbakanlık Osmanlı Arşivi* in Istanbul.

17. For an introduction to the Ottoman court registers see Suraiya Faroqhi, part 3 of s.v. "Sidjill," *The Encyclopaedia of Islam*, new edition, vol. 9 (Leiden: Brill, 1997). See also Beshara Doumani, *Rediscovering Palestine: Merchants and Peasants in Jabal Nablus, 1700–1900* (Berkeley, Los Angeles, and London: University of California Press, 1995), 10–11, for a succinct presentation of the limitations of the *sicil* material. It should always be kept in mind that decrees and other material entered in the court registers reflect, above all, the needs and perspectives of their issuers, and that they should be therefore treated cautiously.

18. In an undated *ferman* of probably 1777 it was stated that the inhabitants of Karaferye had always been rough (Ioannes K. Vasdravelles, ed., *Historika Archeia Makedonias. B´. Archeion Veroias–Naouses 1598–1886* [Historical Archives of Macedonia. II. Archive of Veroia–Naoussa 1598–1886] [Thessaloniki: Hetaireia Makedonikon Spoudon, 1954], 207–9).

19. It is not clear from the formulation of the decree whether the last-named was also a brother of Ali and Abdullah (*Elhacmehmedağazade Esseyyid Osman Beg ve Mustafa Ağa'nın oğulları Hafız Ali ve Abdullah Ağa ve diğer Osman Ağa demekle ma'ruf kimesneler*). As will be explained below, Osman Ağa is mentioned in only one of the two *ferman*s about the incident.

20. Imprisonment was not a standard penalty for murder. According to *kanun*, criminals were imprisoned until the sultan decided on their proper penalty (Heyd, *Studies in Old Ottoman Criminal Law*, 301–3). On the other hand, imprisonment and banishment were not unusual penalties for people who had committed what today would have been called political crimes.

21. *Hakk-i abd* (or *hakk adami*) is a technical legal term denoting the right or claim of a human being as opposed to the right of God (*hakk Allah*). Murder, bodily harm, and damage to property as well as the punishment demanded for them (retaliation, blood money, damages) fall under the "*hakk adami*" category (Joseph Schacht, *An Introduction to Islamic Law* [Oxford: Oxford University Press, 1964], 113, 176–77; Heyd, *Studies in Old Ottoman Criminal Law*, 204–7). In the Redhouse dictionary, *hukuk-i ibad* is translated as "rights due from man to man" (s.v. "ḥuqūq," *A Turkish and English Lexicon by Sir James W. Redhouse* [Istanbul: Printed for the American Mission by A. H. Boyajian, 1890]). I believe that in the present context the term is best rendered in English as "claims" or "damages."

22. KS 98/131/2; a simplified Greek translation of this entry has appeared in Vasdravelles, *Historika Archeia Makedonias*, 223–24. It is important to know who the recipients of a decree were, because those were presumably the authorities and individuals that its issuer considered to be legally qualified to handle an affair.

23. Cf. Sadat, "Rumeli Ayanlari," 351; İnalcık, "Centralization and Decentralization," 41–42.

24. The phrase *ayan-i vilayet ve zabitan ve iş erleri* is largely formulaic, as it appears in many decrees of that time. Usually the officials who really were expected to play a part in the handling of an affair were singled out and their names were placed before the *ayan*s and functionaries in the opening section of a decree.

25. A local *ayan* called Abdurrahman Ağa is known to have been repeatedly *mütesellim* of Salonica from the 1740s at least to the early 1770s (Antonios Anastasopoulos, "Imperial Institutions and Local Communities: Ottoman Karaferye, 1758–1774," Ph.D. diss., University of Cambridge, 1999, 107–8). Eighteenth-century *mütesellim*s were often selected from among local notables (İnalcık, "Centralization and Decentralization," 31–35).

26. The term *eşkiya* was not reserved for robbers or bandits, but for outlaws in the wider sense. For instance, the janissaries were termed *eşkiya* in the decree concerning the suppression of the corps in 1826 (Butrus Abu-Manneh, "The Naqshbandiyya-Mujaddidiyya in the Ottoman Lands in the Early 19th Cen-

tury," *Die Welt des Islams* 22 [1982]: 27), and, generally speaking, everybody outside the bounds of legality was called so. Bandits were usually specified in the entries of the Ottoman registers of Karaferye as *haydut eşkiyası* (see also Eyal Ginio, "The Administration of Criminal Justice in Ottoman Selânik (Salonica) during the Eighteenth Century," *Turcica* 30 [1998]: 201). Gerber renders "fitne" as "civil war" and "social disturbance" (Gerber, *State, Society, and Law*, 106, 228).

27. KS 98/143. A Greek translation (with some mistakes) of this entry, too, has appeared in Vasdravelles, *Historika Archeia Makedonias*, 224–25.

28. The *ayan*s were included among the addressees of most *buyruldu*s issued by the authorities of Salonica, but were absent from most *ferman*s.

29. The meaning is not very clear at this point. The *ilam* was sent initially to a *vekil* and then to the Porte (. . . *kaza-i mezbur naibi mevlana-i mumaileyhin vekilin tarafına vürud edüb bu defa deraliyeme irsal olunan bir kıt'a ilamından müsteban olmağla . . .*). Could this *vekil* be the former *mütesellim*?

30. Depending on how threatening a situation was assessed to be, the state might express its concern by sending troops to the region. Cf. Anastasopoulos, "Imperial Institutions and Local Communities," ch. 5 (pp. 91–119). A somewhat modified version of this chapter has been published (unfortunately with some mistakes, mostly in definitions of terms) as "Lighting the Flame of Disorder: *Ayan* Infighting and State Intervention in Ottoman Karaferye, 1758–59," *International Journal of Turkish Studies* 8 (2002): 73–88.

31. At least in the sixteenth century, the Porte often had its decrees delivered to their recipients by officials who were experts on the particular topic that the decree was about (J. E. Matuz, "Transmission of Directives from the Center to the Periphery in the Ottoman State from the Beginning until the Seventeenth Century," in *Decision Making and Change in the Ottoman Empire*, ed. Caesar E. Farah [Kirksville, Missouri: Thomas Jefferson University Press, 1993], 21).

32. See telling examples of the tenacity of legalism in the Ottoman context in Ergene, "On Ottoman Justice," 84, and Gerber, *State, Society, and Law*, 114, 138–40.

33. The *ferman* refers to oppression and abuses contrary to the sultan's will but also to the illustrious sharia (*mugayir-i şeriat-i garra*). Even though the state was aware of the undesirable side effects of dispatching officials to the provinces, it did not have any other mechanism of intervention in crises nor any means of preventing their misbehavior. The system relied on the right of the people to denounce such phenomena to the imperial council.

34. KS 98/158/2. Osman Ağa, the fourth member of the group, is not mentioned in this decree.

35. The name of the Islamic judge of Karaferye was never stated in state decrees of the second half of the eighteenth century. Some decrees referred to the *naib*

of the town and others to the *kadı*. It is not certain that the authorities paid attention to who was actually serving at the time of issuing a decree.

36. The report submitted by the *mubayaacı* to the Porte was called *kaime* in the document. According to Pakalın, this type of document was issued by those higher in rank and sent to those lower in the hierarchy (Mehmet Zeki Pakalın, s.v. "kaime," *Osmanlı Tarih Deyimleri ve Terimleri Sözlüğü* [Dictionary of Ottoman Historical Expressions and Terms], vol. 2 [Istanbul: Milli Eğitim Basımevi, 1951]). However, here the *kaime* clearly followed the opposite direction.

37. The three men not only had landed property, but also belonged to the aristocracy of the region. They pointed this out in their petition and the central authorities reproduced the term that the three men had used for themselves (*hanedanzade*) in the summary of their petition in the *ferman*.

38. It was pointed out repeatedly in this section of the document that guilt should be proved in accordance with the sharia.

39. The usual form of response to a simple private petition was not a *ferman*, but a rather short note on top of the text of the petition, and this is the way both texts were copied in the *kadı*'s register.

40. The 1780s belonged to an era of economic instability and inflation (Mehmet Genç, "L'économie ottomane et la guerre au XVIIIe siècle," *Turcica* 27 [1995]: 177, 180–82).

41. For large-scale operations against Albanians in 1779, see Nicolas G. Svoronos, *Le commerce de Salonique au XVIIIe siècle* (Paris: Presses Universitaires de France, 1956), 30–31.

42. This incident has been studied and analyzed by Eleni Gara, "Dolophonoi kai Dikastes sten Othomanike Veroia" [Murderers and Judges in Ottoman Veroia (Kara Ferye)], *IMEros* 1 (2001): 113–30.

43. The *subaşı* was in fact a sort of deputy governor of Karaferye, since he was sitting in for the *voyvoda-emin* appointed by the state to supervise its estate in the area.

44. Cf. Gerber's comments about when the Ottoman state intervened in local affairs in his *State, Society, and Law*, 125–26.

45. A case from Salonica seems to confirm that not every impressive murder of a powerful individual generated a crisis. Eyal Ginio's account of the incident gives the impression that the murder of a tax farmer and his retinue by their hosts near Salonica around 1740 did not require recourse to the provincial or central authorities until the heirs of the deceased sued the legal representatives of the inhabitants of the *kaza* not for the murder, but for the stolen money that was still missing. The two sides eventually reached a compromise through the agency of the *kethüda* of the governor of Salonica (Ginio, "The Administration of Criminal Justice in Ottoman Selânik," 206).

46. Schacht, *An Introduction to Islamic Law*, 177, 181; Heyd, *Studies in Old Ot-*

toman Criminal Law, 205, 209, 241–42. In late-seventeenth-century Hızırlı village near Salonica, the *ehl-i örf* detained a man in whose granary a murdered man was found, and set him free after the payment of a fine (Ginio, "The Administration of Criminal Justice in Ottoman Selânik," 204).

47. Suraiya Faroqhi, "The Life and Death of Outlaws in Çorum," in *Armağan-Festschrift für Andreas Tietze*, ed. Ingeborg Baldauf and Suraiya Faroqhi with Rudolf Veselý (Prague: Enigma Corporation, 1994), 67.

48. Ibid., 70–72.

49. See footnote 30.

50. Marcus, *The Middle East on the Eve of Modernity*, 87–89.

51. Ali Rüşdi was in earlier years the official *ayan* of Karaferye (KS 85/770/2 [12 July 1765]).

52. See Marcus, *The Middle East on the Eve of Modernity*, 85, for exile as a penalty for influential local figures who clashed with the state and its representatives or fell from grace, but also for the temporary nature of that measure. See also M. Çağatay Uluçay, "Sürgünler" [Exiles], *Belleten* 15 (1951): 511–32, for the reasons for which one could be banished and many relevant examples.

53. KS 98/145/2 (30 July 1782).

54. Cf. Karen Barkey, *Bandits and Bureaucrats: The Ottoman Route to State Centralization* (Ithaca, N.Y. and London: Cornell University Press, 1994), 189 ff.

55. Issues connected with the setup of provincial administration were the least negotiable. Marcus has observed that, even though the state put great emphasis on the protection of the *reaya* from abuses, only one of the several petitions that the inhabitants of Aleppo sent to the central government against oppressive governors over the years resulted in the removal of a governor (Marcus, *The Middle East on the Eve of Modernity*, 98).

56. See Ariel Salzmann, "An Ancien Régime Revisited: 'Privatization' and Political Economy in the Eighteenth-Century Ottoman Empire," *Politics and Society* 21 (1993): 406–11. The late eighteenth century coincides with the crisis of the malikânization process which had contributed to winning provincial loyalties for the state.

57. Speaking of a seventeenth-century *Book of Complaints*, Gerber stresses the contractual nature of the obligation of the sultan to guarantee conditions of social justice to his subjects (Gerber, *State, Society, and Law*, 154).

58. The fact that most surviving sources have been issued by the state and its representatives poses another problem, because we only learn the official view on how institutions worked, and cannot assess the importance of informal procedures and behind-the-scenes contacts or confirm the real weight of the *kadı* court.

Homicide in Ottoman Bosnia

MICHAEL R. HICKOK

An examination of murder in eighteenth-century Bosnia raises a complex set of questions about relations between law and the state, and between competing visions of justice and social stability. The nature of the crime brought it within the purview of both Islamic *şeriat* and Ottoman *kanun* law, and its investigation thus could stoke tension between judge (*kadı*) and provincial governor (*vali*). It also became an issue of foreign relations, with the interests of outsiders threatening to disrupt local proceedings. To judge from reports of some of these investigations, however, the Ottoman system successfully demonstrated a flexibility of response in maintaining law and order in the Balkans, in spite of the competing pressures.

The crime itself fell under the jurisdictions of Islamic law (*şeriat*), Ottoman criminal law as set out in the *kanunname*, and customary law practiced by the various communities living in Bosnia. The claims of all three of these interpretive systems shaped the evolution of given cases. At the same time,

This article is a revised version of a paper first presented at the conference on Ottoman Bosnia held in Sarajevo in 2001. The original paper has been published in the conference proceedings: Michael Hickok, "Homicide Investigations in Ottoman Bosnia: The Tension Between Legality and Stability," *International Journal of Turkish Studies* 10/1–2 (Fall 2004): 205–24.

the interests of the relevant parties in a homicide were frequently at odds with the state's concerns. The victims' families and friends usually sought revenge or compensation; the Ottoman government—though in nominal sympathy—needed to assert its continued monopoly over the right to kill. To complicate matters further, the reality of Bosnia's geographic position on the frontiers of the Ottoman state made the involvement of foreigners, and thus foreign governments, a continuing concern in local homicides. During the eighteenth century, there were incidents of Venetian citizens and Hapsburg subjects being murdered while traveling in Bosnia. These occurrences sparked correspondence amongst the administrative centers in Travnik, Istanbul, Venice, and Vienna. Provincial crime turned into foreign affair, resulting in an increased level of state scrutiny and a fourth layer of interpretation for investigators. Yet even in cases that were pedestrian by comparison, the imperial government in Istanbul occasionally took an unusual interest in local crime. Thus, the records of murder investigations in Bosnia during this period are relatively rich.

It is possible to show that the homicide investigation itself often obscured the line between the strict legality of theory and the practice of maintaining social order, that the governors' concerns for stability at times preempted the *kadı*s' legal authority, and that the populace manipulated the ambiguities in the system to its own advantage. In addition, the extant records indicate why there was often difficulty distinguishing between the specific crime of murder and the more indeterminate category of brigandage. The investigators' reports suggest why this distinction was not clarified.

A Note on Law and Government in the Ottoman Context

Scholars in the field of Bosnian history have used dialectic reasoning in their depiction of Ottoman provincial administration, resulting in an overly simplified understanding of Bosnian social expectations in the eighteenth century and of the possible range of Ottoman governmental policy. The operative paradigm demands that events be shown to benefit exclusively either Bosnians or the imperial center in Istanbul, which precludes any understanding of joint interests and beliefs. As historians of the Ottoman empire have become uneasy about depicting the state as merely absolute and despotic, so too have they become increasingly aware that the oppositional construction of policy alternatives has masked the sophistication and the suppleness of

administrative conduct. In particular, the study of Ottoman law and its relationship to the maintenance of corporate order has been shackled by this
conception of oppositional extremes.

> This theme is the disruptive tension between the ideals of the
> Holy Law of Islam, the *şeriat* in Ottoman usage, and the practical
> needs of sovereign states. Inquiries based on the theme conclude
> from comparisons of Islamic political theory and isolated examp-
> les of actual practice that Islamic governments have consistently
> failed to be "Islamic" and that Islamic society has failed to be
> "political". This succinct version borders on equivocation, per-
> haps inevitably in view of the heavy theoretical bias of research
> supporting the theme. The research closes in on the legal theory
> and executive practice, demanding purity of the first, corruption
> of the second.[1]

Efforts to restore social tranquility to eighteenth-century Bosnia in the
course of a homicide investigation fell somewhere between the clear but opposed absolutes, pure legal theory, and corrupt executive practice. Far from
being in disruptive tension, these two extremes helped guide the search for
justice and order in an imperfect society.

The attempt to balance legal principles and state needs into an effective means of sustaining order within a community was not unique to the
Ottomans during this period. Contemporary legal professionals in England
commented on a rise in the crimes of robbery and brigandage throughout the
eighteenth century. In part, they attributed the increase to the rising availabi-
lity among the population of material wealth and to a subsequent rise in the
general population's expectations for a higher standard of material culture.
A justice of the peace in Middlesex, Henry Fielding, however, suggested
that the fundamental cause of this growth was the English state's failure to
complete the transformation from traditional forms of social control—oversight by local nobles through coercion—to the newly expanding role of law
courts whose legitimacy rested on legal statutes. He asked:

> What of the ancient conservators of peace? Have the Justices, on
> whom this whole power devolves, an authority sufficient for the
> purpose? In some countries, perhaps, you may find an overgrown
> tyrant, who lords over his neighbors and tenants with despotic
> sway, and who is regardless of the law as he is ignorant of it; but as
> to the magistrate of a less fortune, and of more knowledge, every

riotous independent butcher or baker, with two or three thousand
pounds in his pocket, laughs at his power, and every pettyfogger
makes him tremble. It is a common and popular complaint, that
the Justice of Peace have already too much power. Indeed a very
little is too much, if it be abused; but, in truth, this complaint pro-
ceeds from a mistake of the business of power: The business of
the Justice is indeed multiplied by a great number of statutes; but
I know not of any which has enlarged his power.[2]

This passage underlines the relationship between law and order in the
pursuit of justice in eighteenth-century Europe. Legal statutes derive their
authority from custom, knowledge, and regular application but lack legitimacy if the state is deficient in enforcement capability. As Fielding claimed,
it is the functional equivalent of a capricious despot who had the power but
not the legal authority to force his will on the populace.

The Ottoman search for justice in eighteenth-century Bosnia faced similar limitations. The administration in Travnik and the people of the province
shared an understanding of justice based on corporate order and stability
within the various legal and customary parameters of the Ottoman state. In
instances where disagreements arose over incompatible interpretations of
rights, the *şeriat* courts served as adequate venues for arbitration. Some disturbances required more than arbitration to bring a conclusion, however. The
historical records indicate an agreement that homicides in principle should
be tried before the *kadı*, but not every murder suspect was willing to appear
in a court where, if found guilty, the punishment was death. Such circumstances required the Bosnian governor to step in and fulfill his role as defender
of social order, providing the coercive power lacking in the law courts.

A Note on Sources Concerning Murder

The difficulties of drawing conclusions about criminal activities within a
given society from information stored in legal records—whether legal statutes, court records, or indictment lists—have been well recognized by legal
historians in non-Ottoman fields.[3] A qualitative examination of legal records
has proven more feasible than quantitative analysis for social and cultural
history. This is certainly true in the case of Ottoman homicide records. For
example, Suraiya Faroqhi contends that the thousands of surviving *kadı* registers (*siciller*) "should be regarded as *the* major resource for Ottoman his-

torians," save the Prime Ministry archives in Istanbul.[4] She notes, however, that in the case of murder and other violent crimes these sources are often fragmentary and fail to describe the judgments issued and the manner of their execution. Faroqhi points out that the absence of most homicide cases from the *siciller* is linked to the multifaceted nature of the crime, which was subject to overlapping legal and administrative jurisdictions.

The complicated nature of murder in Bosnia can be compared to the situation in eighteenth-century England, where a similar dichotomy between law and order could be found in law enforcement situations in rural areas.

> [Many historians have sought] to portray the inferior officers of law enforcement as typically inefficient, illiterate and stupid. Many of the inferior officers' problems, however, arose from their ambiguous position in relation to both the machinery of the law and their neighbors . . . The parish officers were forced to mediate between two concepts of order: that of the state law, and that of the village, where order often meant little more than a conformity to a fairly malleable local custom which was considerably more flexible than statute law.[5]

The English state also struggled with its authority over the populace regarding the court's right to determine the nature of punishment in the face of popular resistance.[6] The continued threat of retaliatory violence by the populace competed with the state's interest in a legally correct solution to criminal cases. Legal historians have been cautious about drawing conclusions from the official legal records in such cases in England. In Ottoman Bosnia, the pressure to circumvent the formal legal system often left the remnants of homicide investigations outside the *siciller*. Although there are records of murder cases found in the provincial court records, they occur most often in situations where the nature of the death itself was in question.[7]

A partial record of homicide investigations in Ottoman Bosnia remains, however, in the official correspondence between the sultan's court in Istanbul and the governor's administration in Travnik. The very location of these documents underscores the unusual status of the crime within Ottoman administrative jurisdictions. These records also demonstrate that the Ottoman government in Bosnia had specific officials—similar to the parish officers in contemporary England—who worked between the governor's office and the various *kadı* courts throughout the province. Although the outcome of many of these investigations remains unknown, details of the investigations themselves open many questions about the difficult relationship between law and order in Bosnia.

Governor and *Kadı*, Homicide and Its Investigation

In his study of the Kayseri courts, Ronald Jennings discovered that a *kadı* without soldiers or police at his command had no ability to enforce compliance with the law.[8] *Kadı*s gained their moral authority over the populace and within the broader Ottoman administration through the integrity of the legal tradition they represented. As long as they interpreted the law without prejudice, their legitimacy held. The implied use of physical force as a tool of state coercion remained solely the prerogative of the provincial governor (*vali*). Recognition of this division of roles is necessary in order to understand the division of state supervision over criminal matters in the Ottoman Balkans. The separate but complementary moral and executive powers of *kadı* and *vali* were keys to good governance.

Historians have tended to ignore the resilience and durability of this simple system. Analyzing the differences in the Balkans between peasant rebellions and wars of independence, Dimitrije Djordjević suggests that "the predominance of the agrarian factor can be recognized in upheavals and revolts directed against *local* abuses of power, misfortunes and distresses caused by local authorities."[9] He goes on to conclude that the introduction of a national consciousness by way of an urban elite in the nineteenth century offered Slavic peasants an alternative to Ottoman governance for the first time. This is a narrow interpretation of possible peasant responses to poor governance, however. The Ottoman-Hapsburg frontier was relatively porous, and migration took place throughout the Ottoman period.[10] At the same time, Bosnia's proximity to Montenegro provided another route of escape from Ottoman authority. Dissatisfied peasants could and did vote with their feet. Some emigrated, but many stayed. The people of Bosnia normally accepted the Ottoman governor's authority in part because he was able to meet the expectation for maintaining a degree of justice and political stability. Ottoman rule may have been disciplined, but in theory it was not capricious. Between the populace and the representatives of the Ottoman imperial government there was a set of mutual obligations. The administration's failure to meet these responsibilities provided the impetus for disorder but did not entail resistance to the state as such.[11]

This argument falls within a larger movement in Ottoman historiography toward a view of the Ottoman period as part of a long continuum in Balkan history rather than as an aberration, as argued by many nationalist scholars. The conquest of the Balkans was undoubtedly predicated on the use of overwhelming force, but the foundation of the five centuries of administration was built with an eye toward durability, not temporary occupation. Its endurance may well have partially resulted from the belief among the variegated Balkan populace—at least until the nineteenth century—that the Ottoman way was the best conceivable manner for organizing a multi-ethnic, multi-confessional society.[12] It was not the only choice, but for a long time it retained its legitimacy as the preferred option. This enduring Ottoman way in the provinces was personified first and foremost by the judge (*kadı*) and the governor (*vali*). They arbitrated the mutual rights and obligations between the sultan and his subjects in Bosnia, in particular in matters of criminal justice.

The contrast between judges and governors relating to homicide investigations is particularly revealing. Traditionally scholars have considered these officials as rivals for power and authority within a province or as a conscious attempt by the sultans to provide a system of regional checks and balances. Jennings goes so far as to assert that "in Ottoman history the provincial governor was the *kadı*'s chief rival for power. Whenever provincial governors stood unchecked by imperial authority, they encroached on the legitimate sphere of the *kadı*. It has been shown that this historic and traditional rivalry was extremely acute."[13] Uriel Heyd in his study of criminal law offers a slightly different interpretation, arguing that governors represented a secular authority that functioned in a similar manner to the *kadıs*' *şeriat* courts. He points to the frequent instruction to the governors from Istanbul that they administer justice in accordance with Islamic law as evidence that the governors tended toward arbitrary and oppressive behavior.[14] These conclusions, however, assume that, like the *kadıs*, the governors derived their authority and legitimacy from adherence to legal statutes instead of from their ability to enforce their will. In theory issues, such as murder, that straddled administrative jurisdictions should highlight this rivalry. The investigations of homicide in eighteenth-century Bosnia suggest, however, that the assumption of tension between judge and governor has been exaggerated.

In their instructions to the various Bosnian governors, the sultans ordered explicitly that actions conform to standards of Islamic law and Ottoman custom. Yet the governors were not the arbiters of these laws, nor were they meant to be. Istanbul appointed the *kadıs* for this purpose. A contemporary description of a Bosnian governor's typical day demonstrates, however, that his duties did include judicial activities of a particular sort.

> They rise at day break to perform their morning devotions, which are preceded by ablution. Pipes and coffee are then served. The pasha sometimes mounts his horse, and amuses himself with seeing his pages exercise the dgerid [javelin], and sometimes he gives public audience. He then administers justice in person, and pronounces judgement on whatever regards the public government: he imposes fines or penalties, sentences to the bastinado or the gallows, condemns or acquits, according to his pleasure; for all power is in his hands.[15]

This observation was astute in several ways. First, the governor held an audience—referred to in the Ottoman documents as a *divan* or decision-making council—and not a court of law. Second, the governor administered justice; he did not interpret matters of law. Here, the distinction between the roles of the *kadı* and the *vali* is clear. The *kadı* decided legal matters for Bosnians in civil and criminal matters. The governor ensured justice, which in this context meant maintaining social tranquillity. The governor would not have heard a complaint regarding family law or property but did listen to criminal cases. Thorton recognized this peculiarity in the statement "whatever regards public government." Finally, the governor resolved threats to provincial order "according to his pleasure; for all power is in his hands." The actions of governor Kukavica El-hac Mehmed Pasha offer another clear example. Faced with peasant unrest over unjust taxation by local officials in the 1750s, he restored order with the help of local troops and only then went through several hearings to determine the legality of his methods.[16] The *kadı* and the *vali* were neither rivals for authority in Bosnia nor competing sources of jurisprudence. The judge sought to uphold justice through the medium of law, while the governor fulfilled his responsibility for social stability through the coercive power of his office. The efforts were often complementary but rarely analogous.

It is a subtle but critical difference. *Kadıs* determined in the case of criminal acts what was and was not legal according to Islamic law and sultanic edicts (*kanun*). They did not make or implement law; they interpreted it. To further demonstrate this distinction in Ottoman administrative practice between law and order, a quick survey of the imperial judicial registers (*ahkâm defterleri*) for Bosnia is instructive. These registers were compiled in Istanbul to record complaints sent from the provinces and then acted on through judicial decrees (*hükümler*) issued in the name of the sultan.[17] The *ahkâm defterleri* contain information similar to records in the *kadı sicilleri*. The significant difference between the two sets of documents turned on the issue of selectivity. Istanbul received significantly more petitions and complaints from the people of Bosnia than were recorded. Thus, those affairs summarized in the *ahkâm defterleri* reflected only those issues that the imperial center saw fit to act upon. Without further information from the no longer fully extant archives in Sarajevo, it would be difficult to determine how Bosnian authorities responded to Istanbul's instruction or how these legal disputes were settled. Nonetheless, the *ahkâm defterleri* do indicate which parts of the provincial administration involved themselves in each decision and therefore offer evidence on the relationship between the governor and the judge. Certain major trends stand out.

A change in the partnership between the *vali* and the *kadı* occurred between 1752 and 1798, and suggested a decrease in joint jurisdiction over legal matters. When the legal decrees issued in Istanbul in four different years during the eighteenth century are compared, a shift in administrative concerns becomes apparent. The following samples are taken from the tenure of three different governors who held office for at least three consecutive years. The table below indicates, for each *hüküm*, to which branch of the provincial administration it was addressed for action—governor or judge.

Year (*Hicri*)	*Kadı*	*Vali*	*Kadı* and *Vali*	Total
1752–53 (1167)[18]	3	3	39	46
1757–58 (1171)[19]	7	4	63	74
1783–84 (1198)[20]	29	3	39	71
1797–98 (1212)[21]	70	2	16	88

When the *ahkâm defterleri* began in the middle of the century, the majority of decrees were issued jointly to the governor and the relevant judge. Twenty years later about forty-one percent of the decrees were addressed to the judge alone. The trend accelerated and, by the very end of the century, the majority of legal decrees were sent solely to the *kadı*'s court involved in the dispute. The governor's direct participation in general legal matters declined in Bosnia throughout the second half of the eighteenth century. His joint participation also declined, and he seldom found himself instructed to act alone.

In other contexts, the Bosnian governors were consistently active in matters relating to the social stability of the province, growing over the century as pressures within Ottoman society for change evolved during this period. Yet the register of legal decrees from Istanbul to Bosnia shows a substantial decrease in the role played by the *vali* in the legal affairs of the province. This seeming contradiction lends support to the argument that Ottoman political thought and administrative practice considered "law" and "order" as separate but interrelated issues, dealing with them through different institutions. An examination of those few decrees issued to the governors alone demonstrates that these particular affairs concerned problems that may have touched upon a *kadı*'s legal prerogatives but either required the *vali*'s resources to resolve or infringed on matters usually relegated solely to the governor. For example, in April 1754 the Imperial Council instructed the Bosnian governor to capture eleven mischief-makers (*müfsidler*) and promoters of trouble (*muharrik-i fitne*) dwelling in the environs of Sarajevo.[22] These men had already been tried for their parts in the uprisings in the prior years, but had escaped from the *kadı* of Sarajevo, who did not possess the means to recapture them. Istanbul ordered the governor, Kukavica El-hac Mehmed Pasha, to provide the judge with the necessary coercive force to put an end to the problem. A similar predicament occurred when the *kadı* of Izvornik convicted a person for theft in May 1784, only to have the criminal flee the county (*kaza*).[23] The governor received orders to form a posse to capture the fugitive.

Most of the other examples concerned disputes amongst the various members of the Bosnian militia who either felt their salaries to be less than those of their compatriots in other areas of the province or were having difficulty collecting their salaries.[24] The militia officers often pursued these disputes as legal matters, but Istanbul directed such petitions to the financial administration at the provincial level, not the law courts.[25] This policy holds true for the few cases recorded in the *ahkâm defterleri*. The final category of decrees directed specifically to the governor concerned cases of inheritance in which a *kadı*'s legal decision regarding the disposition of an estate had been ignored by the family members in actual possession of the goods.[26] Thus, the register of complaints demonstrates that the governors became increasingly distanced from purely legal matters, and were called upon to participate only in instances where force was required or military issues were in play.

According to the legal codes, arrest and punishment fell under the control of the *kadı*'s court. The judge had a member of his staff, the *muhzır*, whose duty it was to summon the participants to the proceedings.[27] This office has been recognized as an integral part of an Ottoman judicial court, and the *muhzır* was normally recorded as one of the formal witnesses to proceedings (*şuhud ul-hal*).[28] The salary records for Ottoman religious and legal officials in Bosnia testify to the presence of this office in local courts. *Muhzır*s appeared also as witnesses to legal documents produced by the *kadı* courts in Bosnia throughout the century, and can be so found as signatories during the yearly renewal of salaries.[29] Alone, the *muhzır* obviously did not have the power to enforce a *kadı*'s verdict on an unwilling person. The position of *muhzır* might better be understood as a cross between the roles of bailiff and clerk. The *muhzır* had no enforcement or investigative capacity.

Thus the Ottoman law codes stipulated that in cases requiring coercive force, the pursuit of fugitives, or the examination of events, the courts be allowed to engage a member of the governor's administration or even an official from a nearby urban center as an intermediate step prior to turning the matter entirely over to the *vali* himself. Often such an official was referred to in Ottoman documents as a *çavuş* or a *subaşı*, titles usually interpreted in later histories as "police chief." The *ahkâm defterleri* indicate, however, that the Bosnian courts had no automatic recourse to any such officials. The salary records for these same courts corroborate this conclusion. Though there may have been officials called *subaşı* located in the urban centers of the province, there remains recorded in the extant registers in Istanbul no indication of their participation in matters of violent crime. Such members of the *vali*'s administration do appear as signatories on legal documents, but not in an enforcement capacity.

The same salary records which establish the existence of *muhzır*s within the legal system in Bosnia in the eighteenth century also record payments to officials titled *mutasarrıf*s. The term *mutasarrıf* has been understood to mean commander of a *sancak* and, in fact, *mutasarrıf*s with such a function do appear in Ottoman documents as such.[30] The title of *mutasarrıf* also applied to other functionaries, however. Bosnian records describe men as *ada mutasarrıfı* [island warden?] who were clearly not sancak commanders. In the salary registers of provincial religious/legal personnel there are more examples where the holder of this title was clearly not a *sancak* commander. For example, in 1754 Molla İshak confirmed Hafız İbrahim Efendi as *mutasarrıf* in Travnik at a daily salary of 20 *akçe*, and Molla İbrahim confirmed the Bosnian El-hac Mustafa as *mutasarrıf* in Akhisar also at a daily salary of 20 *akçe*.[31] In files from later in the century, it becomes clear that these officials referred to as *mutasarrıf*s must have been active in the *kadı*'s court. Each *kadı* seems to have had at least one, and important provincial cities like Sarajevo had a hierarchical grouping of *mutasarrıf*s. On March 11, 1776, the Molla of Bosnia, Ahmed Efendi, signed five documents which established the following corps of *mutasarrıf*:[32]

Osman Bey *veledeş*	*mutasarrıf*	Daily salary 20 *akçe*
Yusuf	*mutasarrıf*	Daily salary 11 *akçe*
Ahmed Ağa	*mutasarrıf*	Daily salary 6 *akçe*
Hüseyn	*mutasarrıf*	Daily salary 6 *akçe*
Osman	*mutasarrıf* and *müzeyyin*	Daily salary 5 *akçe*

This and other examples suggest that Bosnians of different social and professional backgrounds, as indicated by the titles or epithets added to their names, could hold the office. The overall pay range was extremely wide, ranging from a high of 60 *akçe* to a low of 2.5 *akçe* per day. Though no definite conclusions can be made from the salary records alone, it appears that these officials constituted a small contingent of enforcement and investigative "agents" in the service of the Bosnian provincial government.

Certain *mutasarrıf*s appeared alongside various militia officers as the principal agents of homicide investigation. The institutional basis of an orderly society can, therefore, be seen as shared between the governor and *kadı*. As an interpreter of legal tradition, the *kadı* decided the parameters for appropriate behavior but had little power to enforce his decisions, if those decided against chose to disagree. On the other hand, the governor held sufficient resources to impose his will, but no authority to do so in matters that were not direct threats to public order. The *mutasarrıf*s appear to have acted as the bridge between these two pillars of state authority. Given the investigators' freedom from exclusive oversight by either the judicial or the executive authorities, it warrants a closer look to see whether in extreme circumstances, such as murder, they enjoyed greater freedom of action, as the state and the people favored social stability over abstract legalism.

The Bounds of Investigation

The theoretical parameters within which an agent of the provincial governor and the legal courts might have conducted a murder investigation appear as ambiguous and contextual as the status of the representative himself. At the most refined level, Islamic jurisprudence guided the actions of the courts and their agents. Homicide is included within the category of offenses (Ar. *jināyāt*) in which the punishments are regulated by both the degree of intent and the degree of legal sanction.[33] The important point is that the court does not act to protect society from the murderer, but instead ensures the victim's family the right to revenge or to recompense. This interpretation, in a simplified sense, defines homicide as a tort and not a criminal offense *per se*.[34] In other words, in a strictly Islamic context the state cannot initiate a murder investigation. Only the "avenger of the blood" (Ar. *wāli al-dam*)—the next-of-kin or those allowed revenge—is entitled to prosecute a claim of murder.[35] No place for the state's interest in controlling violence within the community exists.

This explanation of the Islamic penal process for homicide suggests why the Ottoman state tried to develop supplementary criminal codes and to assign homicide investigators distinct from the *muhzir* or other Islamic court functionaries. These developments would have helped enforce the state's interests, as well as those of the victim's family.[36] In the case of outright murder with no extenuating circumstances, Ottoman law stated that "retaliation [by the state] shall be carried out and no fine shall be collected [in place of punishment]."[37] Though this code still allowed the victim's kin to wave retaliation and accept blood money, it was the state's prerogative to prosecute, and only in determining the punishment did it seek direction from the relevant parties. A clearer contrast may be drawn in the hypothetical situation where a slain body is discovered in open country. Islamic law dictates no action—literally, "blood is not avenged"—while the Ottoman code calls for the people in the villages in the vicinity to be examined. Islamic jurisprudence holds that only the deceased's family has the right to demand retaliation, while the Ottoman code expanded that prerogative to the state itself. This in part explains why, in theory, a *kadı* had little need of enforcement power. He could only arbitrate between parties who had already agreed to his authority in the affair, whereas the governor's agent had the power to interfere in criminal matters reflecting his role in asserting the state's rights as an indirect victim of the violence. This split authority over the investigation and trial of a homicide case was later codified in other areas of the Ottoman empire where involvement of the *kadı* courts in a murder case began only after the preliminary investigation and examination by the representatives of the provincial administration had been completed.[38]

Lacking such codification in eighteenth-century Bosnia, the *vali* had one other administrative trick to ensure that the state's interest in social stability was heeded in some murder investigations, namely to transform homicide into another kind of crime, brigandage. For example, in 1773 the Bosnian governor Ali Pasha had defended his disinterest in a murder investigation in Hersek during his previous tenure by arguing that his appointment had not included any judicial authority in that *sancak*.[39] In accepting responsibility for the case two years later, he made what at first appears to be a counter-intuitive proposal. He did not ask for increased judicial authority; instead, he suggested to Istanbul that the homicides were really the work of brigands (*eşkiya*). The Imperial Council accepted this reinterpretation and instructed him to use Bosnian militia companies to find and eradicate the bandits. By turning the murderers into brigands, the governor shifted the matter definitively from the *kadı*'s realm of legal arbitration to his own authority regarding threats to public order, i.e., to Ottoman administrative control. In the same manner, it moved a set of family killings in what had probably been a tribal feud into the much less explosive category of brigandage, where the state could take actions without appearing overly partisan. Thus, it is not surprising to find in the legal records and archival documents that the incidence of brigandage was far greater than that of unqualified homicide.

The distinction made by Ottoman officials in Bosnia regarding these two crimes was not merely a semantic one. Not only did it place the murder squarely under the governor's authority as a matter of public welfare, it also loosened some of the restrictions of the *şeriat*, since brigandage was a more serious crime than homicide in Islamic jurisprudence. Most importantly, banditry (Ar. *haraba*)—used synonymously with brigandage—falls within the category of Islamic criminal law known as *hudud* which includes crimes committed against the public interest and violates those rights assigned to God.[40] Brigandage, unlike murder, does not require a formal "complaint by the victim or his family." The punishment for a murder committed during an act of banditry is death. The usefulness of this concept was clear to any governor facing the tangles of tribal law.

Tribal or customary law added a third sort of legal guideline which could influence the course of a murder investigation, in addition to the competing

Islamic and administrative concepts of order in Bosnia. Particularly in the southwest where Montenegrin, Albanian, and Bosnian tribes co-mingled, the influence of the various rules relating to blood feuds had a significant impact on Bosnian governors' attempts to investigate murders. Homicides within Bosnia might have had their beginnings in a tribal feud involving Montenegrins or Albanians outside the province. In these cases, the revenge killing might be seen as morally necessary by the participants but fail to meet such criteria within either an Islamic court or the governor's administrative court.[41] This threatened to place the state in the precarious position of pursuing a murder investigation not only without the victim's family as plaintiffs, but often against their very wishes. Here, as in the English situation discussed earlier, the state's perception of the crime was less flexible than society's. Yet, the interaction was not as simple as that of a modern centralizing state desiring to extend its authority over marginal groups in the provinces. Tribal members unable to defend themselves after having committed a murder often fled into areas of stronger Ottoman control, knowing full well that the state would object to their own extra-legal murder in revenge.[42] Thus, not only did all three parties affected by a murder—the immediate participants, the state, and the community—have a variety of legal or quasi-legal systems through which to resolve the affair, but each wanted to choose the system that best suited its own agenda. It also complicated the homicide investigators' choice as to which system's rule they were meant to follow.

One of the by-products of this multi-layered approach to justice in murder cases was the confusion it created in non-Ottoman observers. For example, a contemporary French official in Istanbul wrote of Ottoman justice:

> Let us now consider, how the law treats criminals. It is a shocking truth, that these monsters are more favourably used; for the law, which condemns the murderer to lose his life, permits, at the same time, the nearest relations of the murdered, to grant him a pardon. The criminal is conducted to the place of punishment; he who performs the office of execution, takes on him likewise that of mediator, and negotiates [sic], till the last moment; with the next of kin to the deceased, or his wife, who commonly follows, to be present at the execution. If the proposals are refused, the executioner performs the sentence; if they are accepted, he reconducts the criminal to the tribunal to receive his pardon: but

an accommodation rarely takes place, as there is a kind of scandal annexed to selling the blood of one's relations, or husband. It is evident that were there a like law among us [the French], we would frequently see the most execrable assassins peaceably enjoy the fruit of their crimes.[43]

The same writer later suggested that only "paid assassins" were so executed, and that in some cases the "complaintant himself was executioner."[44] These passages demonstrate the degree of confusion caused by the differing legal systems at work. What was seen as a pardon was in fact the right of the victim's kin to demand recompense in place of revenge in given circumstances, reflecting the Ottoman state's partial willingness to negotiate criminal justice when a certain outcome was coveted. The Ottoman state sought to assert its authority in cases where it saw an interest in the resolution. The murderer and the victims attempted to manipulate the systems to their own desired ends where possible. The community at large demanded justice in the form of social stability, which at times seemed at odds with a structuralist reading of the legal codes of the state. In the subsequent examination of several homicide investigations in eighteenth-century Bosnia, it is important to keep these competing and often contradictory parameters in mind.

Reading Selected Cases

At some point in 1762, Istanbul took, for unknown reasons, a special interest in Bosnian homicides that occurred near the Dalmatian border, and ordered the senior *kadı* in the province to provide a summary report on the matter. In June 1762, after corresponding with Venetian officials, the *kadı* in Sarajevo Hafızzade Mustafa Efendi completed his report in which he gave an introductory remark and eleven short descriptions of criminal cases involving murder.[45] It is unclear from this document whether these were the only cases to have occurred during the period requested or whether these eleven were somehow distinct from the others in some manner. Nevertheless, this collection of homicide cases provides examples of how such incidents were perceived and classified by the senior Ottoman legal official in the province. What is more, Mustafa Efendi had the advantage of a much longer experience in Bosnia than might normally have been the case. Most provincial *kadıs* rotated in their assignments with the same frequency as the governors. Yet petitions from his court demonstrate that Mustafa Efendi was the senior *kadı* in Bosnia from at least January 11, 1758, to November 28, 1763.[46] In his report to Istanbul, Mustafa Efendi listed homicides that he would have been informed of personally and was not simply relating information contained in the court's records. Those individuals involved included both Ottomans and foreigners from a variety of confessional communities, and the murders occurred in several places near the border.

What follows is a translation of that document.

[1] It is declared that this list includes slain Muslims who were grazing [their livestock] when killed on the borders of Islam by Venetians, according to the ambassador's report that came from Venice and the translator's deposition that accompanied the report.

[2] Six months previously, three men—Jovan Tosovik from the village of Zirime, Marin Mirasak from the village of Gabela, and Izton who lived in Iselet—had gone to the borders of Islam to sell animals. Near the tower in Prolog, one Salih who was a guard from that tower along with his men Marko and Probi killed the three men and took two hundred Venetian ducats from their persons.

[3] A year ago, Lokaşar Bey and Raniki Milovi Rado Bey had come to the borders of Islam from the fortress of Sinj for the purpose of trade. In the area known as Buşko Blato, Kosna oğlu Numan Bey's men killed Lokaşar Bey and wounded Milovi. It is said they took their goods.

[4] Novorçolu Bey came to the border of Islam from the village of Vrezniçiye for the purpose of trade. Tokla, Ledistiyan, and Oyçovah, who were infidels from Grahovo, killed him. They took his goods from him. The Ehlune *kadı* discovered them. Kolan oğlu *kapudan*'s *odabaşı* recovered the deceased's goods.

[5] A year ago, Ahmed Kars Bey from Kuprez killed Aleya Kovaçov from the village of Vezime on the outskirts of Kuprez.

[6] A year and a half ago, Esteban Kosnar from the village of Vezime was going to Eskobiya with four bags of salt when on the outskirts of Ehlune he was killed by Koloşak and his men who took the salt.

[7] Three years ago, Aleya Koblov Bey, Andreya Frankov Bey, and Kapton Varaç Bey from the fortress of Sinj were attacked in Buşko Blato by Ohrab oğlu Haci Yarov and his men. Two bags of Venetian ducats and their goods were taken. Some days later the men died from the encounter.

[8] A year ago, Ivan Torziç Bey from the fortress of Sinj was killed in Babla.

[9] Eight months ago, Ivan Kovas Bey from the village of Kostlanovo was passing through the borders of Islam. While coming, he stayed in a travelers' house (*han*). He was set upon and attacked by Ali Refalu Bey and his men. Five days later, he died of the attack.

[10] Six months ago, Harambaş Akrab Bey from the fortress of Sinj was killed in the village of Ali Bey by Ali Pasha Golinovo. Six large bags of wheat and barley and fourteen Venetian ducats were taken from him.

[11] Twenty months ago, Bozov and Estevan Marov from the fortress of Sinj were killed by Yozob Graya and Kaher Manoşov from Glamoç on the outskirts of Glamoç. Three Venetian ducats and their goods were taken.

[12] Eşrapayr Anakov from the fortress of Knin was killed in the village of Vrbnik. The Gülhisar *kadı* discovered this and recovered eight hundred *kuruş* from the people of the village.

Though extremely eclectic in composition, Mustafa Efendi's report reveals several things about homicide cases. First, there was a great deal of cross-border travel and commerce between Bosnia and the Dalmatian coast. This trade moved in both directions, and the government was concerned with the safety of both foreign traders in the Ottoman lands and Ottoman peasants and merchants selling their goods in Venetian lands. Secondly, all of these homicides fell into that nebulous category where the state had to initiate legal proceedings.[47] The victims' families were probably either foreigners or not present in the court, and thus it fell to the state to investigate the crimes. With the exception of a single case, Mustafa Efendi was very clear on the identity of both the victims and the attackers and on the circumstances of the crimes themselves. Moreover, a detailed inventory of the goods taken suggests a successful recovery of the stolen money and trade items. In two cases, this conclusion is specifically confirmed. Looking at cases four and twelve, the *kadı*s in Ehlune and Glamoç initiated the investigation into the murders. After determining the truth of the first affair, the Ehlune *kadı* turned over the problem of catching the three villagers in Grahovo to the Bosnian militia commander in the region, who assigned the task to one of his non-commissioned officers. Here, the orders issued by the Imperial Council to the militia officers to participate in legal affairs after the disturbances of the early 1750s were being acted on. The Glamoç *kadı* appears to have needed no such help in the last case, perhaps because only villagers and not a robber's band were involved. There remains no indication of whether the victim's murderer was ever found, only that the cash he was said to have been carrying was recovered from the villagers. Finally, it is noteworthy that all the homicides listed in this document took place either immediately outside settled areas or in the desolate wilds between urban centers, like Buşko Blato. There are examples of Christians killing Muslims, Muslims killing Christians, and Muslims killing Muslims. The Ottoman state seemed to consider them all equally serious in nature. The court treated individual killers and robber bands in a similar context and, in cases where wounds suffered during a theft later proved fatal, was careful to document the fact. Thus, the attackers could not claim later in their defense that they had only injured their victims. Mustafa Efendi's list raises several questions about crime that can be explored in detail using better documented cases.

The issue of safety on the Bosnian frontiers was a long-standing matter of negotiations between Istanbul and Vienna. Violent incidents involving foreign nationals held the potential for escalation into war, and both sides wished no misunderstanding in such cases. Therefore, police activity on either side of the border was monitored to the same degree as military movements. For example, the Bosnian governor Abdi Pasha wrote Istanbul on August 1, 1751, to report the construction of a new "police station" (*karağulhane*) across the river from Bihke [Bihać] in Rakobiçe [Brekovica].[48] The governor was concerned because similar installations already existed in areas north of Izvornik. The Austrian general in Karlofoça [Karlovac or Karlowitz] had sent Abdi a letter explaining that disorder on the Austrian side of the frontier required the addition of new officers and police buildings. Abdi was not satisfied with this explanation, and ordered the Bosnian *defterdar* Mustafa Efendi to cross into Austrian territory with an interpreter to inquire into the matter more closely. Mustafa Efendi returned with news that a great deal of stone and many large trees were being collected for the building in Rakobiçe, but that the building did not appear to be military in design.[49] The governor then related that he had instructed the *kadı* in Kamengrad to keep track of any further developments.

The subsequent passage in Abdi's report, however, indicates that his own concerns were not far different from those of the Austrian general in Karlofoça. He told Istanbul that he had been receiving letters from militia commanders (*kapudan*s) and certain *mutasarrıf*s which indicated an increasing flow of both peasants (*reaya*) and brigands (*şekavet*) to the frontier regions in order to become outlaws. A subsequent rise in violent crime had been noticed by both Abdi and his counterpart in Karlofoça. The Bosnia governor included copies of these letters and translations in his report to Istanbul.

It is interesting that the issue of crime—in particular murder as opposed to property crimes—and of its containment was seen in a similar manner in both Istanbul and Vienna, as in Travnik and Karlofoça. On the frontier, violent crime straddled a very fine line between the jurisdiction of the local military units and of the civil authorities because of its implications for foreign relations, giving homicide investigators yet another influence on their work. Another example can be seen in a set of correspondence from the spring and summer of 1771, when the Ottoman state was at war with Russia and trying desperately to keep Austria neutral.[50] The Austrian ambassador wrote the Imperial Council that merchants traveling from Croatia into Bosnian territory had been murdered and robbed. He acknowledged that the threat of theft was a conventional risk for travelers, but that outright homicide was not acceptable. The Austrian official passed on under his seal the translations of two depositions taken from Croatian peasants relating to these events. In one, the peasants accused the *kapudan* in Ostrokatch [Ostrovac] of turning a blind eye to criminal activities perpetrated in his region, in particular the murder of two livestock traders in June of the previous year.

Istanbul responded by issuing immediate orders to the Bosnian governor and to the Vidin front commander Muhsinzade Mehmed Pasha—who had also previously been governor of Bosnia—instructing them to ensure the safety of Austrian citizens traveling in Ottoman lands, to use militia officers and members of their own households to capture and punish any people known to have committed rape, murder, arson, or theft within their jurisdiction, and to dismiss any officers in their commands who had knowingly allowed such crimes to occur. These orders did not mention any participation by the local *kadıs* in these matters, and suggest that the greater concerns of foreign affairs served to push these problems from the realm of "law" into the more immediate question of "order." This was to be a recurrent theme in eighteenth-century negotiations between Istanbul and Vienna in relation to the Bosnian frontier. Both sides wrangled over the military concerns, of course, but each side equally stressed the right for its people to enjoy safe passage in the region.[51] There is no indication from these documents that either state believed these matters to be under the jurisdiction of the respective law courts. Instead, there is a continued implication that travelers' safety—social tranquility—was the responsibility of the provincial governor and his officers. Thus in the case of murder, the Austrian officials pointed directly at the Bosnian governor and at the regional militia commanders as the parties responsible for obtaining justice, not the respective *kadıs*.

This emphasis in murder cases on those responsible for enforcement as opposed to those looked to for judgment also appeared in affairs involving only Ottomans. The death of two Bosnian merchants in Vidin on their way home in January of 1756 was brought to Istanbul's attention by the *kadı* in Vidin.[52] The Imperial Council directed that the investigation of this incident be handled by a member of the Izvornik *sancak* commander's household, identified by the title *çavuş*. This official was to draw men from the Bosnian militia companies stationed in the fortress of Izvornik, and was specifically told to include a *mutasarrıf* from the Izvornik *kadı*'s court.

Another example that reveals the process of a murder investigation can be seen in the request made by the people of the village of Oluvi in the summer of 1766.[53] The villagers related that the local *imam* had already determined that a murder had taken place, but then they implied that a failure to resolve the case—to punish the murderer—resulted from this man's inability to enforce his will on the guilty parties. The peasants and the *imam* petitioned Istanbul for the appointment of a member of the Bosnian *divan* (the governor's council) to investigate this matter and to punish the guilty. Yet the petition's stress lies most heavily on the enforcement of punishment, as the villagers had already determined to their own satisfaction the truth of the affair. Again in these examples, the various parties invoked different concepts of order to further their own ends in relation to the homicides. In a contest between legality and safety, the latter concern appears to have predominated when it was a question of murder.

Conclusion

The Bosnian governors during the eighteenth century appear to have understood and shared the populace's desire for social stability and corporate order. In addition, these officials more than anyone else recognized the need to avoid incidents on the frontier that might be considered provocative by their neighbors. Yet clearly the difficulty of navigating through three, or even four, disparate concepts of order to identify a homicide investigator and then to guide the actual investigation made dealing with murder in a timely and efficient manner troublesome. Had the representatives of the two main branches of authority, the *vali* and the *kadı*, been in constant conflict, the task would have been practically impossible. What the records reveal, however, is a very practical linking of the different authorities and resources of the legal and executive branches of Ottoman provincial government in order to create an effective method to resolve murder cases. During most of the eighteenth century, an Ottoman homicide investigator had the recognized ability to navigate a path between the *vali* and the *kadı* to bring some degree of justice—the primary interest of Bosnian society in cases of murder.

Notes

1. Joel Shinder, "Early Ottoman Administration in the Wilderness: Some Limits on Comparision," *International Journal of Middle Eastern Studies* 9, no. 4 (1978): 501.
2. Henry Fielding, *An Enquiry into the Causes of Robbers* (London: A. Millar, 1751), xxviii–xxix.
3. J.A. Sharpe, *Crime in Early Modern England, 1550–1750* (London: Longman, 1984), 41–72.
4. Suraiya Faroqhi, *Approaching Ottoman History: An Introduction to the Sources* (London: Cambridge University Press, 1999), 55.
5. Sharpe, *Crime in Early Modern England*, 76–77.
6. Peter Linbaugh, "The Tyburn Riot Against the Surgeons," in *Albion's Fatal Tree: Crime and Society in Eighteenth-Century England* (New York: Pantheon Books, 1975), 65–117.
7. Eyal Ginio, "The Administration of Criminal Justice in Ottoman Selânik (Salonica) During the Eighteenth Century," *Turcica* 30 (1998): 185–87.
8. Ronald C. Jennings, "Limitations of the Judicial Powers of the Kadi in 17th-Century Ottoman Kayseri," *Studia Islamica* 48 (1979): 151–63.

9. Dimitrije Djordjević, "Agrarian Factors in Nineteenth-century Balkan Revolutions," in *War and Society in East Central Europe*, vol. 1 (New York: Brooklyn College Press, 1979), 165.

10. Catherine Wendy Bracewell, *The Uskoks of Senj: Piracy, Banditry, and Holy War in the Sixteenth-century Adriatic* (Ithaca: Cornell University Press, 1992), 19–50. The author uses Austrian, Croatian, and Dalmatian archives to trace the continued ebb and flow of populations across the Bosnian frontier in response to relative changes in state policies.

11. See for example Odile Moreau, "Bosnian Resistance to Conscription in the Nineteenth Century," in *Arming the State: Military Conscription in the Middle East and Central Asia, 1775–1925*, ed. Erich J. Zürcher (New York: I. B. Tauris Publishers, 1999), 129–33. Though arguing that the province embodied "a state within a state," the author is still careful to distinguish Bosnian resistance to what were considered unfair administrative reforms instead of resistance to inclusion within the Ottoman empire.

12. Cemal Kafadar, *Between Two Worlds: The Construction of the Ottoman State* (Berkeley: University of California Press, 1995), 19–28.

13. Jennings, "Judicial Powers of the Kadi," 154.

14. Uriel Heyd, *Studies in Old Ottoman Criminal Law*, edited by V. L. Ménage (Oxford: Clarendon Press, 1973), 208–12.

15. Thomas Thorton, *The Present State of Turkey; or A Description of the Political, Civil, and Religious, Constitution, Government, and Laws of the Ottoman Empire*, vol. 1 (London: Joseph Mawan, 1809), 160–61.

16. Michael Robert Hickok, *Ottoman Military Administration in Eighteenth-century Bosnia* (Leiden: Brill Publishers, 1997), 116–35.

17. Faroqhi, *Approaching Ottoman History*, 49–51, 95–96.

18. Başbakanlık Osmanlı Arşivi (BOA), Bosna Ahkâm 1, 260–84. The collected *hükümler* include a single decree issued only to the officers of the Imperial Janissary troops stationed in Bosnia.

19. BOA, Bosna Ahkâm 2, 39–63.

20. BOA, Bosna Ahkâm 5, 97–122.

21. BOA, Bosna Ahkâm 6, 313–52.

22. BOA, Bosna Ahkâm 1, 267.

23. BOA, Bosna Ahkâm 5, 108.

24. See for example BOA, Bosna Ahkâm 2, 44; BOA, Bosna Ahkâm 5, 103, 107; and BOA, Bosna Ahkâm 6, 335.

25. For a more complete explanation see Hickok, *Military Administration*, 98–112.

26. BOA, Bosna Ahkâm 2, 46; and BOA, Bosna Ahkâm 6, 346. In this final example, the death of a *zeamet* holder Mustafa led to a violent dispute between his sons Mahmud and Ahmed over the possession of an estate worth 20,186 *akçe* per annum. The younger brother Mahmud controlled the lands and pre-

vented Ahmed from entering the estate. Ahmed had been a soldier serving on the Ottoman eastern frontier, who had subsequently returned to claim his inheritance. Because of his legal rights and his service to the state, the *kadı* had ruled in Ahmed's favor but proved unable, without the *vali*'s help, to force Mahmud to relinquish control.

27. Heyd, *Ottoman Criminal Law*, 235–38.

28. Jennings, "Judicial Powers of the Kadi," 161–63.

29. See for example BOA, Bab-i Defteri Başmuhasebe Bosna Hazinesi (D-BŞM-BNH), dosya 4, gömlek 86, 88, and 91. These files recorded the presence from 1754 to 1755 of *muhzır* Hüseyn Bey of Molla Mehmed's court in Mostar, *ser-muhzır* Salih Bey and *muhzır* Abdullah of Molla Abdullah's court in Sarajevo, and *muhzır* İbrahim Bey of Molla İshak's court in Travnik.

30. Mehmet Zeki Pakalın, *Osmanlı Tarih Deyimleri ve Terimleri Sözlüğü*, vol. 2 (Istanbul: Milli Eğitim Basımevi, 1971), 586. "Sancak adı verilen teşekkülün başında bulan memur hakkında unvan olarak kullanılır bir tabirdir." For examples of appointment documents for Bosnia that relate to this position see BOA, Cevdet Dahiliye 4162; BOA, Cevdet Zaptiye 430; BOA, Cevdet Dahiliye 3191; and BOA, Cevdet Dahiliye 13631.

31. BOA, D-BŞM-BNH dosya 4, gömlek 91, 95.

32. BOA, D-BŞM-BNH dosya 4, gömlek 1, 5, 92, 95, 96.

33. Joseph Schacht, *An Introduction to Islamic Law* (Oxford: Clarendon Press, 1964), 181–87.

34. J.N.D. Anderson, "Homicide in Islamic Law," *Bulletin of the School of Oriental and African Studies* 13 (1949–1951): 812–18.

35. Islamic jurisprudence attempts to address situations where the identity of the "avenger of blood" might not be immediately obvious, i.e. an individual without family or traveler. Yet, the nature of the crime in the Islamic context creates the potential for ambiguity, and demonstrates one of the difficulties of Islamic criminal law.

36. The same dynamic was at play in other parts of the Balkans during this period. See for example Ginio, "Administration of Criminal Justice," 194.

37. Heyd, *Ottoman Criminal Law*, 105.

38. Rudolph Peters, "Murder on the Nile: Homicide Trials in 19th Century Egyptian Shari'a Courts," *Die Welt des Islams* 30 (1990): 101.

39. BOA, Cevdet Dahiliye 11486.

40. Nagaty Sanad, *The Theory of Crime and Criminal Responsibility in Islamic Law: Shari'a* (Chicago: Office of International Criminal Justice, 1991), 49–66.

41. Christopher Boehm, *Blood Revenge: The Enactment and Management of Conflict in Montenegro and Other Tribal Societies* (Philadelphia: University of Pennsylvania Press, 1984), 191–97. The author suggests that a similar tension existed in a modern context over the "legality" of revenge killing in Montenegro within the Yugoslav legal system.

42. Mary Edith Durham, *Some Tribal Origins, Laws, and Customs of the Balkans* (London: George Allen & Unwin Ltd., 1928), 66–70.

43. Baron de Tott, *Memoirs of Baron de Tott*, vol. 1, sec. 1 (London: G. G. J. and J. Robinson, 1785), 198–99.

44. Ibid., vol. 1, sec. 1, 217, and sec 2, 96–97.

45. Topkapı Saray Arşivi, evrak 5277.

46. BOA, D-BŞM-BNH dosya 8, gömlek 17, 50.

47. BOA, Bosna Ahkâm 2. This register covers the years 1755 to 1765, and none of the murders listed by Mustafa Efendi are contained in it. This offers further proof that the Ottoman government in Bosnia initiated any kind of legal proceedings in these cases.

48. BOA, Hatt-i Hümâyûn 98. Though *karağulhane* can mean police station or outpost or guard station, the governor used *palanka* or *kale* to talk about strictly military structures. In addition, the context of the report makes it clear that his concern at the moment is criminal activity along the frontier, and, considering that 1751 was a year of "peasant uprisings" in the province, this concern is understandable.

49. This description of activities on the Croatian side of the Bosnian frontier conforms with the information available concerning the drastic reforms being made by the Austrian state in the Karlstadt district after the Ottoman victory in 1740. See Gunther Erich Rothenberg, *The Austrian Military Border in Croatia, 1522–1747* (Urbana: University of Illinois Press, 1960), 120–21; for the impact of these military reforms on civil order, in particular the mutinies of 1751, see Gunther Rothenberg, "The Habsburg Military Border System: Some Reconsiderations," in *War and Society in East Central Europe,* vol. 1, ed. Gunther Rothenberg and Béla Király (New York: Columbia University Press, 1979), 361–92.

50. BOA, Cevdet Hariciye 6517.

51. See for example BOA, Cevdet Hariciye 820, 3174, and 7082.

52. BOA, Cevdet Dahiliye 6565.

53. BOA, Cevdet Dahiliye 13741.

Whose Territory and Whose Peasants? Ottoman Boundaries on the Danube in the 1760s

VIRGINIA H. AKSAN

Introduction

In 1759, an Ottoman commission was sent by the sultan to investigate claims concerning the illegal usurpation of farmland by demobilized soldiers, vagrants, and migrating peasants along the shores of the Danube from Fethülislam to Ismail, which is roughly the present-day frontier of Bulgaria and Romania. We know this because of a report that survives in manuscript, detailing the charges of the commission, its findings and recommendations. The text is a rare instance of Ottoman bureaucrats expressing their understanding of a complex nexus of trade, agriculture, and defense on an imperial frontier, and it prompts further inquiry. Who were the usurpers, why were they there, and how did the commission deal with the problem? Can we understand from this document how the Ottoman dynasty conceived of the

My thanks to the anonymous reader of this paper, for a very careful and judicious critique.

northern frontier? And, what is the significance of such an attempt to impose territorial integrity north and south of the Danube in the latter half of the eighteenth century?

While the document is intriguing because it affords us a glimpse into a very complex, centuries-old ethnic crossroads, it also reminds us that, in spite of multilateral treaties, or tributary Phanariot princes, or Austrian, Ottoman, and Russian administrations, peasants in the early modern world could escape oppression in ways that eluded the rationalization of boundaries. As we shall see, they were assisted in this case by the "timeless" ecology of a particular geographic formation, and by a scarcity of population that increased their value. Nonetheless, it reminds us that "whose territory?" remains a very modern, and perhaps "fleeting," notion of the organization of agricultural systems.[1]

Ottoman imperial strategy drove the investigation, largely for fiscal reasons, but there is more in this text than just the reestablishment of tax status. The manuscript has been recognized as the first Ottoman geography of Wallachia,[2] though it is just as interesting for what it has to say about Ottoman perceptions of treaty and tributary obligations, and about religious frontiers dividing Ottomans (or Muslims), and Europeans (or Christians). We are afforded a snapshot of an empire in a transitional period, when the defense of the frontier became paramount, and before the principalities themselves became fully independent territories. This paper will begin by briefly rehearsing the geopolitical setting of Wallachia, and the Austro-Russian and Ottoman conflicts that had the most impact on the area. A description of the work of the commission will follow, including some later evidence of the insolubility of the problem addressed in the report. In conclusion, we will return to the questions posed above.

Geopolitical context

The territory of most interest here is a microscopic triangle of land in Wallachia formed at its westernmost point by Fethülislam (Kladovo in present-day Serbia), south and east to Vidin (Bulgaria), and north to Craiova (Romania). Fethülislam was an Ottoman fortress downstream from Orsova and the famous Iron Gates of the Danube, both the scene of intense confrontations between Habsburg and Ottoman for the first half of the eighteenth century. Craiova was a town in the province (also district) of Oltenia, bound by the

River Olt on the east, the Carpathian mountain ranges in the north, and the Danube River to the west and south.

The fortress of Vidin, since 1718 one of the pressure points of the northern Ottoman border, was central to the problem under investigation. Large numbers of Ottoman soldiers, perhaps as many as five to six thousand, had gathered there after the Treaty of Belgrade in 1739, if not before. Demobilized or deserting irregulars, local militias, and Janissaries were all involved in a network of agriculture and commerce contrary to the agreements with the principalities of Wallachia and Moldavia, which in theory prohibited the settlement of Muslims on Christian lands. The porosity of an unstable frontier led to frequent outbursts of rebellion along the shores of the Danube, often incited by Janissaries and their fellow travelers. It is this that forms the background of the report of the commission. Anyone familiar with the later history of the region, of course, will know it because of local warlord Osman Pasvantoğlu [var. Pasvanoğlu/Pasvantoğlu/ Pasbanoğlu] (d. 1807), who controlled Vidin and extended his power base into the surrounding areas on the left and right banks of the Danube as far as Belgrade, for over two decades, beginning in the 1790s. His origins lay in precisely the kind of environment evoked in this report.[3]

Governed by a prince (or *voyvoda*), who was elected by the native aristocracy (*boyars*) and confirmed by the Ottoman sultan, Wallachia was a territory that, since the fifteenth century, had been a tributary principality (*haracgüzar*) of the Ottoman Empire.[4] The region has a particularly rich historiography, at least partially because it was disputed territory in the nineteenth-century international crises over the future of the Ottoman Empire, but also because of the multitude of peoples (and historians) for whom it has served as a bellwether of "Balkanism."[5] Eighteenth-century ethnographers were astonished by the range of "scrambled confusion" of peoples to be found in Wallachia and Moldavia. "One must in effect regard these peoples as a mélange of Romans and Greeks, with the Dacians, the Getae, the Gepids, the Jazgyes, the Sarmatians, the Saxons, the Goths, the Huns, the Avars, the Slavs, the Pechenegs, the Turks, and all the Oriental and Septentrional barbarians who have successively occupied the land."[6] The statement embodies eighteenth-century hyperbole, but it is illustrative of the ethnic mix of the region.

The territory in which the triangle is situated was also known as Lesser Wallachia (Kara Eflak, or Küçük Eflak in Turkish) and forms roughly the western one-third of present-day Romania. The western half of Romania, at least the flat plains stretching north from the Danube to the Carpathians, was prized for the fertility that could yield quantities of grains and cereals. In Ottoman history, the territory is routinely described as the "bread-basket" of Istanbul, essential to the well-being of the huge hub of the empire. A report published in 1820, by William Wilkinson, former British Consul of Bucharest, noted the lushness of the Wallachian plains: "The fertility of the soil is such as to procure nourishment for ten times the number of the present population, and leave wherewith to supply other countries besides. . . . Nature has furnished them with every possible means of becoming prosperous."[7]

Without a doubt, armies on horseback, Ottoman, Austrian, or Russian, were equally covetous of the cattle and fodder presumed to be abundantly available in Wallachia. Writing to Catherine the Great in June 1770, just prior to a major confrontation with the Ottomans, Field-Marshal P. A. Rumiantsev's observations about the conditions in the war zones, including Wallachia and Moldavia, are particularly apt. He described the land of the Russian troop passage as wasted, with depopulated villages. The inhabitants, fleeing both the enemy and the plague, had abandoned their fields completely. There was no evidence of their ability to feed themselves, much less supply the troops. Since the previous September, the Russians had deprived the local populations (north of Hotin) of their horses, oxen, and wagons, to transport the only food supply the troops had had over a long and wretched road.[8] Supply problems were only alleviated, he added, as the Russians captured well-stocked Ottoman depots along the Prut River, in their 1770 march to the Danube, suggesting both a sufficiency on the Ottoman side, and a continued ability of Wallachia and Moldavia to produce the needed grain supplies, if effectively managed.[9]

Austro-Russian and Ottoman Conflicts in Wallachia

Situated on the frontiers of the Austro-Ottoman, later Russo-Austrian-Ottoman-struggle, Wallachia figured prominently in the wars and treaties of the eighteenth century. That was especially true after the signing of the Treaty of Karlowitz in 1699, which in effect froze most of the fluctuating Austro-Ottoman border for the next two hundred years. Between 1700 and 1800, the territories of present-day Romania experienced extraordinary levels of disruption from the major conflicts played out largely on the northern shores of the Danube from Belgrade to Ismail. Three are important to this discussion. The first, 1716–18, was the Habsburg-Ottoman quarrel that ended in the Treaty of Passarowitz. The Austrians occupied and kept Belgrade and western Wallachia (Oltenia) by that treaty. The second major conflagration was the Ottoman-Austrian-Russian war of 1736–39, which ended in the Treaty of Belgrade, when Belgrade returned to Ottoman hands and the Wallachian territories reverted to Ottoman tributary status, but subordinate to Istanbul under the Phanariot regime. Finally, the first major Russo-Ottoman war, 1768–74, when Russian penetration south of the Danube threatened the very center of the empire itself, was played out along the strategic line of Ottoman fortresses from Belgrade to Ochakov (Özü).

Wars and frontiers make for an incredible mix of collaborators, loyalists, profiteers, bandits, rebels, and revolutionaries (nationalists) that both enrich and obscure our histories. Such "floating population(s)" have been the subject of a full spectrum of theories about decimation of cultures, mobility and lack thereof, the degree of serfdom imposed, and the nature of the contest over deserted lands.[10] Most historians acknowledge, however, that the eighteenth century was a period of particularly oppressive tax burdens and forced labor (*corvée*) in Wallachia (and Moldavia), directly related to the increasing flow of armies across the territories. That oppression in turn accelerated peasant flight and increased the desertion of villages. Raids by plundering private armies of semi-independent Ottoman pashas from south of the Danube were endemic. The principal cause for much of the oppression of the period is attributed to the Ottoman decision to replace local princes with loyalist Greek (Phanariot) families from Istanbul after 1711.[11]

In 1716, Nicholas Mavrocordat was appointed directly by the Ottoman sultan as the Phanariot *Voyvoda* of Wallachia. His legitimacy was determined primarily by that appointment. The *voyvoda* was forbidden to raise an army, but allowed a Janissary guard of two hundred soldiers. The new governors maintained a court in Bucharest, unique in its Ottoman, Greek, and Romanian blend, an example of what Ehud Toledano has called the "Ottoman-local elite," to describe a similar process in the Arab provinces.[12] Most of the Phanariots managed to remain in power for no more than the original three-year appointment, although reappointment after a hiatus was not uncommon. In the course of such short and uncertain tenure, they extracted a heavy toll from the peasantry, creating a court environment that mirrored Istanbul in its ostentatious and rapacious politics. They continued to pay a tribute to Istanbul, but that was generally understood as a token. Other kinds of routine and/or extraordinary taxes, such as the sale of grain, cattle, or timber at fixed prices, was part of the cost of semi-autonomy. Peasantry caught in the middle of this interplay among imperial courts, local aristocracies, and occupation armies were continuously at the mercy of the current hegemonic force.

In military terms, the Ottoman strategy of expanding dominion over heretofore buffer zones made some sense. The new border with the Habsburgs after 1700 made redefinition of populations who fled to the Ottoman territories imperative. Wallachia served throughout this period as a major source of supplies for campaigns, and its stabilization would guarantee its ability to do so. Demilitarization of the tributary territories did not make as much sense, except as a means of enforcing dependence. Phanariot influence privileged a new class of aristocrats who had little control over the countryside, and little means of subduing rebellions. Small popular, volunteer military units assisted both Austrian and Russian armies throughout the wars of the century.[13] The changing nature of the Ottoman military, its decentralization into locally raised militia and "volunteer" mobs, and the emergence of local centers of power has been the focus of detailed attention elsewhere, but is a central backdrop to this discussion.[14]

Confrontations — 1689–1718

In 1689, no one was more knowledgeable of the vagaries of the Danubian shores than Luigi Ferdinando Marsigli, nobleman, scientist, diplomat, cartographer, and factotum for both Venice and the Habsburgs. That year, in the midst of the long Austro-Ottoman War (1683–99), Austrian troops had penetrated deep into Serbian territory, finding themselves at the end of the campaign season isolated in Nish (Niş). Marsigli led the troops of Commander Lewis of Baden to Fethülislam, where they crossed into Wallachia on a bridge of boats (pontoons). Prince Constantin Brancoveanu was "persuaded" to supply winter quarters for desperate Habsburg soldiers, the opening thrust of a century-long struggle for mastery of western Wallachia.[15] It took another ten years before the war ended, and a cessation of hostilities was signed at Karlowitz. The famous treaty wrested large parts of Hungary from Ottoman sovereignty, but left the province of Temesvár (Timişoara) more or less intact. Ottoman authorities were extremely sensitive to the new defensive environment, and relocated considerable number of soldiers from surrendered fortresses (such as Eger in Hungary) to Ottoman territories. Af-

ter Temesvár fell to the Austrians in 1716, in the renewal of Habsburg-Ottoman hostilities, perhaps as many as 5,300 soldiers moved to fortresses along
the river. As a result, banditry and other abuses of the population increased,
as indicated by the number of complaints in petitions sent to Istanbul. The
sultan and his advisors acknowledged the need for reinforcements in the
area to prevent the subjects from turning themselves into *hayduts*, "resulting
in disorder on the marches."[16]

In fact, that is precisely what was happening. Gradeva points to the
increased militarization of Vidin after the temporary Austrian occupation in
1689, but especially after the fall of Temesvár. By one estimate from 1750,
there were at least 5,440 "Janissaries" in Vidin. Even more striking is the
increase after 1770: 7,863 soldiers listed for 1771, to a high of 9,476 soldiers in 1776. Vidin had become the pivotal fortress of the western defense
system.[17] The consequences of that kind of demobilization and reordering
of the border are analyzed in at least one Ottoman document investigated
by Cvetkova. In 1715, the *reaya* of Vidin had been called on to pledge (by
communal guarantee) not to tolerate the *hayduts*, an ongoing practice of the
Ottoman administration to force collective responsibility onto its subjects.
Border insurrections in the Vidin-Lom area in 1716/17 forced, in addition,
an Ottoman investigation into a revolt that appears to have been an armed
insurrection of a small band of *hayduts,* who had (re-)crossed over the Danube into Ottoman territory. The rebellion was curtailed only after mobili-
zing the "loyal" countryside.[18]

Restoration of the fortress and surrounding area of Orsova on the Danube also became a priority, and indicates the degree to which the Ottomans
had begun to rely on Wallachia for war supplies. Timber, oxcarts, and saltpe-
ter were in scant supply in the territories recently the site of major battles.[19]
The Istanbul archives and the *kadı* court records of Vidin abound with the
give and take of Ottoman commanders and local officials over the question
of war supplies, a constant throughout the eighteenth century. The pressure
on northern Bulgaria became particularly acute after the Russians occupied
Moldavia and major fortresses on the mouth of the Danube in 1770.[20]

Confrontations — 1718–39

By the treaty of Passarowitz in 1718, the Austrians occupied and retained
Belgrade, Temesvár, and Wallachia west of the Olt River, including Crai-

ova. The capture of Belgrade and Temesvár province meant a further dis-
location of soldiers, mercenaries, and their followers, who crowded below
the new frontier on the south shores of the Danube, especially, as noted
above, at the fortress at Vidin. Oltenia entered a period Chirot has called "A
Premature Experiment in Modern Colonialism," during which the Austrians
carried out a census, and attempted to rationalize the *corvée* obligations
of free, landless peasants, in order to increase agricultural production for
the army of occupation. By 1722, the burden was increased to as many as
fifty-two days a year, as contrasted to three to nine days normal to other
parts of Wallachia at the time. The brief period of Austrian occupation also
began the clarification of the role and number of *boyar*s, as they relied on
a small number of families to rule.[21] After the reversion to Ottoman control
in 1739–40, the Austrian work rules in Oltenia were abolished, and such
forced labor was stabilized at twelve days a year for most of the century.[22]
Corvée was certainly one source of rural disruption, as it is not hard to
imagine how semi-independent villagers would react to an increase in such
obligations.

Orsova and its environs were a major focus of much of the campaigning
of the 1736–39 War, leaving the territory deserted and depleted, "terrorized
by runaway villagers mixed in with assorted Turkish deserters, Albanians,
Serbs, Bulgars, and Gypsies who lived by brigandage (the Haiduci)."[23] By
one estimate, 77,000 of 147,000 peasant families emigrated from the whole
of Wallachia in the period 1741–46.[24]

Phanariot *Voyvoda* Constantin Mavrocordat, appointed six times betwe-
en 1730 and 1763, undertook a series of reforms in the period 1739–46 in
order to resettle scattered populations. These included tax relief initiatives
as well as attempts to redefine the relations between peasant and landlord.
The significance of his reforms is much debated, either as representing the
empowerment of the peasantry in the age of the enlightenment, or the beginning of its enserfment.[25] Mavrocordat also created a Russian-style service
class of high and low *boyar*s, the former with court offices and tax-exempt.
Both the Austrian colonialism and the Mavrocordat efforts at reform would
have generated much criss-crossing of the Danube, the subject of the investigation below. Under the Mavrocordats and their successors, Phanariot
Wallachia was characterized by increased grain (cereal) production for export, but also by a monetarized system of governance requiring rapid accu-
mulations for tributary payments, the buying of offices and bribery. Thus,
the nature of the reforms and their implications and consequences continue

to be rehearsed by historians. It is worth a reminder that Mavrocordat's reforms concerning peasant-landlord relations had received the blessing of the sultan.[26]

Description of the Ottoman Commission

The work of the commission built on perceptions of the problem of agricultural production and property usurpation that probably dated from the reversion of Austrian Oltenia to Turkish suzerainty in 1739. Without a doubt, the above-mentioned reforms bear on the events as well, but in 1756, the Ottomans extended their *zahire* ("provisioning") regime to the principalities. The *zahire* system estimated specific amounts of grain (barley, flour, wheat) to be delivered to Istanbul twice a year, spring and autumn, at fixed, below market, prices, and was already the practice in Bulgaria and elsewhere in the Balkans. Its imposition in Wallachia has been argued as an Ottoman attempt at a colonial regime similar to that of the Austrian occupation. The imposition was likely caused by the increasing difficulty of raising such supplies elsewhere in the empire, an Ottoman attempt to regularize the flow of basic foodstuffs as access to European markets increasingly threatened the grain trade to Istanbul altogether.[27]

Craiova was important enough to the Phanariots to be the seat of a *kaymakam*, an official appointed by the princes in Bucharest to oversee the district of Craiova on their behalf, itself divided into five administrative districts, each with two *Ispravnik*s (or deputies) appointed annually by the prince. Their task was collection of taxes and tributary payments.[28] The findings of the Ottoman commission sent to investigate the disruption in the principalities make it clear that the Vidin-Craiova connections were complex. The local residents had the potential for resisting the claims and exactions of local *boyar*s as well as the Bucharest court, by exploiting the competing claims of the Ottoman border administration in Fethülislam and Vidin.

An officially sanctioned commission was appointed only after a decade of complaints from a variety of sources, as recorded in the provincial records at the archives in Istanbul. Several are prefaced with the reiteration of the obligations of the sultan (Mahmud I, 1730–54) to then *voyvoda* Scarlat Ghica of Wallachia (1758–61 and again in 1765–66), who had filed a complaint in Istanbul about Janissary abuses in the Craiova plain. His was apparently just one of the petitions that had been brought to the sultan's

attention, as the document refers to the metropolitan of the Romanian Orthodox Church, the bishops, priests, and *boyars*, as authors of individual or
collective petitions.[29] Wallachia is characterized in these sultanic proclamations both as enjoying "full freedom" and as the "pantry," or "larder" (*kiler*),
of the sultan. It was the sultan's duty and sovereign right to guard against the
oppression of Wallachia's people. This document acknowledged the repeated failure to do so, citing previous efforts to investigate the abuses of the
soldiers (*asker taifesi*) on the north shores of the Danube as part of treaty arrangements. Since then, soldiers and others, characterized as "not-soldiers"
(*gayri-asker*), "oppressors" (*mütegallibe*), and "vagrants" (*serseri gezer*),
had invaded Wallachia, with the collaboration of their officers, especially
in Craiova, where they had established [illegal] quarters (*kışla*), farms, and
beehives. They had thrown the *reaya* off their land, and enslaved their children.[30] Furthermore, they were extorting protection from Muslim merchants
in Wallachian territories and engaging in illegal trade.[31]

The head of the commission, Giridi Ahmed (Ahmed of Crete), described himself as a teacher (*müderris*). He had been appointed by *Şeyhülislam*
İsmail Asım and the grand vezir to carry out the imperial orders to restore
order. He was specifically to: 1) relieve the people of Wallachia of the tyranny of bandits and scoundrels (*eşkiya* and *erazil*); 2) seize and surrender
usurped land and properties to their rightful owners; and 3) return beehives
and animals to their owners by means of arbitration by a judge.[32]

Giridi Ahmed took his job very seriously, to judge from the tenor and
passion of the narrative.[33] After three to four pages of encomiums to his su-
periors (Sultan Mustafa III [1757–74], Grand Vezir Koca Ragıb [1757–63],
and *Şeyhülislam* Veliyüddin [Feb. 1760–61, 1767–68], who replaced İsmail
Asım [1759–60] upon the latter's death),[34] Giridi Ahmed began the report
with a detailed geography of Wallachia (as summarized in the Orhonlu articles), that consumes twenty folios of the manuscript. Of special note is
the description of Craiova. It was one of the five districts (*kaza*) of Lesser
Wallachia on the west side of the Olt river: the other four being Çerniç, Tir-
gûzi (Tirgu-Jiu), Hokna, and Karakal (Caracal) (folio 6a). Craiova was a big
town that could be circumnavigated in an hour and a half. It was the headquarters of the administration of a "*bann*" (ancient name for local governor),
who along with the chief *boyars* and their entourages resided there. Each
of their residences was of four to five thousand cubits, built of imported
stone inside and out, and included outbuildings and gardens and orchards.
The residences were separated by farmlands, so they resembled palaces.

The poor lived in hollowed-out mud.[35] There were at the time two *oda*s of *ocaklı* (presumably Janissaries, fortress guards). A big building like the *khan* of a *vezir* had served as the headquarters for the commander during the occupation [Austrian] and now was on the verge of ruin. It was similar to a castle, situated in a secure place, with towers and wall (10b). The castle had been well fortified and stocked by the Austrians with guns and supplies. The walls had since, of necessity, been rebuilt, but the rooms were left in ruins. As an aside, the author noted: rebuilt as a *khan*, they would make a very worthy protected shelter for merchants. (11a) Craiova had fifteen churches, of which the oldest had been built three hundred years before. The length of the town was taken up with a market, split into two: the commodity market and that of the merchants. The shops had stone storerooms to protect the goods, such as the cloth and other stuffs that came from Leipzig and other places, and were bought and sold here and there. Right in the middle of the market was a space for the Friday market, which in some seasons, on some days, experienced 25 *keselik* (purses)[36] sales of local animals, grains, clarified butter, and honey among other produce (11a). Two stone *khan*s, with many rooms, remained. Four others, wooden, for Muslims, had been destroyed (11b).[37]

The report proper begins on folio 21 of the manuscript. Since the time of the conquest [likely meaning 1739], the author began, the people of this region had been living in peace and prosperity, without external interference. More recently, the rabble, bandits and plunderers, especially Albanians (*Arnavut*s) and fugitives, had entered the region little by little, with the connivance of officers (*zabitan*), negligent *ayan*s, indulgent and willfully blind *voyvoda*s, and *boyar*s. Such types had descended on Wallachia, stirring up terror and misery, capturing their lands, enslaving the poor, their wives and children, and generally wreaking havoc across the land, in violation of the sharia (21a). The exaggerated tone of Giridi Ahmed is completely in keeping with the elevated exposition of the earlier encomiums. Much of it was read out loud as part of official ceremonies of allegiance and compliance, as in fact attested by Giridi Ahmed in a number of instances in the text.

The commission left Istanbul in August 1759 (28a). It included former *Cebeci Başı* el-Hac Mehmed Agha and *Turnacı Başı* Hüseyn Pasha, military officials, as well as Giridi Ahmed. When they arrived at Vidin on the Danube, the commander of the fortress officially welcomed them. The investigation was formally proclaimed, and consultations began. The military men conveyed their understanding of the situation to Istanbul. It seems that the offenders occupying Wallachia were of two sorts: those who were soldiers, and those who were vagrants. The vagrants were dependent on the soldiers in the towns. Furthermore, their leaders resided in Craiova, and they were tied to former *yamakan* of the fortress at Vidin.[38] By early October, the commission had received permission (from the commander of the Janissaries in Istanbul) to proceed against the members of the Janissary *ocak*, believing that the primary cause lay there. Two hundred soldiers residing in Craiova, along with the rest of the Vidin soldiery, were assembled in the fortress. The official declarations of the charges were read out in the presence of the members of the commission, all of the local commanders, and the military judge of the fortress (*kazıasker*) (31b). The judge and two officers oversaw the interrogation of members of the offending group, who reiterated their understanding that they were forbidden to reside permanently in Wallachia. They also pledged to disavow the *serseri*, and to be properly registered (as the legitimate Craiova guard). They further agreed to restrict trade to the designated markets (31b-32a).

The next step was the actual count of the properties and goods in Craiova proper, again following orders from Istanbul to destroy all the illegal properties there. This section of the report, dating from early October 1759, includes petitions that started to emerge from the *yamakan* about outstanding accounts and debts with local *boyar*s and *reaya*. It cannot have been an easy process to disentangle the relationships. The list of the soldiers' properties (described as their own: *kendi mülkleri*) that the officials confiscated included 131 houses, seven shops (*dükkân*), three ovens, three slaughterhouses (*selhane*), three honey works (*balhane*), one three-room house, with a storeroom, and kiosk, and one five-room house, with two sheds and two storehouses. In addition 685 *çiftlik* (farms) and 112 flourmills were confiscated from the surrounding areas. Of 450 of an estimated 1000 *moşye* in Oltenia, judged illegally occupied, 393 had been restored to their owners, with the expectation that the 57 remaining ones would soon be as well.[39] A great deal of controversy concerning moveable belongings, such as beehives and animals and grain (*hayvanat ve hububat*) spills off the pages of the manuscript. Such items were at first hidden from the authorities by the offending soldiers. Once discovered, their redistribution involved considerable adjudication and restitution by the commission and the authorities in Istanbul.

The commission was also called upon to investigate the complaints of peasants of Fethülislam, in a further complication of the relationships reflected in this manuscript. Although not explicitly stated, the trouble arose precisely as the commission was at work.[40] It appears that there had been considerable, recent traffic between Fethülislam and the Craiova plain that had erupted in a fracas among older and more recent immigrants. This in turn was raised to the level of disputation between the governor in Fethülislam and the Wallachian *voyvoda*, concerning the rights of taxation and enforcement on the right and left banks of the Danube. In other words, whose territory and whose sovereignty? The state was faced with the fundamental question of peasants who were exercising their rights of usufruct in two different jurisdictions, possibly three, because of the proximity of the new Austrian border around Orsova. Complaints from Fethülislam (from the governor, also called *voyvoda*) stated that the *boyars* were taxing the peasants excessively and unjustly in Wallachia, forcing them to flee for refuge. The Wallachian *voyvoda,* represented in Istanbul by his *kapı kethüda,* along with the judge from Vidin, denied the claim. In fact, they asserted, the Fethülislam governor had forced the peasants to cross over, and given them *ispence* papers.[41]

The commission interviewed residents from up and down the Danube around Vidin concerning the legitimacy of the claims. Their sense of the matter was expressed as follows: tilling the soil by peasant families on two sides of the Danube was a long-term practice. Up until seven or eight years previously (1752–53), many had moved across the Danube, established themselves in villages along the southern shores, and cut off connections with Wallachia. They had no quarrel with their situation. The new problem had arisen only in the past two years, when Wallachian *reaya*, who continued to pay tithes (*aşar*) for holdings in their home territories, crossed over (*rihlet*—migrate, immigrate) to the Ottoman side. Recent reforms by the *voyvoda*, designed to encourage their return to Wallachia, had these so-called Fethülislam *reaya* claiming their rights to Wallachian lands. As a result, many among them were conniving at establishing connections, claiming of some: "this is our shepherd"; or of others: "This is our brother, or our uncle." Then there were those who were trying to escape taxes in Fethülislam, by desiring to return to their original home.

The governor of Fethülislam makes an appearance in the report, claiming that if the *ispenceli* were his *reaya*, then they should not be obligated to pay tax (actually, he was unwilling to let them pay taxes) to the Wallachian *voyvoda*. The *voyvoda* then weighed in with his arguments. "These *reaya* are mine of old, and I have the rights over their disposal, subsistence, and obedience, even of those who cross over. As long as I possess the imperial edict of the sultan, the rights and obligations of the *reaya* are mine to dispense. Those who have immigrated [and, by extension, wish to return], *ispenceli* or not, will not be molested by me." As a further argument, the *voyvoda* continued: "The taxes the Fethülislam governor has extracted rightly belong to me. By paying only the *ispence*, these *reaya* do not pay the customary taxes of the region owed to the imperial treasury. Moreover, *reaya* who remain behind find their tax burden increased." The solution recommended by the commission was simply to forbid the passage by an imperial order preventing the movement of the peasantry. Wallachian *reaya* who crossed over must cut all connections with Wallachia, while those from Fethülislam who wished to return must cut all ties to Fethülislam.[42]

The *voyvoda* had the right of it, according to traditional Ottoman practice, and drew on the language of the limited sovereignty exercised by him. Since the fifteenth century, a treaty between Wallachia and Istanbul had established a tributary relationship that persisted into the eighteenth century. The Ottomans recognized the right of the *voyvoda* to collect the *cizye* (poll tax on non-Muslims) on behalf of the sultan. A moveable, likely multi-ethnic, and multi-religious population was also accustomed to the trans-Danubian passage, and to being assessed an *ispence* tax or fee when they left the suzerainty of the Wallachian *voyvoda*. This was one of the most frequent impositions on such populations who crossed at all the fortresses along the Danube. The trouble was that the two jurisdictions wanted the right of taxation, whereas, by the mid-eighteenth century, the Wallachian exemption from paying the *cizye* a second time when resident in Ottoman lands was well-established by customary law, as frequently mentioned in petitions to the sultan. In Istanbul, the tributary principalities were assumed to be part of Ottoman dominion, and their inhabitants treated as *zimmi*s for tax collection purposes.[43] The commission ruled according to precedent and custom, restricting the movement of peasants across the Danube to restore order to a taxation regime: a boundary, however unenforceable.

Historians' description of the "classical" Ottoman conceptions of legitimacy and suzerainty agree on the consistency with which the Ottomans reiterated their concern for peasant subsistence and well-being, clearly appealed to by the wily *voyvoda*. Similarly, the same concern is reflected in the commission's charge to remove peasant holdings from the Vidin guards and their cohorts in Craiova, and restore them to their proper owners. The solutions looked like justice in action, even though enactment may have proved impossible on the ground. The rulings called for the imposition of idealized tax categories, and the restoration of *nizam* (order) over *fitne* (disorder, or revolt) that was caused by bandits or rebels (*hayduts*, or *eşkiya*; here *serseri*). Implicit in the language is an assumption that the commission was also resetting the boundary between Muslim (*askeri*) and Christian (*reaya*). The claims made by both the peasants and the soldiers themselves, operating with families and deep connections among the three locales, make one suspect that it was far more complex. I speculate that both the *reaya* and the so-called *serseri*, under the "protection" of the soldiers, were of mixed ethnic and religious origins, and dissimulation was part of the arsenal of survival. The region of Oltenia had an ancient agricultural history and a character all of its own, which did not fit well with the attempt to impose modern lines of territorial or religious demarcation.

Conclusions

That brings us to the final question posed at the beginning of this paper, about the significance of the report and its findings. I have already argued that the "frontier" in question was a historically idealized boundary, reconstituted by the commission along the binaries *askeri* (Muslim) and *reaya* (Christian). There are two further points that I would like to raise that may have prompted the investigation at this particular moment. One concerns evolving international legal instruments, the other the military strategy that lay at the heart of Ottoman initiatives on the Danube after Karlowitz (1699).

I believe it is possible to see in these documents a discussion of the question of "subjects" and their rights and obligations to "sovereigns," which had become part of the arsenal of Ottoman diplomacy. The Belgrade treaty contains three articles (XV, XVI, and XVIII) referring to the resolution of problems arising from incursions across borders by hostile forces or rebellious subjects. Article XVIII, referring to "*haydones*" has already been mentioned. Article XV refers to the appointment of "commissaries" on respective borders to settle "disputes, differences, and disagreements." They were to be looked after by those ". . . who shall not be difficult men but serious, honest, prudent, able, and peaceable . . . to listen to each and every dispute, to discuss them and to settle them amicably." Article XVI speaks of "devastation or depopulation of either territory" as "expressly and strictly forbidden" and the necessity of prompt seizure and return of "all things stolen" in all equity to those to whom they belong.[44]

Grand Vezir Koca Ragıb, who along with the *şeyhülislam* had approved the sending of the commission, was part of the negotiating team at Nemirov in 1738, and then at the Belgrade treaty negotiations in 1739. Giridi Ahmed was a protegé of the grand vezir, and the misfortunate signer of the later, disastrous 1774 Küçük Kaynarca treaty, an experienced diplomat and ambassador sent to Vienna (1757–58) and Berlin (1763–64). Both were Ottoman bureaucrats who were used to the new language and conditions of multilateral treaties. They may have been implicitly trying to stabilize a "border" in keeping with European practice, even though the language of the text refers explicitly to the sharia, and to the traditional understanding between *voyvoda* and sultan. The tributary territories of the Ottoman Empire operated as zones of influence under Ottoman suzerainty, but the imposition of the Phanariot regime after 1711 argues for the attempt to clarify or extend Ottoman power into the territory in more concrete ways.[45] I propose this interpretation because the recently signed multilateral treaties required Ottoman bureaucrats to abandon (or modify) the idealized image of the boundless (ever-expanding) borders of empire, and the idea of "temporary" and unilateral peace treaties, for fixed boundaries driven by "permanent" peace and trade instruments that essentially lasted until the end of the empire. Lesser Wallachia, as we have seen, had been (briefly) Austrian, and Russian claims to it became increasingly pressing after 1760, especially from their bases in Jassy and Bucharest. Just where "Ottoman" land began and ended in 1760, as argued out of such documents, needs far further study. Fierce Ottoman resistance to later treaty demands by victorious Russians, especially after the war of 1806–12, reinforces the impression that the Ottomans not only recognized the changes to definitions of "frontier" environment, but also became adept at exploiting the international diplomatic environment, even in moments of great weakness.

What must have concerned the Ottomans most, however, was manpower and supplies for the defense of the fortress line from Belgrade to the mouth of the Danube. Ottoman historian Vasıf Efendi tells us of the complications for local residents in having Russian soldiers on Wallachian soil after 1769, in the course of the 1768–74 war. The Russians occupied Bucharest for the five years of that war. Since the Russians had entered Wallachia, Vasıf explained, "they had actively tried to seduce the subjects of the sultan. A number sided with them and provided the enemy with supplies. Such was the case in Slatina (on the River Olt). A small corps of the enemy was harbored in that village and threatened Craiova. The *bann* of the village was a

Greek called Manolaki, who had been appointed by the *voyvoda*, himself a traitor who had fled to the Russians. This Manolaki, incensed by the treason of his Prince, requested aid from the pasha of Vidin. Gathering around him the Albanians scattered throughout Wallachia, and with some help from the Vidin pasha, he successfully defended Craiova. His fame reached the ears of the grand vezir, who was persuaded that any individual, no matter his religion, merited compensation for his loyalty, and commanded his appearance at Babadağı headquarters in order to be recognized."[46] Vasıf's account suggests the continued complex relationship of Vidin and Craiova ten years on from the date of the commission.

Similarly, the grain supply for both the army and Istanbul was particularly worrisome, as blockades of the Dardanelles increased. The *zahire* regime imposed in 1756 is one piece of evidence of the attempt to regulate the supply from the Balkans. The need became especially acute when Wallachia became a war zone, making grain increasingly scarce.[47] In March 1769 orders to the *voyvoda* for 100,000 *kile* of flour and 225,000 of barley, are included in the estimates for the upcoming campaign, for the bivouacs (*menzils*) of the army passage.[48] These are reiterated, with increasing stridency, as order after order remains unfulfilled. Obviously, part of the reason was the ongoing battles over the Danubian fortresses. Russian regiments harried the Danube fortresses, especially around Giurgiu, during the winter of 1769–70. In early February 1770, Ottoman troops from Craiova, Nikopol, Rusçuk (Ruse), and Giurgiu, perhaps as many as twenty thousand men, confronted the Russians at Bucharest, and were routed. By mid-February, General Stoffeln had occupied Giurgiu. Three thousand Ottomans reputedly were killed in the attempt to defend the town before they abandoned it. Russians troops were subsequently withdrawn from Giurgiu because of a lack of supplies. General Stoffeln reported the firing of the town, warehouses and magazines, and some hundred vessels, along with all the surrounding villages, before pulling back to Bucharest. By spring 1774, when hostilities resumed after an extended truce, Russian Field-Marshal Rumiantsev reported that the Ottomans had assembled fifteen thousand troops in Vidin, Ostrova, Orsova, and Kladovo (and Belgrade) with the intention of invading Craiova *banat* in order to drive the Russians beyond the Olt.[49]

By February 1770, interestingly enough, Giridi Ahmed himself had been ordered into the Bulgarian countryside to purchase (at market prices) 120,000 *kile* of flour and 345,000 *kile* of barley for the upcoming campaign season, because of the impossibility of delivery from Danubian sources.[50] A hint as to why it had become impossible is found in a cancelled order in another document: The people of Vidin, Fethülislam, and the surrounding villages, had refused consent (*rizadade olmayub*), and had resisted (expelled) the officer sent to carry out the purchase.[51]

These samples from the 1768–74 war indicate a deteriorating condition of the region that was exacerbated by subsequent conflicts, and gave rise to warlords such as Osman Pasvantoğlu. Osman was born in Vidin in 1758, son of Ömer, a Bosnian, then one of the wealthiest aghas of the area, and a Christian mother. Ömer and his son Osman were sentenced to death by Abdülhamid I (r. 1774–89) in 1787 for extortion and rebellion, in an attempt to restore order to the area surrounding Vidin. Ömer was executed, but Osman escaped into Serbia, where he distinguished himself in the war against Austria 1787–91 in Wallachia, having "turned" Albanian and gathered around him his own band. The sultan in gratitude allowed him to return to Vidin and reacquire part of his family property. His personal army consisted of bandits (*eşkiya, haydut*s), dissatisfied Janissaries, and irregulars (*yamak*s). Osman besieged Vidin itself, taking possession in 1792. He established an extensive and impregnable power base in Vidin by raiding and acquiring control of villages in Wallachia as far as Craiova. In the course of the next decade, Pasvantoğlu became one the most powerful *ayan*s of Rumeli, by manipulation of the pattern of population movement and survival strategies described in the text we have studied. Even an Ottoman army of some forty to fifty thousand sent against him in 1797–98 failed to unseat him from his power base in the city, and his reign of power continued until 1804–1805, when Selim III (r. 1789–1807) was finally able to break his hold over Vidin and Belgrade.[52]

In conclusion, 1759–60 appears to have been a moment when Ottoman bureaucrats attempted to reassert sultanic legitimacy on the northern frontier, and called on a range of contractual precedents, from classical Ottoman models to multilateral treaties. They were responding to multiple complaints from their proxy rulers, the Phanariot *voyvoda*s, and their ruling elites. The reasons for restoring order were overtly fiscal, but based on an understanding that Vidin had become an important border fortress for the defense of the empire, and pivotal to the well-being of the Danubian supply system. Their failure to impose a fiscal and disciplinary regime is evident in subsequent events, and in the rise of the great *ayan*s by the end of the century.

Notes

1. The report of the commission itself is in an untitled manuscript (Topkapı H 445), dated internally to 1760. Another untitled copy is in the British Museum collection, Ms Or 11156, n.d. Both are designated *Eflakeyn* or *Eflak ve Bogdan*. There are two copies reportedly in Romania, as discussed by M. Guboğlu, "Doua manuscrise turcesti de Ahmed Resmi Efendi, in Biblioteca 'V. A. Urecchia' din Galați privand tarile române," in *100 de ani de la infintarea primei biblioteci publice din judetul* (Galați, 1974), 15–49.
2. By Cengiz Orhonlu; see explanation below, notes 30 and 32.
3. See F. Bajraktarevic Ast, "Paswanoghlu," *Encyclopedia of Islam,* 2d ed. (CD version). Also, Robert Zens, "Pasvanoğlu Osman Paşa and the Paşalık of Belgrade, 1791–1807," *International Journal of Turkish Studies* 8 (2002): 89–104, and the contribution by Rossitsa Gradeva in this volume.
4. Viorel Panaite, "The *Re'ayas* of the Tributary-Protected Principalities: The Sixteenth to the Eighteenth Century," *International Journal of Turkish Studies* 9 (2003): 79–117, as well as "The Voivodes of the Danubian Principalities— as *Harâcgüzarlar* of the Ottoman Sultans," 59–78, in the same issue of *IJTS,* for the pre-1700 period. He points out how many titles the Ottomans used for the prince: *domn, tekfür* (from Armenian *takhavor*), *kral (kiral), bey* ("Power Relationships in the Ottoman Empire: The Sultans and the Tribute-Paying Princes of Wallachia and Moldavia from the Sixteenth to the Eighteenth Century," *International Journal of Turkish Studies* 7 [2001]: 26–53). *Hospodar,* or governor, was attached to the Phanariots in western works to indicate the changed relationship after 1711. The Ottoman preference in documents I have examined is *voyvoda.* Panaite is also author of *The Ottoman Law of War and Peace: The Ottoman Empire and Tribute Payers* (Boulder, Colo: East European Monographs; New York: distributed by Columbia University Press, 2000). I am grateful for all the help Panaite has given me.
5. As effectively critiqued by Maria Todorova, *Imagining the Balkans* (New York: Oxford University Press, 1997).
6. An observation made by Charles Peyssonel (the elder), from *Observations historiques et géographiques* (Paris, 1765), 30, as quoted in Larry Wolff, *Inventing Eastern Europe: The Map of Civilization on the Mind of the Enlightenment* (Stanford: Stanford University Press, 1994), 286 and 399.
7. William Wilkinson, *An Account of the Principalities of Wallachia and Moldavia* (London: Longman, 1820; reprint New York: Arno Press, 1971), 85. He adds: "Men have ever proved themselves the determined enemies of their prosperity."
8. He was writing from headquarters on the Prut River just prior to the confrontation with the main Ottoman army at Falça/Larga and Kartal/Kagul, sometime in late July/early August 1770. (P. A. Rumiantsev [Collected Documents]

(Moscow, 1953), vol. 1, #145, dated June 24, 1770) — with thanks to Maryna Kravets for the translation from Russian.

9. Rumiantsev, reporting in November 1770, [Collected Documents], vol. 1, #190. The subject of war supplies forms part of my manuscript: "Ottoman Warfare 1700–1870," scheduled for publication in 2005.

10. Conflicting economic and political systems in Eastern Europe, at least until the collapse of the Soviets, have resulted in an extraordinary diversity of histories of oppression and liberation, in Russian, Turkish, Greek, Romanian, Bulgarian, German, and English. Daniel Chirot, *Social Change in a Peripheral Society: The Creation of a Balkan Colony* (New York: Academic Press, 1976), 72. See also: N. Beldiceanu, "Eflak" *Encyclopedia of Islam* 2d ed. (CD version); Aurel Decei, "Eflak," *İslam Ansiklopedisi*, vol. 4, 178-89.

11. Phanariot refers to the section of Istanbul, residence of the Greek Orthodox Patriarch, called Fener. Imperial armies, Catholic, Orthodox, or Muslim, made up of co-religionists or not, required the cooperation of local leaders. In the eighteenth century, the hardening of boundaries ended in the death of remarkable leaders, such as the Austrian arrest and imprisonment of potential Serbian ally George Brankovic in 1689. Or, even more disastrously, in terms of its implications for Wallachian rule, the Ottoman execution of Constantin Brancoveanu (1688–1714). The latter was accused with conspiring with Dimitrie Cantemir to supply Peter the Great upon the Russian advance at Prut in 1711. This in part stimulated the Ottoman decision to impose a proxy regime in the two principalities.

12. See Ehud Toledano, "The Emergence of Ottoman-Local Elites (1700–1900): A Framework for Research," in Ilan Pappé and Moshe Ma'oz, eds., *Middle Eastern Politics and Ideas: A History from Within* (London; New York: Tauris Academic Studies; dist. in the U. S. and Canada by St. Martin's Press, 1997), 45–62.

13. These uprisings have been widely read as early expressions of nationalism, but it is hard to sustain such an interpretation. See Peter F. Sugar, "Unity and Diversity in the Lands of Southeastern Europe in the Eighteenth Century," 262; see also Ilie Ceauşescu, "Military Aspects of the National Struggle of the Rumanian Principalities in the Eighteenth Century," 371–85, and Florin Constantiniu, "Tradition and Innovation in the Eighteenth-Century Military Structures of the Rumanian Lands," 387–99, all in Gunther E. Rothenberg, Béla A. Király and Peter F. Sugar, eds., *East Central European Society and War in the Pre-Revolutionary Eighteenth Century* (Boulder, Colo.: Social Science Monographs; New York: dist. by Columbia University Press, 1982). In spite of remarkable scholarly efforts in recent decades, "the centuries of Ottoman domination are [still] conceived as a period of intense resistance to the foreign 'occupier,'" per Fikret Adanır, "Balkan Historiography Related to the Ottoman Empire Since 1945," in Kemal H. Karpat, ed., *Ottoman Past*

and Today's Turkey, (Leiden: Brill, 2000), 252. Adanır concurs with a similar conclusion by Maria Todorova, "Bulgarian Historical Writing, on the Ottoman Empire," *New Perspectives on Turkey* 12 (1995): 97–118, here, 116–17. For the most recent and comprehensive review of Balkan historiography, see: Fikret Adanır and Suraiya Faroqhi, eds., *The Ottomans and the Balkans: A Discussion of the Historiography* (Leiden: Brill, 2002), especially the editors' introduction, 1–55.

14. V. Aksan, "Whatever Happened to the Janissaries?" *War in History* 5 (1998): 23–36, and "Ottoman War and Warfare 1453–1812," in Jeremy Black, ed., *War in the Early Modern World, 1450–1815* (London: UCL Press, 1999), 147–76, and "Ottoman Military Recruitment Strategies in the Late Eighteenth Century," in E. Zurcher, ed., *Arming the State* (London: I. B. Tauris, 1999), 21–39.

15. Marsigli went on to map the territories around Orsova and Belgrade, one of the first to do so with accuracy. Marsigli and Ottoman Commissioner İbrahim later officially paced the new border following the treaty of Karlowitz in 1699 (literally, with markers at every 300 paces). John Stoye, *Marsigli's Europe, 1680–1730* (New Haven: Yale University Press, 1994), 182. Marsigli is the author of the famous *L'État militaire de l'Empire ottoman* (La Haye, 1732).

16. Géza Dávid, "The *Eyalet* of Temesvár in the Eighteenth Century," *Oriente Moderno* n.s. 18 (1999): 114. He points out that this was a very large number, even for the highly militarized zone. *Hayduks* (*haiduci*) is the term presently used all over the Balkans for "freedom-fighters," and just as consistently by the Turks as "rebels, bandits" (*haydut*s). Articles XIV of the 1718 Treaty of Passarowitz and XVIII of the 1739 Treaty of Belgrade refer to "haydones" as "brigands" who live by "plunder" or "rapine." (Fred L. Israel, ed., *Major Peace Treaties of Modern History, 1648–1967*, vol. 2 [New York: Chelsea House Publishers, 1980]). The treaties agreed that it was illegal to give refuge or comfort to such "evil men, subject rebels, or malcontents" (from the Passarowitz treaty); to "evildoers, or to rebellious and disaffected subjects" (Belgrade).

17. Rossitsa Gradeva, "War and Peace Along the Danube: Vidin at the End of the Seventeenth Century," in Kate Fleet, ed., *The Ottomans and the Sea, Oriente Moderno* 20 (81), n.s. (2001), 149–75. The figure 5,440 comes from Ahmed Cevad, *Tarih-i Askeri-i Osmani* (Istanbul, 1880), 105. Contrast Belgrade at 5,039 Janissaries, and Bender at 4,134 for the same date 1750; also in French: A. Djevad, *L'Etat militaire Ottoman depuis la fondation de l'Empire jusqu'à nos jours,"* (Constantinople, 1882), 167. The rest of the figures are drawn from an official Ottoman document recording the source of the salaries for all the border fortresses: Istanbul Başbakanlık Archives D.BSM # 4274, dated 1771–80, 7–9. Compare Belgrade, reproduced in the same document: 4,917 Janissaries in 1770, and 6,196 in 1776; or Bender: 6,435 Janissaries in 1770, when it fell to the Russians.

18. Bistra A. Cvetkova, "Un document turc inédit concernant un mouvement de résistance en Bulgarie du Nord-Ouest au XVIIIe siècle," *Rocznik Orientaliztyczny* 36 (1976): 93–100. In Cvetkova's view, this is representative of continual opposition to the "Turkish" oppression. The insurgents are referred to in the Ottoman documents as "unbelievers," the countryside troops as "brave Muslims."

19. Dávid, "The *Eyalet* of Temesvár," 116–18. The recovery of Belgrade was the chief Ottoman strategic aim of that war zone in the 1736–39 War.

20. See Gradeva, "War and Peace," for an article full of information about the military supply question for the seventeenth and early eighteenth centuries, and especially interesting about the Danube fleet.

21. Two families in fact: Balaceanu and Cantacuzine (Decei, "Eflak," 186).

22. Chirot, *Social Change*, 74–75. How free they actually were is the subject of much debate, as is the question of "who owned the land."

23. Chirot, *Social Change*, 86.

24. Peter F. Sugar, *Southeastern Europe Under Ottoman Rule 1354–1804* (Seattle and London: University of Washington Press, 1977), 137. Most of the families moved south into Bulgaria. His source is David Mitrany, *The Land & the Peasant in Rumania* (London: Oxford University Press, 1930; reprint, New York: Greenwood Press, 1968), 16. It seems a highly suspect (large?) figure.

25. Chirot, *Social Change*, 78–80, reviews the argument. Sugar, *Southeastern Europe*, 136–38, prefers the latter interpretation: "Serious flaws in the reforms themselves made the peasantry's small gains illusory" (137).

26. Chirot, *Social Change*, 76, includes the text of the 1746 reform decree by Mavrocordat.

27. The *zahire* system, normally applied during campaigns, was extended year round in the principalities after 1756, till at least 1769, and abolished in 1774. It was later extended to sheep. (M. M. Alexandrescu-Dersca Bulgaru, "L'Approvisionnement d'Istanbul par les Principautés roumaines aux XIIIe Siècle," *Revue de l'Occident Musulman et de la Méditerranée* (1988): 73–78.) Concerning the problem of supplies for the Ottomans during the 1768–74 war, see also: V. Aksan, "Feeding the Ottoman Troops on the Danube," *War and Society* 13 (1995): 1–14, and below.

28. Wilkinson, *An Account of the Principalities*, 58–59.

29. There are many scattered throughout the catalogues, but the events generating this response can be found discussed in the Başbakanlık Archives series *Ecnebi defterleri* (Romania), 77/1, 152–56. Reports of the actions taken by the committee are summarized in Başbakanlık CH 6557 and CD 11367, July and August 1760, respectively.

30. This is an abridged version of pages 155–56 of the *Ecnebi defterleri* 77/1, as transcribed into modern Turkish characters by Cengiz Orhonlu in "Ahmed Resmi Efendi'nin Eflâk Coğrafyası," *Güney Doğu Avrupa Araştırmaları Der-*

gisi 4/5 (1975/76): 1–14. *Kışla* normally refers to winter quarters, or barracks, for troops. It should be noted here, for the sake of completion, that non-Muslims living in lands south of the Danube were similarly prohibited from owning property. See Panaite, *"Re'ayas,"* 103, for an example from 1741.

31. Bulgaru, "L'Approvissionement d'Istanbul," especially p. 74, contains documentary evidence of abuses of the Muslim community of merchants in Moldavia (predominantly Laz from Trabzon), who had usurped property there, illegal according to the customary practice that prohibited Muslim residence (more especially ownership) in the territories. In 1731, the number of merchants allowed to legally reside in Wallachia was fixed at 20–25. By 1733, Mahmud I was ordering the expulsion of the Laz merchants altogether. This parallels the kinds of actions taken by our committee concerning similar Janissary abuses.

32. See Virginia H. Aksan, *An Ottoman Statesman in War and Peace: Ahmed Resmi Efendi, 1700–1783* (Leiden: Brill 1995), 37–38, where the question of authorship and the identity of the head of the commission, Giridi Ahmed, is covered in some detail. The verdict is still out whether Ahmed Resmi Efendi, also of Crete, the well-known historian and statesman, was in fact the author. Orhonlu argues that Ahmed Resmi's acquaintance with geography, and his embassy to Vienna (1757–58), could have given him the idea to include what is in effect an Ottoman geography of Wallachia in the routine report. Ahmed Resmi, however, is not identified as a *müderris* in any other source, or even as a member of the *ulema*. (Cengiz Orhonlu, "The Geography of Wallachia Written by A Turkish Politician," *Revue des études sud-est européenes* 13 (1975): 447–52, here 451), translated from his article cited above, which includes the transcriptions of important documents. There is an additional important piece of evidence on authorship in the *Eflakeyn* manuscript, folio 25b, where the author states that he was a long-time member of Koca Ragıb's entourage, which confirms that he may well have been Ahmed Resmi.

33. The content of the report must be treated with considerable caution in assessing the impact of the mission, until further evidence surfaces. The text is just as interesting for its self-representation of the Ottoman dynasty and its connections to far-flung territory. Much of the text is a reproduction of relevant orders, petitions, and requests for action. There is a great deal that is informative, and a sense throughout that the mission was as much about public performance as about the resolution of the problem.

34. İ. H. Uzunçarşılı, *Osmanlı Tarihi*, 2d printing (Ankara: Türk Tarih Kurumu 1983), vol. 4/2, 48–91.

35. These dwellings were also described by Wilkinson, *An Account of the Principalities*, 157: "The walls are of clay, and the roofs thatched with straw . . . in winter, they retire to cells under ground, easily kept warm by means of a little fired made of dried dung and some branches of trees."

36. The author also uses the word *panayir* (or weekly market). He is probably making an estimate of the worth at roughly 12,500 *kuruş*, as a *kese* (or *kise*) was normally calculated as 500 *kuruş* in the eighteenth century.

37. This is just a sample of what the manuscript contains concerning Wallachian agriculture. As far as I know, it has not been explored fully for its potential.

38. This information is found in an *arzuhal* (petition) included in the report, *Eflakeyn*, folio 30. *Yamakan* is an infinitely elastic term, which could refer to recruits, or volunteers, or both, in Janissary ranks, or aspiring to join them. They had a semi-official status as associates of the *askeri* class. They figure prominently in all fortresses of the empire after 1700 as a source of trouble. There are often references to *eski* (old, or former; sometimes the synonym *atik* is used) or *cedid* (new)—my surmise is that the reference is to previous and newly enrolled recruits, hired on as campaigns loomed, or to replace deserters.

39. *Eflakeyn*, folio 34b. The number 1,000 is mentioned on folio 6a. Moşye or moshie (in Romanian—with thanks to Viorel Panaite) means a "large field." The Arabic term *musha'* was used to connote communally distributed lands (or common lands held in shares) at least in nineteenth-century Greater Syria. (See Martha Mundy, "Village Land and Individual Title: *Musha'* and Ottoman Land Registration in the 'Ajlun District," in Eugene L. Rogan and Tariq Tell, eds., *Village, Steppe and State: The Social Origins of Modern Jordan* (London: British Academic Press, 1994), 66–67. Chirot uses the term the *moşneni*: "free villager with traditional rights to land" (Chirot, *Social Change*, 78). He notes the term came into widespread use in the eighteenth century for the Oltenia part of Romania. The Austrian census of 1722 listed 47% of the peasant villages as free in Oltenia (Chirot, *Social Change*, 25). Other words routinely cited in these documents: orchard/vineyard (*bağ*); garden (*bahçe*); field (*tarla*).

40. Başbakanlık CH 1733, May/June 1760, is an official notice to the commission of the Fethülislam "quarrel" (*niza*) which was sent by courier. The investigation is recorded in the manuscript, 43b–46a.

41. *İspence* is being used here as "residence" permit—but with the implication that those with *ispence* were not liable to the head tax (*cizye*) or land tax (*haraç*) of long-term residents. The term *ispence* is understood by historians to be variously a poll tax applied to Christians, prisoners of war, or slaves, but the discussion here is free of any designation other than *reaya*, clearly agriculturalists, perhaps in our present-day understanding of migrant workers.

42. This represents a very loose summation of folio 45–46 of *Eflakeyn*. The two officials do "speak" as I have indicated. It is clear that the *voyvoda* had more experience with Istanbul from the appeal he makes to the imperial treasury (*mal-i miri*) to which, in theory, the taxes of Wallachia contributed. The document thus represented is dated mid-July 1760.

43. Wilkinson, *An Account of the Principalities*, 20. See also above for the works of Panaite, especially "The *Re'ayas*," 84–5, and 93ff. He includes multiple examples from Ottoman chancery documents which frequently reiterated the illegality of imposing the *cizye* more than once on populations from the principalities who moved across Ottoman frontiers along the Danube.

44. See note 16. It is language expanded from similar texts in both the Karlowitz and Passarowitz treaties. The Ottoman version of the treaty refers to disputes, differences and disagreements as "*dava*" and "*niza*" (*Muahedat mecmuası* [Istanbul(?), 1880], vol. 3, 132–33). For general discussion of such trends, see William H. McNeill, *Europe's Steppe Frontier, 1500–1800* (Chicago: Chicago University Press, 1966); J. C. Hurewitz, "The Europeanization of Ottoman Diplomacy: The Conversion from Unilateralism to Reciprocity in the Nineteenth Century," *Middle East Journal* 23 (1961): 741–52; Rifaat Ali Abou El Haj, "Ottoman Attitudes Towards Peace Making: The Karlowitz Case," *Der Islam* 51 (1974), 131–7; see also Virginia H. Aksan, "Locating the Ottomans Among Early Modern Empires," *Journal of Early Modern History* 3 (1999): 103–34.

45. Rossitsa Gradeva offers that explanation for a Vidin-Craiova set of cross-Danube connections in Ruse (Rusçuk) and Giurgiu. Giurgiu was initially part of a *kaza* (district) centered in Bulgaria, but then became a *kaza* itself, with the *kadı* dependent on his equivalent in Ruse (personal communication, December, 2001).

46. Ahmed Vasıf Efendi, *Précis historique de la guerre des turcs contres les russes* (Paris, 1872), 80–84. My paraphrase.

47. That shipments were substantial can be verified by the reforms of the Grain Administration (1793) under Selim III (r. 1789–1807). Among its stipulations was the order to see to the stocking of the Istanbul (Arsenal) granary with a minimum of 2,000,000 *kile* of grain from the shipments from Wallachia and Moldavia. Lynne M. Şaşmazer, "Policing Bread Price and Production in Ottoman Istanbul, 1793–1807," *The Turkish Studies Association Bulletin* 24 (2000): 28. A *kile* is generally estimated as the equivalent of 24–25 kilograms. I am speaking here only of grain—the need for peasant labor and wagons for transport become an acute problem during the two Russo-Ottoman Wars of the eighteenth century. One petition of 1783 complains of the diversion of one thousand poor peasants and their wagons and tools to repair the fortresses, as well as another one thousand to transport grain over long distances, no doubt routine impositions. (Florin Marinescu, "The Trade of Wallachia with the Ottoman Empire Between 1791 and 1821," *Balkan Studies* 22 [1981]: 292–93.) This article, a translation from Romanian, is very badly mangled, but full of useful information.

48. These are likely the *zahire* imposition described above. Başbakanlık CA 2642, 2 March 1769. Similarly, for comparison, for the villages of Rusçuk (Ruse),

Hezargrad (Razgrad), Şumnu (Shumen), and Eski Cuma (Tărgovishte), 118,600 *kile* barley and 43,750 *kile dakik* (flour) was estimated/requisitioned in July 1769 (Başbakanlık D.MKF 30413, 2).

49. Rumiantsev [Collected Documents] vol. 2, #115 and #121, pp. 224–25 and 256. On the numbers of the Ottoman forces and deaths, military historians beware. The struggle for the Danubian fortresses, such as Silistre and Nikopolis, continued throughout the war. (Rumiantsev [Collected Documents] vol. 2, #360, p. 724). Skirmishes downstream from Kladovo and raids on Ottoman outposts are recorded in May of 1774: 40 Albanians (under Russian command) captured one large vessel loaded with 800 *okka*s of butter, 600 *okka*s of honey, and 1,000 *okka*s of dried fish (Rumiantsev [Collected Documents], vol. 2, #374, p. 751). 1 *okka*=1.28 kilograms. The Vidin-Craiova axis figures very largely in battles in the 1806–12 war and again in 1828–29.

50. 8 February, Başbakanlık KK 2929, 5–6.

51. Başbakanlık D.MKF 30413, p. 4. That order was for 300,000 *kile* barley, from September 1769.

52. As detailed in articles by Zens and Gradeva, note 3.

Albanians and "Mountain Bandits"

FREDERICK F. ANSCOMBE

While numerous historians have recognized the problems which "Mountain Bandits"[1] (*Dağlı Eşkiyaları*) and other outlaw groups caused in the Balkans before and during the reign of Selim III (r. 1789–1807), few have given much attention to the brigands themselves, their origins, and their reasons for taking up banditry. Ottomanists have tended to focus on Istanbul's efforts to control the problem and on the role of provincial notables in the troubles.[2] The national tradition in Balkan historiography, on the other hand, has often tended to lump Muslims together as "Turks," incomprehensible, incorrigible, intolerable. It also has been prone to consider banditry as a self-contained, "national" problem (i.e., Bulgaria suffered from the rampages of *kărdzhalis/kırcalıs*, Serbia endured Janissary and *dahi* oppression, Wallachia and Romania faced rapacious Janissaries), rather than recognizing it as a problem unconfined by then-unknown national borders. Yet banditry was a problem which affected most of the Ottoman Balkans, and those choosing a life outside the law did so for a wide range of reasons and came from a variety of backgrounds. A great many bandits were not ethnic "Turks" but rather were Albanians.[3]

This article will offer a preliminary assessment of the Albanian elements in the Mountain Bandit and parallel outlaw phenomena, the reasons leading so many Albanians to brigandage, and the steps taken by the government to control the problem. Ottoman records from other periods regularly reveal Albanian engagement in "banditry" (an elastic term in Ottoman usage, including everything from highway robbery to local feuds to struggles between regional political factions),[4] with variations in locale and intensity, but generally at a tolerable level. Such extralegal violence could be expected, given a generally well-armed population governed by a limited, pre-modern state, especially in a case where the population inhabited rough terrain. This Albanian participation in brigandage is easier to track than for many other social groups in Ottoman lands, because Albanian (*Arnavud*) was one of the relatively few ethnic markers regularly added to the usual religious (Muslim–*Zimmi*) tags used to identify people in state records.[5] These records show that the magnitude of banditry involving Albanians grew through the 1770s and 1780s to reach crisis proportions in the 1790s and 1800s.

The reasons for this extended rise in brigandage are rather less elegant or heroic than some theorists of Ottoman banditry would suggest. Karen Barkey, discussing the Anatolian *celali*s of the seventeenth century, made a provocative claim for seeing this banditry as a tool of negotiation between the government and provincial groups feeling pressure from a centralizing state.[6] While some bidders for provincial office did hire mercenary bands to try to seize power (as in the case of Matlı Osman cited below), in the 1790s the general lack of bandit interest in bargaining for state favors is striking: most brigands showed a clear understanding that the real, immediate rewards were to be won by taking advantage of the state's weakness. Those who did try to seize provincial offices seem to have been motivated more by the obvious opportunities for immediate enrichment through abuse of office in a time of weak oversight, rather than by a desire to gain rewards from the state for service.

Still less did these brigands demonstrate the slightest affinity to the "*hajduk*" – "social bandit" ideal hypothesized by Eric Hobsbawm (and in more extreme form by some Balkan historians), featuring Christian *hajduk*s (Tr. *haydud*) or *klepht*s as "*national*" (Howbsbawm's italics) proto-revolutionaries fighting against an oppressive, alien, "Turkish" system.[7] As far as can be determined, the great majority of the Albanian brigands (and all of their leaders) were Muslim and certainly plundered whoever was vulnerable, both Muslims and non-Muslims. Rather than motivated by ideology, most simply sought even marginal profit. Small though the rewards often were, they nevertheless offered an escape from the often dreadful poverty and living conditions found in the brigands' homelands. This was true also for those subgroups usually identified in recent histories of this period as the bandits, namely soldiers discharged after the end of the war with Austria and Russia in 1792, or mercenary troops who had deserted from the private retinues of local notables in the eastern Balkans.[8] To live securely and comfortably was rarely an easily achieved goal in Albania, but the pressures created by repeated wars made it much tougher in this period. One of the most damaging war-induced problems was Istanbul's loss of control over provincial authorities, who quickly discovered that the government would turn a blind eye to almost any unjust act, as long as these notables continued to send men to serve in the army. Like the bandits themselves, the notables took advantage of the state's distractions to seize land, wealth, and power. The Ottoman government proved unable to reestablish effective control over these notables, let alone to improve conditions in the Albanian provinces, and thus poor, armed Albanians continued to emigrate to seek a living in any way possible throughout the reign of Selim III.

Bandits! Bandits! Bandits!

Istanbul received a seemingly unending stream of reports in the 1780s, 1790s, and 1800s which detailed the depredations of marauders in all corners of Ottoman Europe. Taken to suggest the scale of the problems faced by both the government and the inhabitants of the Balkans, the following examples describe the activities of Albanian bands and bandits in different places, years, and situations.

In June 1792 the Sublime Porte learned from several sources that a number of Albanian bandit groups were roaming western and central Macedonia, creating havoc.[9] A certain Matlı Osman (from today's Mat, in central Albania[10]) marched to Pirlepe (Prilep, western Republic of Macedonia) with a band of three hundred Albanians to claim the position of local military commander. The residents of Pirlepe refused them entry, and the leading administrator of the town sent a request for help to a notable of Dibre (Debar, western Macedonia). One Mulla Yunus, a resident of Peşkipa (Peshkopi, central Albania) and an ally of this notable, duly arrived outside Pirlepe, accompanied by eight hundred Albanians, only to discover that Matlı Osman's men had departed. They had vanquished the defenders of Pirlepe and, after being paid 25 *kese akçe* (12,500 silver coins, worth roughly £10) to leave, had gone on to find employment with a claimant to the position of *ayan* (chief local notable) of İştip (Štip, eastern Macedonia). Under his direction they were to harry this and surrounding districts.[11] The luckless leader of Pirlepe tried to send away Mulla Yunus and his men, since they were no longer needed, but they demanded their wages. As all these groups did, they lived off the land until they were paid, in this case another twelve *kese akçe*, as the people of Pirlepe were by now too poor to pay more. Mulla Yunus and his men subsequently headed toward Dibre. Other bands of Albanians from Kırçova (Kičevo, western Macedonia) and Dibre now entered the free-for-all, some joining Matlı Osman outside İştip, while others swarmed around Köprülü (Veles, central Macedonia). In all, some 1,500–2,000 Albanians from central Albania and western Macedonia were ranging across much of the rest of the present-day Republic of Macedonia, as far as Köstendil (Kyustendil, western Bulgaria), stripping the land of both money and food and causing much of the population to flee their homes.

The violent struggle over the *ayanlık* of İştip had drawn Matlı Osman and others to eastern Macedonia, and disputes over provincial offices or provincial officeholders there and elsewhere offered opportunities to many other hired guns in this period. In July 1795 two administrators of İstefe (district of Thebes, southern Greece), themselves Albanian, were called to court in Athens to settle a conflict involving theft of property and murder. One of them showed up, as did a representative of the other party. His partner, however, gathered a band of Albanians under his command and refused to submit. He then joined forces with the local *ayan* and *kocabaşıs* (local notables, Muslim and Christian, respectively), who themselves faced charges of levying an illegal "second tithe" on crops. Albanians seem to have provided the backbone of something akin to a local legal defiance bloc.[12]

As the legal system in the provinces became less effective in this period of turmoil, those who lost positions and possessions to powerful local notables also recruited Albanians to strike back at those above the law. Late in 1788 the powerful *ayan* of Siroz (Serres, northern Greece), İsmail Bey, returned home after the first campaign season of the 1787–92 war against Austria and Russia, only to find that a number of his properties had been sacked by bandits. The destruction affected not just the district of Siroz but that of Demir Hisar (Siderokastro, Greece) as well. The main force of the bandits consisted of two thousand Albanian followers of a certain Orhan Bey of Beraştan, near Permed (Përmet, southern Albania). One of the leading disturbers of the peace, who had recruited Orhan and his men, however, also sent a complaint to Istanbul, charging that İsmail Bey had illegally seized his estates (*çiftlik*s).[13] That İsmail confronted a similar outburst of violence ten years later suggests that his noteworthy personal authority did not rest easily on the region. In 1799 the brother of the *nazır* (supervisor of revenues) of Drama (Greece) joined forces with one of the most notorious leaders of Albanian Mountain Bandits, Manav İbrahim, to pillage the district of Nevrekop (Gotse Delchev, Bulgaria) as part of a long struggle against İsmail's domination. İsmail naturally "managed" the problem by recruiting his own gang from Albania.[14]

Large, independent, roving gangs such as those of Manav İbrahim, Ali Zot,[15] and the other leading figures of the Mountain Bandit phenomenon were an even greater concern for Istanbul than were such localized, recruited bands as those of Orhan Bey or Mulla Yunus. A great many of the rank-and-file bandits were Albanian,[16] which presented the government's officers an additional potential problem, because so many of their own soldiers were also Albanian. Sometimes these government irregular troops (*levend*s or *sekban*s) fought determinedly against the bandits, but on other occasions they cooperated with, or even deserted to, the outlaws.[17] This can be illustrated by the experiences of but one provincial notable who held a succession of important posts, Hasan Pasha of Zihne (Zihna, northern Greece). In the early 1790s he served as governor of Silistre (Silistra, northeastern Bulgaria), an important post for the defense of the Danube and for the struggle against the Mountain Bandits. His position caused him to be given the primary responsibility for battling the bandits in 1792–93, a task in which he was ultimately unsuccessful, at least in part because many of his own men, Albanians, joined the brigands. As was often the case, arrears of pay due for service probably boosted such desertions. Hasan Pasha nevertheless continued to rely heavily upon Albanians thereafter. When he was dismissed from a later office in 1794, he was ordered to make sure that the one thousand Albanians in his retinue received all of the pay due them and were sent directly home, lest they, too, were to seek to recover back wages by joining the Mountain Bandits.[18]

Although ethnic, or more likely clan, ties may have played a role in some Albanians' changing sides in the struggle, it was this desire to be paid that appears to have driven the actions of so many of them on both sides of the government-bandit divide. In June 1800 the brigand Bayraktar Arnavud Hüseyn, besieged with his men in Bana (Soko Banja, north of Niš, Serbia), persuaded a number of the besiegers to join his group in the town. It was no doubt meaningful that both bandits and turncoats were Tosks[19] from southern

Albania—but Hüseyn's distribution of money may well have been as important as the commonality of background.[20] Under such conditions, switching
masters thus did not always have to go against the state. This could be seen
in Vidin (Bulgaria), the base of the rebellious pasha Osman Pasvanoğlu [var.
Pasvanoğlu/Pasvantoğlu/ Pasbanoğlu] and one of the great centers of unrest
in the Ottoman Balkans at the turn of the century. When Osman did not pay
his own Albanian troops, some offered to come over to the government's
side, provided that the state could demonstrate its ability to pay wages.[21] The
state treasury being perennially empty, gaining the loyalty of its employees
through prompt payment of wages was a tremendous challenge, however.[22]

As this limited selection of examples indicates, practically no region of
the Balkans escaped problems involving Albanians operating outside of the
law. Some particularly severely affected areas, such as geographic Macedonia, faced depopulation, while others, such as the Morea, southern Greece,
and Serbia, would later be centers of insurrection.[23] Yet it is also true that
much of the government's remaining ability to control the Balkan provinces
rested in the hands of Albanian officers and troops. Albanians were certainly not irrevocably doomed to a life of banditry, with all legal options
unthinkable. What, then, were the causes for the unusually severe outbreak
of violence during this period?

Underlying Problems

Conditions throughout the Balkans in this era encouraged or forced many
men to take up arms, either as brigands or as irregular soldiers who might
not be much better than bandits. Bosnians and other Muslims of the region
took part in the chaos, yet Albanians played an especially prominent role.[24]
This suggests that it was not only the conditions felt throughout the peninsula
during and after the 1787–92 war that drew in Albanians, but also circumstances peculiar to those districts in the western Balkans which had significant Albanian populations. It appears that those conditions were particularly
severe.

A) Environment and Agriculture

Even in the best of times, the conditions of life found in regions inhabited
primarily by Albanians were tough. The population density in these areas

was relatively high—strikingly so, when the nature of the land is taken into consideration. Remarkably little of the land now within the borders of the Republic of Albania was ideally suited to agriculture in the Ottoman period. Almost three-quarters of the area was forested mountain and, until the advent of modern drainage techniques, much of the remainder was wetland.[25] While some Albanian-inhabited lands in present-day northern Greece, western Macedonia, and Kosovo were slightly less forbidding, they, too, fit the general description of a region ill-suited to intensive and extensive agriculture. Throughout the Ottoman period, Albanians had to migrate to find farmland or other means of making a living, because the population so frequently tested the limits of what their rural homelands could support.

Endemic infectious diseases added to the precariousness of life and thus doubtless also helped to push many to migrate. Albania and Epirus were known centers of infectious diseases, especially in the eighteenth century.[26] The marshy flatlands surrounding such important settlements as Avlonya (Vlorë, southern Albania) and Dıraç (Durrës, central Albania) were breeding-grounds for mosquitoes carrying malaria. The highlands of Albania, whose population depended heavily upon pastoralism, suffered from other threats associated more clearly with animals. Plague was a particularly dangerous recurring problem, reported regularly in an arc from Yanya (Ioannina, Greece) in the south to İşkodra (Shkodër, Albania) and Prizren (Kosovo) in the north. Foreign consular reports noted the presence of plague in Albania-Epirus in 42 years of the eighteenth century—almost certainly an undercount, given limited consular access to the rugged interior.[27]

During the period of rising banditry, disease was but one of the hazards that became critical in the western Balkans. In Yanya, for example, the French consul reported a plague epidemic lasting from 1784 to 1787. Venetian records note plague in İşkodra in 1798–99 and 1803–4.[28] The disease indeed appears to have become a severe problem throughout the peninsula, spread no doubt by Albanian brigands and soldiers, as well as soldiers returning from the Danubian principalities. In 1795, for example, Orthodox residents of Zağra (Stara Zagora, Bulgaria) were accused of trying to take advantage of the government's preoccupation with controlling both plague and bandits to build an unsanctioned new church.[29] Shortages of food also appear to have been a severe problem at times, particularly in the first half of the 1790s.[30] In the case of Matlı Osman and the various brigands encamped around Pirlepe, described above, it was by no means incidental that food was one of their primary demands, and that the local population quickly faced the specter of starvation themselves. A decade later, the *vali* (governor) of Rumeli, who enlisted Albanian highlanders to track down mountain bandit groups, was shocked by his recruits' abject poverty, describing them as little better than naked.[31]

The difficulties encountered in ensuring a sufficient food supply for the Albanian population were probably aggravated by the continuing spread of *çiftlik*s throughout the region. *Çiftlik*s were estates considered and treated as essentially private property, rather than as lands at the free disposition of the sultan, as was the case with land assigned as *dirlik* (prebend, such as the *timar*s designed to support cavalrymen) to members of the military class, who were to use the revenue to equip themselves for campaign. In and of itself, estate formation was not necessarily a bad thing. Previously unproductive land could become the *çiftlik* of the person who brought it under cultivation, for example. Even the transformation of state *dirlik* into private *çiftlik* might be beneficial to the military, as long as the estate-holder made sure that the army gained a dependable source of the ever-more-critical irregular *sekban* infantry instead of the cavalry previously supported by the *timar-dirlik*.[32] This was especially true in the western Balkans, given the exemplary reputation of Albanian *sekban*s, and indeed it had long been understood that notables appointed to office in Albanian provinces would use revenue from lands under their control to outfit *sekban*s for Ottoman service. While some land in the region remained in the *dirlik* category even after the end of the *timar* system in the 1830s, much more became *çiftlik* through this conversion process in the eighteenth century, as well as through that of land reclamation.[33]

More damaging and more common than these, however, were the other means of creating private estates on already-worked land during this extended time of chaos. These generally involved the use of force to acquire rights over privileged lands and peasants. A number of areas in the region had never been fully incorporated into the *dirlik* system, which meant that many villages, farms and pastures enjoyed freedom from close oversight and from some of the usual tax burden borne by peasants on a *timar*. The sultan and his family, for example, retained control over broad swathes of land, appointing their own agents to collect the revenue. Other lands were set aside as *vakıf* (pious endowment), with revenue again collected by the administrator of each endowment or his agent. *Derbend* (highland pass) villages also were a quite common feature in a region as mountainous as the western Balkans. The *derbend* villagers enjoyed significant relief from

taxes in return for their service policing the roads and passes near their settlements. Other villages had similar rights in return for guarding the coast.
Throughout this period of wars and turmoil, a growing number of such privileged villages and farms (in addition to nominally *dirlik* lands) fell under
the control of powerful local notables.

The procedure adopted was frequently some variation of the following.[34]
Given the lack of close oversight of a privileged village by any influential
protector, a locally powerful man—military officer, *ayan*, tax farmer, self-
appointed police chief—would demand the payment of taxes from which
the villagers were excused, or which they had already paid to the properly-
appointed agent. The villagers could not easily refuse. Given the generally
low level of wealth possible for peasants on often marginal land, soon they
fell deeply into debt. Unable to meet the rising demands for money, they
eventually would offer to place themselves under the control of someone
who could pay the debts and protect them from such arbitrary, illegal taxation. Whether or not the legal status of the land changed to *çiftlik* or remained as before (as would be the case with *vakıf*, for example), however, the
peasants thereafter often continued to have to pay higher taxes than the laws
prescribed.

The state often could offer little help to those who appealed for assistance beyond refusing to grant *post facto* legality to land grabs. In a village in
Yanya district, for example, pasturelands were taken illegally as *çiftlik* by a
local notable, but the state's officers could not reverse the seizure. The best
that could be done for the dispossessed villagers was to refuse to sanction the
transfer of the new *çiftlik* to the notable's heirs after his death.[35] In this extended era of state weakness, the fact that one powerful notable, Tepedelenli
Ali Pasha of Yanya, was able to accumulate up to one thousand *çiftlik*s by the
end of his career in 1822 gives an idea of the spread of estates, although it is
impossible to determine the number of these that were new or illegal.[36] Yet it
is clear that the spread of *çiftlik*s, with the often accompanying heavier taxation, helped to impoverish many who worked the land, pushed others off it,
and contributed to the problems of feeding the population in troubled times.

B) Provincial Authorities

Integral to the widespread, recurring destitution seen in the Balkan provinces
were the stresses produced by war from 1787 to 1792, in addition to those
caused by the mountain bandits themselves thereafter. While banditry was

always to some degree a problem in the Albanian-inhabited lands, much of the region escaped the most obvious effects of military campaigning against either Habsburgs or Russians, since no armies passed through on the way to the front lines. This had also been the case during the disastrous 1768–74 war with Russia. Yet both of these wars and the ensuing internal disturbances did affect the region, helping to push many Albanians into joining brigand bands. The link between distant war fronts and local turbulence lay in provincial leadership.

One of the most significant ways in which even distant campaigning promoted penury and chaos, and then brigandage, among Albanian groups was that it gave *ayan* effective *carte blanche* to break the law. Along with Osman Pasvanoğlu of Vidin, the most commonly cited examples of *ayan* who crippled Istanbul's authority by acting violently and disobeying orders are Buşatlı Kara Mahmud Pasha of İşkodra and Tepedelenli Ali Pasha of Yanya. What is much less commonly recognized is that the two Albanian pashas initially established their local autonomy by serving Istanbul's war-induced, temporary critical interests, especially in providing invaluable men to fight the Austrians and Russians. In serving the state in this limited sense, in effect they earned the privilege to demand that Istanbul turn a blind eye to their own plans for self-aggrandizement.

During much of the period between 1699 and 1768, Istanbul had been able to keep the violence-prone rivalries that commonly feature in a kinship-based society such as Albania's under some degree of control. From the early days of Ottoman rule, the empire had tried to manage the region by tying the interests of its leading families to the well-being of the state, incorporating many of them into the ruling *askeri* class.[37] In return for titles, offices, and control of some land, a number of these families became effective servants of the sultan, guarding the region against Venice and sending soldiers when needed elsewhere. Should these *ayan* and other office-holders abuse their positions of influence, however, or fail to deliver tax revenues and soldiers to Istanbul, they were dismissed. This system was not unlike that found in provinces elsewhere in the eighteenth century, the "Age of Ayans."[38] It usually worked reasonably well. Ali Pasha himself, born of a notable Tosk family, lost his first important office after five months of ruthless "service"—and he was not the first member of his family to suffer such quick dismissal for misconduct.[39]

Istanbul's interest in, and therefore capacity for, keeping aggressive notables in check slipped in the era of repeated wars after 1768. The state's reaction to reports of one *ayan*'s misdeeds in 1772 offers an illuminating example of the change of priorities. The activities of a notable of Fılorina (Florina, Greece) aroused complaints, but Istanbul chose to ignore them. The *ayan* was expected to equip and lead five hundred soldiers on the upcoming campaign against Russia; if he were made to answer the complaints, he would naturally be unable to show up with those valuable troops. It was decided, therefore, to delay justice until the campaign finished.[40] "Justice delayed" might not unreasonably be considered "justice denied," however, especially when the state, defeated, emerged from the war in such a weakened condition. The lesson would be hard to miss. Indeed, the 1770s saw very energetic struggles between ambitious Albanian notables.[41]

These struggles did not die away before 1787, and the renewal of war in that year only encouraged the competing *ayan* to new efforts. True to its form in earlier times of crisis, the state did not show its usual interest in investigating matters of justice, preferring to opt for the immediately rewarding expedient in the interests of finding soldiers. After Austria showed its readiness to withdraw from the war in 1790, for example, the *vali* of Rumeli began preparations for raising an army against Russia in the next campaign season. When he looked at Albania, the view frustrated him: a great pool of potential soldiers, but most of them (and most of the provincial revenues) were tied up in *ayan* squabbles. Each district (*sancak*) governor felt threatened by his neighbor, poured money into strengthening his own defenses—and then wanted to annex another *sancak* in order to be able to afford the arms race. The result was that, if the governor of a district were ordered to join the army with one thousand men, plus his household troops, he either would ignore the directive completely or, his attention and resources engaged elsewhere, would show up briefly with one or two hundred men, proving to be of no help to anyone. The *vali*'s solution was to have the state make clear to each recalcitrant notable that it wanted the levy of soldiers which his *sancak* was assigned to raise, preferably with the help of the notable, but, if a neighboring rival showed greater willingness, then Istanbul would be happy to give the rival control over the *sancak*.[42]

As before, this policy of expediency had shortcomings, and now there were particularly aggressive men, such as Tepedelenli Ali Pasha, to exploit them. The *vali* thought it particularly important to bring about a reconciliation between Ali and his bitterest rival, İbrahim Pasha of Avlonya. Their rivalry was to continue for many years, but already it was widely known for its intensity. Peace between the two men thus could not fail but to have a good effect on other *ayan* rivalries. The problem with Ali Pasha, however, was that he adhered to peace agreements only until he saw a good opportunity to strike again at his original target.[43] And whenever he struck, he did so with devastating consequences to both rivals and general population.[44] He also was ready to back other *ayan* who might be useful to him, working more indirectly to increase his own wealth and influence.[45] Whatever the means chosen to enlarge his own power, the net result was to threaten the lives and livelihood of others, driving both peasants and notables to seek their living out of his reach. Ali managed to get away with this kind of behavior for thirty years, however, because he also usually did take care to answer the state's demands for fighting men. Indeed, that is how he won his position in Yanya in 1787. He was appointed governor there in order to raise and lead an army against Kara Mahmud Pasha of İşkodra, who had himself caused so many problems for his neighbors that Istanbul felt obliged to remove him by military means.[46]

Kara Mahmud was such a disruptive force in these years that it really should be no surprise that the western Balkans fell into lasting turmoil.[47] In listing the *sancak*s included in Ottoman Albania in 1790, the *vali* did not even bother to include İşkodra, perhaps because it was a district so completely dominated by its difficult governor that its resources could be tapped only by separate agreement with him. By that time Kara Mahmud had already faced more than one military expedition sent to punish him for his forays into adjacent territories; the threat of Istanbul throwing its support to one of his rivals would not impress him overmuch. He did have many men at his disposal, however, and when Istanbul desperately needed soldiers, it did try to persuade him to deliver them. On more than one occasion, he did so. Following the Austrian advance into the province of Bosnia in 1788, for example, Kara Mahmud was promoted to the rank of *vezir*, given the *eyalet* of Anadolu (Anatolia, essentially a lucrative financial reward), and assigned the responsiblity of defending Yeni Pazar (Novi Pazar, Serbia).[48] Kara Mahmud fulfilled his new duties for a time but, like Ali Pasha, proved unable to give up for long his designs on neighboring territories, resuming his raids by the end of the war.[49]

One of the primary objects of desire for Kara Mahmud, as for other notables, was the port of Dıraç, whose customs duties were a valuable source of revenue normally worked by a tax farmer. It was one of a number of properties in the vicinity of the *sancak* of İşkodra controlled by Asma Sultan, the sister of Sultan Abdülhamid I. Asma Sultan became one of Kara

Mahmud's determined enemies in Istanbul because of the threat he posed to her holdings.[50] Dıraç was particularly important for consideration of the reasons behind emigration from Albania, however, not only because of the general turmoil engendered by the struggles for control over it, but more specifically because its insecure, embattled position represents the difficulties which faced anyone wishing to make a living from commerce.

C) Commerce

Trade, both internal and external, had grown in importance in the western Balkans during much of the eighteenth century. This growth was simply part of the expansion of commerce seen through much of the empire.[51] The rise in external trade, at least, must have been aided by the opening of ports such as Dıraç and Avlonya to European consuls after 1699. Within the peninsula, the development of a network of local and regional trade fairs (*panayır*) helped the growth of commerce, as did the increase in use of financial tools such as bills of exchange.[52] Given the relative poverty and limited opportunities for agriculture in their provinces, it is not surprising that many Albanians turned to trading both local goods and the produce of distant lands. Among the most important exports were wool, hides, livestock, tobacco, rice, olive oil, salt, cotton, and silk. Artisan guilds also produced manufactures, including weapons, which were traded elsewhere in the Balkans. While maritime trade with Europe passed through ports such as Avlonya, Dıraç, Ülgün (Ulcinj, Montenegro), and Arta (Greece), the overland trade centers were spread throughout the interior, including important ones at Yanya, Elbasan (central Albania), Arnavud Belgrad (Berat, central Albania), Kavaya (Kavajë, central Albania), and Prizren and Priştina (Kosovo). The two with perhaps the strongest claims to importance, however, were İşkodra and İskopol/Oskopol (Voskopojë, southeast Albania, commonly known as Moschopolis).[53]

Both of these leading inland centers of commerce suffered badly from the unsettled conditions of this time. The thriving commercial and cultural center of İskopol offered a tempting target to nearby notables who needed money quickly, since it had little protection or oversight by any powerful governor or *ayan*.[54] Late in the seventeenth century it had been a village included in a *zeamet* held by a secretary in the imperial land registry in Istanbul.[55] By the 1780s it had become part of the imperial properties (*emlak-i hümayun*), still dependent upon Istanbul, and vulnerable to repeated harrassment from neighboring villages and more distant powers.[56] The town was sacked three times during the Ottoman wars with Russia and Austria, in 1769, 1772, and 1789, but not by foreign raiders. The last attack, by Ali Pasha's men, practically destroyed the town. Some of its commerce shifted to Görice (Korçë, Albania) and Arnavud Belgrad, but those towns could not make good the losses suffered by İskopol.[57]

The fate of İşkodra was rather different, although it, too, suffered from some of the same factors to be seen in Ali's lands to the south. Once Ali secured his control over tax farms, towns, and large swathes of land in Yanya and neighboring districts, he encouraged commerce. Charging high prices for goods and levying high taxes, he could command great profits from practically every transaction. Merchants accepted this in part because they had little choice, in part because Ali tried seriously to maintain public security, and in part because it was becoming ever clearer that fortunes might be made by all in neutral-flag trade during the Napoleonic period. Kara Mahmud also established his pervasive influence on commerce in the north, given his own notable collection of *çiftlik*s and tax farms. He gained a dominant voice in the grain and pitch trades, for example, and in shipping out of Ülgün. With his accumulated power and wealth, he, too, could charge high prices and fees, although he seemed to take greater care to foster good relations with merchants than did Ali Pasha in the south and almost certainly enjoyed much stronger popular backing in his domains than did the pasha of Yanya. One reason for Kara Mahmud's support among the important merchant community of İşkodra, as well as among the city's artisans, was his willingness to provide "services" in return. Like Ali Pasha, he tried to keep the various unruly groups within his domains in check. Since the degree of Istanbul's direct writ of authority within the province was limited by distractions elsewhere and by the strength of a governor as entrenched as Kara Mahmud, moreover, İşkodra's merchants could more safely ignore imperial restrictions on trade, including the standing orders against the export of critical commodities to Christian countries or restrictions on the use of foreign currency.[58] In short, Kara Mahmud was a defender against both disorder at home and predatory authorities outside of the *sancak*.[59]

Some, at least, of the problems with external authorities thrown in the way of İşkodra's traders could accurately be blamed upon Kara Mahmud himself, however. The menace he posed to neighboring notables and to the state's authority prompted them to try to apply pressure on him by squeezing his merchants. His apparently tireless (and sometimes violent) efforts to acquire land and tax farms left those threatened feeling that İşkodra owed them a debt, which they duly tried to collect by seizing its merchants' goods and money whenever they came within reach. For example, the losses to İşkodran traders in Dıraç were one factor explaining why Kara Mahmud could not give up his hopes of acquiring control over it.[60] The threat of interference in the grain and pitch trades, based around Elbasan and Arnavud Belgrad, also helped to push him to attack mid-Albania's leading notable of the 1770s and 1780s, Kurd Ahmed Pasha, then the governor of Avlonya and one of his leading rivals. This campaign in 1785 eventually brought him yet another Ottoman army, sent to strip him of office, title, and property. When Kara Mahmud fell afoul of Istanbul, as in his conflicts with neighboring *ayan*, it was İşkodra's merchants who paid the stiffest penalty. In 1793–94, when its governor was declared yet again in rebellion against the sultan following renewed incursions into Elbasan, Istanbul ordered that İşkodra was to be completely blockaded, and any of its natives found trading elsewhere were to be imprisoned, as were those with whom they traded.[61] And even if the traders managed to avoid arrest, they too had to be on guard against bandits, who regularly robbed merchants and attacked *panayır*s in the western as in the eastern Balkans. While the changes in value and volume of trade throughout the Albanian provinces in the 1790s and 1800s are impossible to measure, the overall trend cannot have been ever-upward under conditions such as these.

D) Emigration

If both commerce and farming were particularly hazardous or onerous in this period, then what other alternative means of earning a livelihood still existed? Albanians throughout the eighteenth century, and earlier, had migrated in search of work.[62] Except for those engaged in trade or war, many (but by no means all) of the jobs they found were semi- or unskilled. Patrona Halil, a seller of used clothing in Istanbul and the leader of the revolt which overthrew Sultan Ahmed III in 1730, is particularly well known but otherwise not atypical. Sultans periodically issued decrees barring such unskilled job-seekers from migrating to Istanbul.[63] The bans were never completely effective, however, and there always was a large Albanian community in the imperial capital, and indeed in the sultan's palace. When war broke out in 1787, all non-Muslims in the Balkans were to turn in any weapons they might have, in return for fair compensation; any non-Muslim found armed thereafter was to lose his weapons without compensation.[64] The sultan issued an exemption from this restriction to merchants and others who needed to protect themselves against bandits while traveling—including thirty caretakers of the palace water pipes and drains, who were going to visit their families in the district of Ergiri Kasrı (Gjirokastër, southern Albania).[65]

Other groups of Albanian émigrés, however, saw their employment opportunities in the capital and other areas limited sharply. Albanians had come to monopolize the lime-burning trade around Istanbul, for example, but the government ordered them sent home and for lime to be brought from Selanik (Salonica, Greece), an old source of supply.[66] Albanians were hardly more welcome in provinces such as Selanik or Yenişehir (Larissa, Greece), since they had come to be associated with troubles, and not only with banditry. Standing orders had been issued in the 1770s against Albanians taking up tax farms outside of their native provinces, for example.[67] The orders had little lasting effect, of course; the enduring banditry problems of the 1790s led to the renewal of wishful calls for barring Albanians from holding sensitive tax farms.[68] Whether tax farmers or not, almost all Albanians came to be viewed with suspicion and resentment. An incident from Yenişehir may serve as an example of what might result. A large group of local people, both Muslim and Christian, took the orders against the tax farmers as a license to attack other Albanians and thus assaulted those guarding a nearby *derbend*, killing six. Such an act shocked the government in Istanbul, and perhaps as a result the restrictions of the 1770s may have been enforced only loosely.[69] Yet migration for Albanians remained difficult in the following decades, as the state tried ever harder to control the movements of poor, desperate people.

Although the state might reasonably guess that its restrictions on movement would simply increase the poverty and deprivation felt by so much of the Albanian population, it did have equally valid reasons for tightening them. The Albanians' bravery and skill with weapons created many job opportunities for them as watchmen or guards, not only in *derbend*s but in any valued place. The fact that Muslim Albanians long acted as guards and caretakers for important Orthodox sites in Kosovo excited curiosity amongst outside observers of the recent troubles there—but this kind of arrangement was replicated throughout the Balkans.[70] The sites protected naturally were much more often secular than religious, and the owners also often wished to use Albanian guards to win immediate earthly rewards rather than to wait for the heavenly. The Khans of Crimea, for instance, gained a series of *çiftlik*s near Burgos (Burgas, Bulgaria) in the early 1780s and set up shops in the newly-acquired villages, placing Albanians in the shops. One of the Albanians' important duties apparently was to make sure that villagers did not go elsewhere to buy necessities to avoid the high prices in the shops. This was bad enough, but with the rise of banditry in the region, the Albanians also seemed to be too ready to shelter brigands in the *çiftlik*s. Istanbul ordered the shops closed to resolve the issue.[71] A problem on a much larger scale was that, given Albanians' reputation as superb warriors, they could always find employment in the army or, following the conclusion of peace in 1792, in the private retinues of the rich and powerful throughout the empire. Demand for them among *ayan* remained strong for fifteen years after the end of the war, as these notables fought each other over territory and revenues.[72] Being little more than mercenaries in these struggles, many Albanians switched sides when offered better or prompter pay, or, as has been noted, joined the ranks of the Mountain Bandits.[73]

The government of the Ottoman empire thus found itself confronting a multifaceted problem which proved to be remarkably stubborn. In order to resolve the Mountain Bandit crisis and restore peace in the Balkans, the movement of Albanian mercenaries had to be controlled. This required not only effective control over land and sea routes, but also stabilization and improvement of conditions in the Albanian districts. This, in turn, depended on the state's assertion of effective authority in the teeth of resistance from such increasingly wealthy and powerful notables as Tepedelenli Ali Pasha and Buşatlı Kara Mahmud Pasha. Could the Ottoman government accomplish any of these formidable tasks during the reign of Selim III? Its performance certainly suggests that it could not, in spite of prolonged efforts.

The State's Methods of Restoring Peace and Justice

Selim III's government did not have the strength or resiliency needed to rescue the Balkan provinces from the tremendous disorders of the 1790s and 1800s. In the wake of the war lost to Russia, Istanbul lacked the money necessary to raise, equip, and maintain a force large enough to crush the brigands; as one contemporary analyst pointed out, it would take twenty thousand men to hunt down four thousand bandits, given the rough and wild terrain in which they hid.[74] Even with enough men, the state lacked capable military commanders. As a result, the efforts to control the brigands depended upon cooperation from all of the *ayan*, which some gave, while others did not. This is hardly surprising, given the strength of rivalries among provincial notables. These problems should not suggest that progress was never made: forces led by various *ayan* clashed with lawless gangs regularly, and a steady stream of messengers brought heads of bandits to Istanbul to prove that vigorous action was being taken. Yet as long as some brigand bands survived, and as long as the government outfitted forces to chase them, Albanians would be drawn to the arena of action. Unable to control the bandits effectively, Istanbul never managed to address adequately the issue of Albanian migration, let alone those even tougher tasks involved in bringing more order and prosperity to the western Balkans.

The most constant measures applied, as suggested above, involved the setting up of a system to police transportation routes across the Balkans. A regime under which Albanians were allowed through passes and along roads only with written permission from district governors was well established by the second half of the 1790s, if not earlier.[75] Istanbul also applied a measure commonly essayed in order to check the wilder impulses of possible troublemakers, including *sekban*s: the requirement of naming guarantors (*kefil*), or indeed the taking of hostages. Sometimes these methods worked, but none offered a perfect solution. One energetic *vezir* who campaigned against the Mountain Bandits, Hakkı Pasha, wanted Tepedelenli Ali Pasha to seize as hostages relatives of leading southern Albanian bandits operating in present-day Bulgaria. Ali replied that he was willing to do so but pointed out, quite reasonably, that the measure would be unlikely to accomplish anything, since the brigands would know nothing of their far-off relatives' new plight.[76] When Ali himself was later given the responsibility of quelling the Mountain Bandits, however, he did take hostages, apparently with some effect.[77] Yet guarantors and hostages could not halt the flow of so many disparate groups and individuals from the region.

The system of restrictions thus was intensified after the turn of the century, as part of a general tightening of restraints on movements by all and sundry in Ottoman Europe.[78] By mid-1803 no Albanians—even the soldiers so needed by those fighting the brigands—were to be allowed out of their homelands, even with the permission papers.[79] Any responsible official who allowed such men to pass was threatened with dire consequences. Not all listened to orders, however. Tepedelenli Ali was often singled out by other frustrated officers of the state as bearing great responsibility for the continuation of the Mountain Bandit problem because of his reluctance to close the mountain passes under his control.[80] One of the offices which he held was *derbendler başbuğu*, or supervisor of the system of guards watching the highland passes throughout much of the Balkans. His unwillingness to apply the rules restricting the movement of Albanians thus was particularly damaging to their effectiveness, which makes the frustration of other officers quite understandable. Given that Ali himself was in charge of the operations against the Mountain Bandits in 1802 and did well in persuading many to settle down, why did he not cooperate in closing the passes?

Ali had more to fear from closing the passes than from supervising them laxly and risking Istanbul's displeasure. Although his own status and authority amongst the Tosks of the south was great, it was by no means unchallenged. He always had to struggle to control banditry even in the districts most under his control, let alone those still being absorbed after violent campaigns against other notables. Ali would much rather see the kinsmen and followers of defeated rivals, as well as those who lost *çiftliks* or other property to him, go elsewhere to try to mend their fortunes, rather than stay bottled up in or near his territory. The degree of his mastery over the passes is also debatable. The *derbend* system did not cover all of the Balkans (which in itself suggests that he did not bear sole responsibility for allowing disreputable bands to slip through) but did extend over a very large area. While he exercised greater mastery over the system than did his several predecessors, it seems likely that his ability to ensure complete closure of distant passes was less than absolute, even had he wished to. Ali was rarely, if ever, accused of sending bands of brigands far from Albania, since his interests were focused on neighboring lands, but it does seem all too understandable that he did not spend much of his influence and resources on keeping those who wished to migrate from doing so.

In light of Istanbul's demonstrated inability to bend Ali and other Balkan notables to its will and of the limited efficacy of its road-policing system, it is difficult to explain conclusively the ending of the Mountain Bandit era after Selim III's overthrow in 1807, and especially the dwindling of the Albanian threat to public order. The deaths of several of the most powerful and willful *ayan*, including most notably Osman Pasvanoğlu, certainly helped.[81] No one of equal stature could rise to such levels of influence in lands which were exhausted by 1807. In some senses the Albanian provinces perhaps gained some stability, as trade boomed during the Napoleonic period and the successors to Kara Mahmud in İşkodra showed themselves to be less troublesome to their neighbors and the state.[82] Plague also subsided for a number of years after 1804. Another probable factor, however, was the renewed outbreak of war with Russia in 1806, which offered to many Albanians once again the opportunity to find employment in the Ottoman army. It is ironic that renewed warfare might have helped to reduce the problem of banditry, after having been so important in promoting it in the previous century.

Conclusion

Ottoman Europe suffered turmoil in the late eighteenth century that shook to its foundations Istanbul's structure of provincial authority. Violence and lawlessness are symptoms of frictions or tensions within a society, and no state has ever been entirely free of them. In this case, the veritable epidemic of brigandage points to the existence of widespread, fundamental problems. For the Albanian provinces of the western Balkans, the 1780s, 1790s, and 1800s brought the most intense stretch of an extended period of turbulence, as rival notables became ever more aggressive in their attempts to secure for themselves wealth and power. Their actions caused rising impoverishment and misery in both town and country, both by outright destruction resulting from raid and counter-raid, and by promoting significant changes in the urban and rural economy. Notables gained control over ever more land through threats and force, imposing thereafter heavy revenue burdens upon the remaining peasants. Commerce, in turn, suffered from the insecurity promoted by the conflicts, and by the *de facto* creation of internal borders defended by rival *ayan*. The local notables were taking advantage of the imperial government's preoccupation with immediate threats to its own existence, and many Albanians who had no secure place in this environment chose to emigrate. Given both the lack of viable peaceful opportunities and the plunder to be taken in other chaotic, ill-defended provinces, it is no surprise that so many chose the option of banditry. For the state, pressed by severe external threats, mounting internal challenges, and suffering a visible loss of domestic authority and power, little could be done quickly to repair the damage suffered by the Albanian provinces. Many years would pass before Istanbul could muster the resources needed to crush the last of the powerful *ayan* of the Balkans, Tepedelenli Ali Pasha.[83] The move came too late to repair the old system, as the various layers of lawlessness eventually provoked successful revolts against Ottoman rule amongst first Serbs and then Greeks. These revolts, of course, were to push the Ottoman state toward the full-scale reform or modernization projects of the nineteenth century.

Notes

1. The term refers to brigands or "outlaws" who, based in the Balkan and Rhodope mountain chains of Bulgaria, ravaged surrounding areas as far as northern Greece, southern Romania, and western Macedonia from ca. 1791 to ca. 1808.

2. Stanford Shaw, *Between Old and New: The Ottoman Empire under Sultan Selim III, 1789–1807* (Cambridge: Harvard University, 1971); Yücel Özkaya, *Osmanlı İmperatorluğunda Dağlı İsyanları (1791–1808)* (Ankara: Dil ve Tarih-Coğrafya Fakültesi, 1983); Bruce McGowan, "The Age of the *Ayans*, 1699–1812," in Halil İnalcık et al., *An Economic and Social History of the Ottoman Empire, 1300–1914* (New York: Cambridge University Press, 1994), 663. Halil İnalcık ("Arnawutluk," in *The Encyclopedia of Islam* [Leiden: Brill, 1960], 656–57) is one of the few to make even a passing reference to the large numbers of Albanians among the Mountain Bandits.

3. In light of the recent violent troubles in Kosovo and Macedonia and the strong emotions tied to them, readers are urged most emphatically not to draw either of two unwarranted conclusions from this article: that Albanians are somehow inherently inclined to banditry, or that the extent of Ottoman "Albania" or *Arnavudluk* (which included parts of present-day northern Greece, western Macedonia, southern Montenegro, Kosovo, and southern Serbia) gives any historical "justification" for the creation of a "Greater Albania" today.

4. For further comment on the breadth of activities considered as "banditry," see discussion of the term "*eşkiya*" in Anastasopoulos's contribution to this volume.

5. The reasons for the Ottomans' enduring readiness to use a non-religious identifier are obscure but perhaps are related to Albanians' mobility as both pastoralists and migrants, which brought them and their noticeably clannish or tribal social mores into frequent and extended contact with settled groups of different social and ethnic backgrounds. Other groups sharing these characteristics (and not by coincidence also from very mountainous regions, in the majority of cases), such as people from the Caucasus (Georgians, Abkhaz, Circassians), Kurds, and Gypsies/Roma, were also more often identified by an ethnic marker than was the case with Greeks, Bulgars, or non-tribal Turks and Arabs. Indeed, the word "Arab" was most commonly applied to desert nomads, rather than the much larger category of Arabic speakers.

6. Karen Barkey, *Bandits and Bureaucrats: The Ottoman Route to State Centralization* (Ithaca: Cornell University Press, 1994).

7. In the most recent edition of his book on banditry, Hobsbawm acknowledged criticism of his reliance on mythical folklore in his discussion of *hayduds*—but nevertheless changed remarkably little of his original theoretical model (Eric Hobsbawm, *Bandits* [London: Weidenfeld and Nicolson, 2000], xi, 171–72, ch. 7). Katherine Fleming recently attempted to link together the Hobsbawm and Barkey theories in discussing Tepedelenli Ali Pasha's career. Terming this time as a period of increasing centralization of the state and strengthening of its institutions, and drawing upon much the same flimsy material used by Hobsbawm, her picture also fails to persuade (K. E. Fleming, *The Muslim Bonaparte: Diplomacy and Orientalism in Ali Pasha's Greece* [Princeton: Princeton University Press, 1999], 40–44). For a purer "Balkanist" view of bandits as national heroes, see Bistra Cvetkova, "The Bulgarian Haiduk Movement in the 15th to 18th Centuries," in Gunther Rothenberg, Béla Király, and Peter Sugar, eds., *East Central European Society in the Pre-Revolutionary Eighteenth Century* (Boulder, Colo: Social Science Monographs, 1982), 301–38. For the best account of banditry in the Ottoman Balkans, with particular attention paid to exposing many of the common misperceptions about *haydud* bands operating as national-Christian freedom fighters, see Fikret Adanır, "Heiduckentum und Osmanische Herrschaft," *Südost-Forschungen* 41 (1982): 43–116.

8. For example, McGowan, "Age of the *Ayans*," pp. 665–66, and İnalcık, "Arnawutluk," 657.

9. Başbakanlık Arşivi, Istanbul (BA), Cevdet Dahiliye (C.DH) 427, 8 June 1792; BA, C.DH 1340, 25 June 1792.

10. The current place-name and country (including Kosovo, for the sake of simplicity, in spite of its present hazy status) henceforth will be given in brackets following the Ottoman name.

11. BA, C.DH 6365, 12–16 June 1792.

12. BA, C.DH 1452, 13 August 1795.

13. BA, C.DH 7850, various reports dated November 1788.

14. BA, C.DH 534, orders dated March–April 1799; BA, Mühimme Defteri (MD) 210/30, late February 1800.

15. Ali Zot came from a notable family in the district of Yanya which had entered into the violent struggles for wealth and power afflicting the area in the 1780s. Ali emigrated to become one of the leading figures of the Mountain Bandit problem in the 1790s.

16. Of the more than three thousand Mountain Bandits in the vicinity of Filibe (Plovdiv, Bulgaria) and Zağra (Stara Zagora, Bulgaria) in September 1791, half were Albanian. BA, Hatt-i Hümayun (HH) 10420, 2 October 1791.

17. BA, HH 2844-A, 1799–1800; BA, C.DH 326, late December 1794; BA, Cevdet Adliye (C.ADL) 703, 6 April 1802.

18. BA, C.DH 1832, 1793–94; BA, HH 5239-A, 1792–93; Özkaya, *Dağlı İsyanları*, pp. 23–24; BA, C.DH 326.

19. Among the various Albanian linguistic-social groups, the two most important were the Tosks of the south and the Ghegs of the north. In this case, without more information it is impossible to determine whether just the Tosk background or some closer tie inclined the brigands and deserters toward each other.

20. BA, HH 3742-A, June–July 1800. John Koliopoulos, *Brigands with a Cause: Brigandage and Irredentism in Modern Greece, 1821–1912* (New York: Oxford University Press, 1987), 58–60, also notes such an overtly mercenary streak demonstrated by bands from "northern Greece" (including Epirus and Macedonia) during the Greek revolt of the 1820s.

21. BA, HH 3434-D, 12 January 1801.

22. BA, HH 2889-B, 17 July 1802; Deena Sadat, "Ayan and Ağa: The Transformation of the Bektashi Corps in the Eighteenth Century," *Muslim World* 63 (July 1973): 206–219.

23. The Morea suffered repeated raids and other abuse, particularly after 1770, in spite of Istanbul's efforts to keep Albanians out of the peninsula. See, for example, BA, HH 1285, 1778; BA, C.DH 900, 5 April 1782; BA, Cevdet Zabtiye (C.ZB) 4236, 26 May 1795; BA, C.DH 281, 13 January 1800; BA, C.DH 521, 29 August 1803.

24. For references to Bosnians, see BA, C.DH 4126, 18 May 1800; BA, HH 3049, 1801–2.

25. Machiel Kiel, *Ottoman Architecture in Albania (1385–1912)* (Istanbul: Research Center for Islamic History, Art and Culture, 1990), 14.

26. Gilles Veinstein, "Les Provinces Balkaniques (1606–1774)," in Robert Mantran, ed., *Histoire de l'Empire Ottoman* (Paris: Fayard, 1989), 321.

27. Daniel Panzac, *La Peste dans l'Empire Ottoman, 1700–1850* (Leuven: Editions Peeters, 1985), 109–115, 198.

28. Panzac, *La Peste*, 67, 111–12.

29. BA, C.ADL 1053, 1 November 1795.

30. Özkaya, *Dağlı İsyanları*, 25, for references to famine in 1794; BA, HH 6163-F, for grain shortage in Prizren in 1806; BA, C.DH 13425, undated (probably shortly before 1798) for lack of grain shipments from Selanik due to drought. Ahmed Cevdet, *Tarih-i Cevdet* (Istanbul, 1886), vol. 5, 211, for grain shortages in Istanbul in 1791, and vol. 6, 86, for shortages in Manastir in 1794.

31. BA, HH 6907, 17 December 1803.

32. Since it has been customary since the seventeenth century to deplore the decline of the *sipahi-dirlik* system and to point to this development as evidence of "decline," it is worth repeating that the system could not continue unchanged in an era of military requirements much changed since the *sipahi* system was first instituted. It is noteworthy that Russia started to move away from its own system of landed service-cavalry (and its "Janissaries", the *strel'tsi*) in the eighteenth century for similar reasons. See Donald Ostrowski, *Muscovy and the*

Mongols: Cross-Cultural Influences on the Steppe Frontier, 1304–1589 (New York: Cambridge University Press, 1998), and Simon Dixon, *The Modernisation of Russia 1676–1825* (New York: Cambridge University Press, 1999).

33. Conversion of *dirlik* to *çiftlik* in Albanian territory was already well advanced by the mid-eighteenth century. BA, MD 154, 308/1, late April–early May 1750. See also Ligor Mile, "De l'extension du système des *çiftlig* sur les territoires albanais," *Deuxieme Conférence des Études Albanologiques* (Tirana, 1970), 101–108. For continuation of the *dirlik* system long after its formal abolition in the 1830s, see Nathalie Clayer, "Note sur la survivance du système des *timâr* dans la région de Shkodër au début du XXe siècle," *Turcica* 29 (1997), 423–31.

34. Records of irregular taxation and disputes over *çiftlik*s abound. For a selection from different years, places, and tactics, see: BA, C.ADL 446, 1 November 1768; BA, C.DH 10372, November–December 1785; BA, Rumeli Ahkâm 42/773, mid-April 1788; BA, Rumeli Ahkâm 47/275, mid-November 1793; BA, Rumeli Ahkâm 50/149, April 1796; BA, MD 210/678, mid-May 1800.

35. BA, C.DH 10372, 1786.

36. Dennis Skiotis, "From Bandit to Pasha: First Steps in the Rise to Power of Ali of Tepelen, 1750–1784," *International Journal of Middle East Studies* 2 (1971): 221, note 1; McGowan, "Age of the *Ayans*," 668, 688. McGowan notes that Ali also took advantage of Istanbul's preoccupation with the Ottoman-Russian war of 1806–1812 to seize more lands. For references to the seizure of *çiftlik*s by Ali and his family during that war, see William Leake, *Travels in Northern Greece* (London, 1835), vol. 4, ch. 38.

37. Halil İnalcık, "Stefan Duşan'dan Osmanlı İmparatorluğuna," in *Fuad Köprülü Armağanı, Mélanges Fuad Köprülü* (Istanbul: Dil ve Tarih-Coğrafya Fakültesi, 1953), 85–90; Kiel, *Ottoman Architecture*, 18.

38. For an example from Anatolia, see Yuzo Nagata, "The Role of Ayans in Regional Development during the Pre-Tanzimat Period in Turkey: A Case Study of the Karaosmanoğlu Family," in his *Studies on the Social and Economic History of the Ottoman Empire* (Izmir: Akademi Kitabevi, 1995), 120–21.

39. Skiotis, "From Bandit to Pasha," 226, 234–36.

40. BA, C.DH 980, February 1772. For a similar case from 1790, see BA, Cevdet Askeri 3850.

41. Skiotis, "Bandit to Pasha," 230–31; Kristo Frashëri, *The History of Albania (a Brief Survey)* (Tirana, 1964), 101–4.

42. BA, HH 2058, 18 November 1790.

43. BA, HH 15326, 1800–1801.

44. BA, MD 210/380, mid-April 1800.

45. BA, C.DH 1570, late August 1799.

46. BA, C.DH 334, 6 March 1787; BA, C.DH 3815, undated but almost certainly from the same year.

47. For a good example of Kara Mahmud in action, see Michael Hickok, *Ottoman Military Administration in Eighteenth-Century Bosnia* (New York: Brill, 1997), 152–75.

48. BA, HH 1106-C, 14 February 1789; Cevdet, *Tarih*, vol. 5, 17.

49. Peter Bartl, "Albanien im Russisch-Österreichischen Türkenkrieg, 1787–1792," in Klaus-Detlev Grothusen, ed., *Albanien in Vergangenheit und Gegenwart* (Munich: Südosteuropa-Studien, 1991), 57–60; Cevdet, *Tarih*, vol. 6, pp. 84–86; BA, HH 3318, 1 April 1793.

50. Stavri Naçi, *Pashallëku i Shkodrës nën sundimin e Bushatllive në gjysmën e dytë të shek. XVIII* (Tirana: University of Tirana, 1964), chapter 4; Cevdet, *Tarih*, vol. 6, 197–98; BA, HH 742, 27 January 1788; BA, HH 7922 and 10913, 1789.

51. McGowan, "Age of the *Ayans*," 724–25.

52. See Ömer Şen, *Osmanlı Panayırları (18. –19. Yüzyıl)* (Istanbul: Eren, 1996) for information on selected fairs in the Balkans, particularly for the nineteenth century.

53. McGowan, "Age of the *Ayans*," 736; Stavri Naçi, "Le Facteur Albanais dans la Commerce Balkanique au XVIIIe Siecle," *Studia Albanica* VII/2 (1970), 37–42.

54. On İskopol see Max Peyfuss, *Die Druckerei von Moschopolis, 1731–1769: Buchdruck und Heiligenverehrung im Erzbistum Achrida* (Vienna: Böhlau, 1989).

55. BA, MD 104/470, mid-August 1693.

56. BA, C.DH 16315, August–September 1782.

57. Veinstein, "Provinces Balkaniques," 332; Frashëri, *History of Albania*, 102, 108; Peyfuss, *Druckerei*, 43, 45. İskopol did not disappear completely from the map of Albanian commerce, but it certainly never regained its previous prosperity. See Ferit Duka, *Berati në Kohën Osmane (shek. XVI–XVIII)* (Tirana: Toena, 2001), 137. It continued to be vulnerable to outside threats: by the end of the Greek revolt of the 1820s, most of İskopol's residents had fled to safer places. BA, C.DH 8285, mid-September 1829.

58. Both of these restrictions were honored haphazardly, at best, in other Albanian *ayans*' territories. For the widespread use of non-Ottoman currency in Ali Pasha's Yanya, see BA, MD 220/208, mid-March 1803.

59. Shaw, *Between Old and New*, 230; Naçi, *Pashallëku i Shkodrës*, ch. 4; Stavri Naçi, "Le Pachalik de Shkodër considéré dans son développement économique et social au XVIIIe s.," *Studia Albanica* III/1 (1966): 137–42; McGowan, "Age of the *Ayans*," 667; Fleming, *Muslim Bonaparte*, 46–49, 51–54.

60. BA, C.DH 4496, 24 and 28 July 1780. İşkodra's traders were not the only ones to suffer such losses, of course. For an early example of confiscation of goods from a trader from Arnavud Belgrad, carried out in 1775 by İşkodran officers in Bar (Montenegro), see Duka, *Berati*, 145.

61. BA, C.DH 543, April 1794; BA, C.DH 1280, 26 March 1794.
62. The migration of Albanians in search of work has been noted frequently, at least in passing. For a recent discussion of this phenomenon, see Suraiya Faroqhi, "Migration into Eighteenth-Century 'Greater Istanbul' as Reflected in the Kadi Registers of Eyüp," *Turcica* 30 (1998): 171, 173–75.
63. Robert Olson, "Jews, Janissaries, Esnaf and the Revolt of 1740 in Istanbul," *Journal of the Economic and Social History of the Orient* 20/2 (1977): 187–88, 194–98.
64. As with many still-popular beliefs about the oppressiveness of Ottoman rule over non-Muslims in the Balkans (e.g., drastic curbs placed upon churches, bans on riding horses, numerous sumptuary restrictions), the idea that *zimmi*s could not have weapons certainly does not reflect the reality of all times and all places. One of the empire's defense and security tactics was the *nefir-i amm*, which called all capable men of a district to arms. BA, C.DH 560, 21 June 1796, for example, calls all local men, including *reaya* (non-military men including, but not necessarily limited to, Christian peasants), to arms against Mountain Bandits active in central Bulgaria. Those who fought against the bandits were permitted to keep whatever spoils they captured—not just money and goods, but also weapons.
65. BA, Rumeli Ahkâm 42/424, late October 1787.
66. BA, Rumeli Ahkâm 42/829, early June 1788.
67. BA, C.DH 3291, 1779.
68. BA, C.DH 430, undated but apparently from the period 1798–1801, for example, decried the continuing practice of awarding important positions, such as the *nezaret*s (supervisor of revenue collection) of Üsküb (Skopje, Macedonia) and Filibe (Plovdiv, Bulgaria) or the *cizyedarlık* (collector of the poll-tax paid by non-Muslims) of Edirne (Turkey), to Albanians or any other locals who lacked clear dependence upon Istanbul.
69. BA, C.DH 8776 records the presence of Albanian tax farmers in Yenişehir in 1793–94—and both they and other Albanians continued to be viewed frequently with suspicion. In Domenik district in northern Greece, Albanian traders as well as tax farmers preferred to demand food and lodging from Orthodox villagers as they passed through, rather than to arrange their own supplies. BA, C.DH 2501, 12 November 1795. For an earlier case in Yenişehir, see BA, C.DH 8196, 1782.
70. See, for instance, Noel Malcolm, *Kosovo: A Short History* (New York: New York University Press, 1998), xxviii, the best history of the background to the recent conflict. For a summary of explanations of the role of guards, see Ger Duijzings, *Religion and the Politics of Identity in Kosovo* (New York: Columbia University Press, 2000), 72, n. 6.
71. BA, C.ZB 425, May and August 1790.
72. Albanians fighting for ambitious *ayan* was certainly not a phenomenon reser-

ved solely for the Balkans. The retinue of the Bosnian Ahmed Cezzar Pasha ("The Butcher"), *ayan* of Acre on the Syrian coast (1775–1804), had a large Albanian component—as of course did that of the Albanian Mehmed Ali Pasha of Egypt (1805–49).

73. BA, MD 210, mid-April 1800; BA, C.DH 430. The latter document, a detailed analysis of the Mountain Bandit problem, has been published in transliteration (but with numerous errors): Yücel Özkaya, "XVIII. Yüzyılın İkinci Yarısına Ait Sosyal Yaşantıyı Ortaya Koyan bir Belge," *OTAM* 2 (Ankara, 1991): 303–34.

74. BA, C.DH 430.

75. BA, C.DH 7377, late November 1797.

76. BA, HH 2168, 18 March 1797.

77. BA, MD 220/658, early June 1803.

78. BA, C.DH 430 includes details of a wide-ranging scheme to police all movement in the regions affected by the Mountain Bandits.

79. BA, MD 220/643–656, early June 1803. These restrictions, however, did not prevent the *vali* of Rumeli from recruiting Albanians to serve in his army in the following winter (see note 31).

80. BA, HH 2168, 18 March 1797; BA, HH 13256, undated but presumably 1800–1801.

81. Özkaya, *Dağlı İsyanları*, 101–03.

82. Norman Saul, *Russia and the Mediterranean, 1797–1807* (Chicago: University of Chicago Press, 1970), 221, for example, notes that Black Sea trade through Odessa saw strong growth in 1808, promoted in part by the Continental System of Napoleon's newly-expanded European empire.

83. Istanbul never could manage to crush that other famous Albanian provincial notable, Mehmed Ali Pasha, a *sekban* leader who left Kavala (Greece) to establish his dominance in Egypt. Mehmed Ali's actions and mindset bear a number of important similarities to those of Tepedelenli Ali. The best critical work on Mehmed Ali is Khaled Fahmy, *All the Pasha's Men: Mehmed Ali, His Army and the Making of Modern Egypt* (New York: Cambridge University Press, 1997).

Osman Pazvantoğlu of Vidin: Between Old and New[1]

Rossitsa Gradeva

O sman Pazvantoğlu's star rose in the midst of the anarchy which spread in the central Balkan provinces of the Ottoman empire in the last
decades of the eighteenth, and descended almost simultaneously with the
subsidence of chaos at the beginning of the nineteenth century. His secession from the empire was an integral part of a social phenomenon that left
a lasting imprint on the historical memory of the people living in these territories during the period labelled as the "*kırcalı* time."[2] This period was
marked by considerable disruption in the functioning of the institutions
of central authority in the provinces. Power in Rumeli was parcelled out
among numerous local *ayan*s who ruled over smaller or larger territories
with varying degrees of independence. Against this backdrop of chaos and
autocracy, there rose in numerous centers of power (but also of lawlessness
and anarchy, which overlapped in the central Balkan lands) local despots
who established almost unrestrained rule: the Buşatlıs in northern Albania
and some adjacent regions, Ali Paşa of Tepedelen in Yanya [Ioannina] and
much of modern continental Greece, Osman Pazvantoğlu [var. Pasvanoğlu/
Pasvantoğlu/ Pasbanoğlu] of Vidin in modern northwestern Bulgaria and
eastern Serbia, İsmail Tırseniklioğlu in Rusçuk [Ruse] and part of modern

northeastern Bulgaria, İsmail Bey of Serrai [Serres], in modern northeastern Greece, and others.[3] They all achieved some level of independence from central authority, but two—Osman Pazvantoğlu and Ali Paşa—seem to have gone beyond mere attempts to ensure financial and administrative autonomy under the Ottoman cloak and constructed "proto-states."[4] The process of fragmentation was closely intertwined with the first serious attempt at modernization in the Ottoman state, the reforms in the ruling and military systems undertaken by Sultan Selim III (r. 1789–1807). Finding support mainly among the circles which openly opposed these reforms, Osman Paşa and Ali Paşa themselves actually introduced reforms in their own possessions, acting in many ways as predecessors of the policy of Mehmed Ali in Egypt. However, their activities met with opposition, and not only from the still very strong empire. They also had to reckon with the very complicated international situation after the outbreak of the French Revolution and the successful march of French armies eastward to the Balkan boundaries of the Ottoman empire. The two had little chance for success in a situation where the traditional enemies of the Ottoman state, the Russians and the Austrians, supported legitimism and the integrity of the Ottoman state. Finally, the ultimate success of their secession from the empire was highly dependent on, and in general complicated by, the effect of the ideas of the French Revolution on the Balkan peoples (the Greeks, in particular), the first signs of the "National Awakening," and the first attempts at political liberation of Balkan peoples.

While interesting as an historical phenomenon in itself, Osman Pazvantoğlu's secession also provides an interesting angle in the discussion of contemporary events in several directions. In the first place it offers a glimpse into the reaction to Selim III's reforms among rank-and-file Muslims and Christians in the Balkan provinces, and into the roots and the reasons for the opposition to their introduction among all strata of Ottoman society. Of particular interest is the fact that, like the other noteworthy secessionists, Osman Pazvantoğlu found wide support in various Christian circles. During his short life the Vidin rebel came in contact with some of the first leaders of several Balkan peoples' Awakening. Legendary and historical evidence relates him to the Greek revolutionary Rhigas Velestinlis, to the Bulgarian bishop of Vratsa, Sofronii, and even to Kara George, the leader of the First Serbian Uprising. None of these Balkan leaders can be regarded as a close associate of Osman Pazvantoğlu, as each followed his own path. Yet these paths at some point crossed that of the Vidin *paşa*

and ran parallel with his for a shorter or longer while. Driven by sometimes contradictory motives, many non-Muslims—including members of
Rhigas's *hetairia*, high Orthodox clergy, and local merchants—were active
participants in Pazvantoğlu's diplomatic and political moves. The geographic location and the complex international relations in the region contributed to the considerable interest in his personality manifested by the Great
Powers. In this context, it is difficult to name all famous personalities of the
time who came to know Pazvantoğlu and established contact with him, but
they included the French foreign minister Talleyrand and even Napoleon
himself, the Russian tsar, his ministers and generals, and high Austrian state
officials. Diplomatic correspondence of the 1790s and 1800s from and to
the Ottoman empire abounds in information about his deeds and conjectures
concerning his further moves.

Despite the considerable interest in Pazvantoğlu shown by his contemporaries, his life has rarely been the object of study, the only two works being published several decades ago.[5] It seems that the subsequent events—the
First Serbian Uprising, the Russo-Turkish War of 1806–12, the Napoleonic
wars, the rise of Ali Paşa of Yanya (whose longer rule brought him the recognition to which Osman Pazvantoğlu aspired),[6] the strong philhellenism
dominating Western society during the eighteenth and nineteenth centuries,
and the Greek War of Independence—have overshadowed the image of the
Vidin rebel in fiction and scholarly works.

This paper does not aim to provide a biography of Osman Paşa of
Vidin—a task that has yet to be undertaken and requires further research in various Ottoman and diplomatic archives. The purpose here is
more limited and is concentrated around two major circles of problems.
In the first place, I analyse the views and the "domestic policy" of Osman Pazvantoğlu in his possessions, as revealed in available Ottoman
and diplomatic sources. This should contribute to a clearer picture of Ottoman decentralization at the end of the eighteenth and beginning of the
nineteenth centuries, to a better understanding of the processes at work
in Ottoman society at the time, and to the reasons for the fierce opposition to the reforms undertaken by Selim III. It should also provide firmer
ground for discussion of the reasons for the popularity of Pazvantoğlu and
other significant separatists who applied similar methods in government,
among various circles of Ottoman Muslim society and, to some extent,
among the Christians living in their territories. The latter forms the second area of focus. Particular attention is devoted to the relations between

Pazvantoğlu and various groups among the non-Muslim population. Here I analyze the attitude of the "speechless" masses who have left practically no explicit expression of their views. This is done on the basis of indirect evidence found mainly in Ottoman official documentation and in diplomatic sources. Another level of this attitude is displayed in the relations between Pazvantoğlu and his closest associates, who helped him in his diplomatic relations with the Ottoman authorities, with the princes of the Danube Principalities and with the representatives of the Great Powers in the region: wholesale merchants, high Orthodox clergy, and physicians, who often served more than one master. Of particular interest here are his relations with the leaders of the young national movements of the Balkan peoples—Rhigas, Bishop Sofronii, and the Serbs after the outbreak of the First Serbian Uprising.

The aims of the paper require a note on sources and their shortcomings. Ottoman court records (*kadı sicill*s) have great value,[7] as do diplomatic correspondence[8] and travellers' accounts.[9] All shed light on the shaping of policies regarding events in the Ottoman empire, on the prejudices and fears of governments, but also on the moods reigning among the relatively "speechless" multitude of the lower ranks of Ottoman society. The diplomatic reports vary in terms of reliability because of the circulation of numerous rumors about Pazvantoğlu. Of further interest are, of course, the works of Rhigas and his associates or adherents,[10] of Bishop Sofronii,[11] and the short inscriptions in manuscript and early printed books reflecting the views and feelings of his Bulgarian contemporaries living through the hell of the *kırcalı* time.[12] We must admit that our information about Pazvantoğlu's views and deeds originates mainly from circles openly hostile to him. When sources claim to express his views, usually through an intermediary, they vary greatly depending on the addressee. Even his so-called proclamations are known only by the trace they have left in the diplomatic correspondence. Though French, Austrian, and Russian sources mention them,[13] and they were apparently sent to the respective foreign office bureaus, we have been unable to retrieve any original document of the kind. No other documents have been preserved revealing Pazvantoğlu's direct relations with any of the above-mentioned groups, traces of which surface in the diplomatic correspondence. Of course all this leaves grounds for speculation regarding his real motivation and aims. Unfortunately, at present, we can only make educated guesses about them.

Some notes on Vidin and its district at the end of the eighteenth century

The area of Vidin had enjoyed a specific status and agrarian regime ever since its conquest by the Ottomans at the end of the fourteenth century. One of the main features was the sweeping introduction of the *miri* regime, without any sigificant agrarian *mülk* and *vakıf*. In the course of the subsequent two centuries the *timar* system was in practice gradually abolished in this district, mainly to the benefit of imperial *hass*es. The Vidin *nezaret* founded during the seventeenth century expanded particularly after the war with the Holy League at the end of the century. Afterwards *timar* holders almost entirely disappear from the local records. The *sancak* was divided into several *mukataa*s. Their revenues provided the salaries of the paid troops in the *sancak* and in several other fortresses and provinces, such as Temešvar, Isakçea, and those of the captains and crews of the river ships stationed in several fortified places up the Danube. This regime, combined with the displacement of villagers during the wars at the end of the seventeenth and in the first half of the eighteenth century, led to the formation of a specific system of land ownership in the area. *Tapu* deeds were no longer in the possession of peasants cultivating the land, but in the hands of new agents who intervened between the *nazır*s, acting as representatives of the sultan, and the direct cultivators. The *tapu*s were bought usually by citizens of Vidin, mainly Janissaries, depriving villagers of their legal possession rights on the land. Towards the end of the eighteenth century this process was given additional impetus by another series of wars, the devastation of the countryside, plagues, and especially by the regime of Osman Pazvantoğlu. The transformation of villages into *gospodarlık* corresponds to the process of *čitlučene* taking place in the adjacent Belgrade *Paşalık*. It meant that the peasants no longer paid the traditional taxes, which were replaced by a single tax to the owner of the *tapu* and one to Pazvantoğlu (in the Vidin area) who had acquired the prerogatives of the former *voyvoda*s of the imperial *hass*es and of the *nazır*. Pazvantoğlu was himself an active participant in the process of divesting the peasants of their ownership rights on cultivable land.[14]

Vidin as a city and fortress also underwent considerable changes, especially after the war with the Holy League. In 1689–90 it fell into Austrian hands for about ten months. This occupation apparently caused considerable problems for local Muslims, and twenty years later they still referred to the "occupation of the city by the infidels" as the reason for the flight of many local people, as well as for the destruction of local places of worship.[15] This shock, along with the even more disastrous war of 1715–18, when the district was once again one of the theaters of military hostilities, laid a lasting imprint on the mentality of the Muslim inhabitants of the town. After the peace treaty of Passarowitz (1718) when the Ottomans lost Banat, the important fortresses of Temešvar and Belgrade, and even two *kaza*s of the Vidin *sancak*, Vidin again became part of the *serhad*. Many fugitives from the lost territories settled there. It was then that, following an application on the part of local Janissaries alluding to the *kanun-i serhad*, Christians were forced to move out of the fortified part of the town. They were required to build houses of wood, not stone, so that these could not serve as a shelter for the enemy in case of an attack. The Christians' houses were sold to Muslims, and the two main faiths in the city were spatially separated.[16] Similar attitudes can be detected as late as the first half of the nineteenth century, when Janissaries in Vidin claimed that, in compliance with the old law, property rights on land in the border areas belonged exclusively to Muslim soldiers from these fortresses.[17] Another consequence of these events was the sharp increase in the number of military men, especially those involved in one way or another in the Janissary units in Vidin. In fact, it seems that nearly the whole Muslim population of the town must have been involved in its defense.[18] All these circumstances contributed to the emergence of an atmosphere of militant spirit combined with strong religious feelings among local Muslims. No doubt this climate, the regime of land possession, and the closeness of the border triggered the emergence of secessionist opportunities. Indeed, on several occasions before Pazvantoğlu we hear of Janissary riots in Vidin. However, they became particularly dangerous with the rise of the Pazvantoğlu family.

Osman Pazvantoğlu: sketches from his biography and political career

Despite all that was written at the time of Osman's rise and afterwards, there is still much to be clarified about the family of the rebel and the early history of his rebellion. Here I shall only summarize some facts from his life and rise to power.

Contemporary sources advance several theories of his family's origins. The most popular one, based on the notes of the French officer Mériage and adopted by the majority of scholars who have studied this period, attributes to him Bosnian background and even Slavic and Christian roots.[19] More recently V. Mutafchieva, on the basis of the few Ottoman documents relating to the Pazvantoğlu family before the rise of Osman,[20] advanced a "Vidin" hypothesis—that his parents belonged to well-established Vidin families.[21] It is quite possible to "marry" the two theses: without refuting a more distant Bosnian background, it is indeed possible to claim that by the time of Osman Pazvantoğlu the family was well entrenched in the Ottoman provincial elite in Vidin.

The sources are unanimous about several points in the history of the Pazvantoğlu family. Osman Pazvantoğlu reportedly inherited considerable wealth from his father. Moreover, by the time of Osman's rise to power, the family was an important factor in the military elite in Vidin. His father was *ağa* (in some sources *alemdar*) of the 31st Janissary *orta* (he is mentioned as such in documents of 1764 about events prior to that date, and in 1787). By 1787 Osman, too, had become one of the commanders of the same *orta*. Osman followed the family traditions in yet another direction. Contemporary authors speak of the long record of his father (and even grandfather) as a rebel against Ottoman central authority. The somewhat fabulous stories related by western authors are confirmed to a considerable extent by the scanty Ottoman documentation about the early history of the family. On at least two occasions there was an open conflict between Ömer Pazvantoğlu and the central authority. Prior to 1764, already *ağa* of the 31st Janissary *orta*, he was exiled to Belgrade for unknown misdemeanors. It is not clear when he was allowed to return to Vidin, but in 1787 a *ferman* of the sultan condemned him (as well as Osman and seven other Janissaries from other *orta*s) to capital punishment. They were accused of having conspired against the central authority, planning a general revolt which could open to enemies the road to the Ottoman capital. Within six months (by June 1788) Ömer Pazvantoğlu was executed and his estate divided among his heirs. Strangely, Osman was among them and had apparently been spared by the sultan's justice. This is the time when Osman Pazvantoğlu entered official records, already with some experience in challenging the sultan's authority (even before Selim III's ascension to the throne) and with an important position in the military hierarchy.

From here on, the milestones of Pazvantoğlu's rise are much better known. Documents of various types provide information about Osman's life, mainly from 1792 onwards. In the first place they are related to his creation of an independent power center.[22] All sources of the time consider this power center inseparable from the *kırcalı* unrest. By 1791–92 it had become clear that he was also in alliance with the Janissaries banished from Belgrade, providing them with shelter and support. Not only that, he armed the *reaya* in the regions adjacent to the *Paşalık* of Belgrade and forced them to take part in the military activities on the side of the *kırcalı*s and Janissaries.[23] In 1793, Vidin and its district served as a shelter for the *dağlı* bands and rose as a center of Janissary opposition to the central authorities and the reforms introduced by Selim III, supporting especially the Janissaries banished from Belgrade. In 1794 Osman Pazvantoğlu was already undisputed master of Vidin. His troops and the *kırcalı* bands connected with him started infesting more distant places like Şehirköy [Pirot, Serbia], Belgrade, and Pleven (in north central Bulgaria). His growing popularity and power caused the Ottoman authorities to undertake the first siege of Vidin at the end of 1795. This siege is not well documented but the outcome is clear. In February 1796, the troops of the Porte were forced to withdraw. A year later Pazvantoğlu started a massive offensive against places that were under the rule of hostile *ayan* or were still faithful to the central authority. Tărnovo, Sevlievo, and Niğbolu [Nikopol] were all attacked by Pazvantoğlu's men, and his possessions expanded.

Pazvantoğlu's great popularity and the expansion of his dependencies led to the organization of a second counteroffensive by the Porte. The preparations began in the fall of 1797, but even in early 1798 his troops still besieged İsmail Tırseniklioğlu in Rusçuk, his main adversary and rival in north Bulgaria, and the *ayan* of Hacıoğlu Pazarı [Dobrich, northeastern Bulgaria]. Pazvantoğlu held all of what is today northwestern and north central Bulgaria, as well as some territories of present-day northeastern Serbia and, for a short time, even Sofia. In February 1798 he started to withdraw toward Vidin, keeping only his elite forces. His capital city was well prepared for a long siege by the huge Ottoman army, which according to contemporary sources numbered a hundred thousand men. The siege of 1798 was very strange. Slowly moving toward Vidin, the *paşa*s, each in command of his own troops, finally formed a loose circle around the fortified center of Pazvantoğlu's possessions. By October it had become clear that Osman was the winner. In fact, the Ottoman authorities were rather keen to stop these military activities, as from September the Ottoman state was at war with the French Republic in Egypt. At this time Russia also supported the legitimacy of the sultan in the conflict with Pazvantoğlu, and sultan and rebel had to reach an agreement. After long negotiations Osman received his long-desired rank of *vezir*, or three-tail *paşa* of Vidin, and the Ottoman troops withdrew. The third siege of Vidin took place in 1800, when Pazvantoğlu concluded an alliance with Cengiz Ghiray (in other sources Mehmed), one of the Tatar sultans based in Vărbitsa, northeastern Bulgaria. This presented not just a military but also an ideological menace to the Ottoman dynasty, because of the Ghiray *hans'* legitimacy. Though supported by Austria and Russia, the Ottoman armies could not do more than during the previous sieges.

After 1800 Osman was left almost entirely on his own. From 1802 until his death there emerged some kind of division of the territory of northern Bulgaria between him and İsmail Tırseniklioğlu, succeeded by Mustafa Bayraktar. Blocked in Vidin to the north by Russia and Austria, now eager to come to the rescue of the sultan, by İsmail Tırseniklioğlu to the east and, after the beginning of the First Serbian Uprising, by the Serbs to the west, he had to content himself with the small corner he had had almost from the very beginning of his rise in the region of Vidin. Osman Pazvantoğlu spent his last years in Vidin surrounded by enemies, deserted by most of his supporters and soldiers among the Christian population and actually in open war with the latter. Toward the end of his life he suffered another humiliation. Despite his rank of *vezir*, it was Mustafa Bayraktar who was appointed commander of the Ottoman troops against Russia in the war of 1806–12.

Along with his political career Osman Pazvantoğlu also managed to continue the family traditions in the accumulation of properties.[24] According to some sources he left to his heirs 25 million *akçe*, including gold and precious stones, huge stores of food and arms, and land possessions amounting to almost one third of the territory of his mini-state, a strip of land along the Danube 50 miles long and 20–25 miles wide,[25] comprising two hundred villages, some inherited but the majority his own acquisitions.[26]

He died on 5 February 1807, probably of influenza, leaving behind a small, almost independent territory and properties whose exact dimensions have yet to be delineated. Pazvantoğlu's properties were divided among his wife, son, and aunt.[27] Shortly after his death his widow married his close associate, Molla İdris Paşa, who inherited not only his possessions and family but also the administrative position of Osman. The central Ottoman authorities did not dare to claim any rights over the properties of Osman Pazvantoğlu until after the death of Molla İdris Paşa, in March 1814.[28] Thirty or more years after his death we see Pazvantoğlu's name in the *kadı sicills* as the person who distributed the villages in the region to his *ağa*s and other notables in Vidin.

The attitude of the Ottoman authorities

As mentioned, Osman came to be noticed by the Ottoman authorities as early as 1787, when he was named in a *ferman* as an organizer of a general revolt in Vidin against the sultan. By the beginning of the 1790s, despite the ups and downs in the history of the family, Osman had emerged as one of the greatest dangers to Ottoman centralism, to the dynasty and to the reforms which Sultan Selim III was trying to introduce.

From the very beginning of his open rebellion he was treated as a "rebel" and a "bandit" in all Ottoman documentation originating from the central authorities. He was accused of breaching the laws, opposing the legal authority, and committing crimes whose main victims were the *reaya*. Gradually his revolt became the main concern for the Ottoman authority, leading not only to the three sieges of Vidin and many attempts at creating opposition to his rule among the Vidin notables and at his murder, but also to the need for a religious and legal justification of the military campaigns against him. Such a justification was particularly needed, due to his popularity among Muslims of all ranks. His ideas were bringing together all opponents of Sultan Selim III's reforms and were in agreement with the mentality of pious Muslims, earning him numerous partisans not only among those who suffered most from the reforms, the taxpayers, but also among the highest functionaries of the Ottoman state. It is not surprising that he was always well informed about the decisions of the state council, and that a number of *paşa*s lost their lives on accusation of being his secret supporters. Thus, in 1797 the sultan felt the need to secure *fetva*s from the *şeyhülislam*, appealing to all Muslims to participate in the suppression of the rebellion and in the extermination of the rebel *paşa* and his closest adherents.[29] These four juridical documents provide the ideological basis of the "holy war" against Osman Pazvantoğlu. Those participating in the battles against him were called *gazi*s, and those killed were proclaimed *şehid*s, titles associated with holy war against "infidels." He was accused of being a ringleader and, as such, "of killing people in public, shedding human blood, threatening the sultan's subjects, devastating towns and villages, terrorizing the poor Muslims and the *reaya*, and committing a number of other crimes." The second and more important accusation was of "having proclaimed himself an independent ruler, being disobedient to the sultan, and having settled in one of the sultan's fortresses, attacking the peaceful (Muslim) communities."[30]

A series of *ferman*s addressed to local authorities in Rumeli, read in public in the Sheriat courts, contain "horror stories" about the slaughter of faithful

Muslims and their families by Pazvantoğlu's hordes. They invariably compared his deeds to those of the armies of the "infidels" during the war (of 1787–91), including bombardment of fortresses, taking Muslims prisoner, burning Islamic cult places and eighty villages, roasting alive women and children (Muslims and *reaya* alike), and pillaging the possessions of the population.[31] No doubt these were not just groundless accusations but part of everyday life in Rumeli for the decades of the *kırcalı* time, but the main purpose was to convince Muslims that their religious duty lay with the sultan's cause.

The popularity of Pazvantoğlu among the Janissaries made the sultan resort to yet another measure. The Janissary *ağa* in the capital convened a meeting of the officers and veterans at which were read all the reports and requests for help from the administrative bodies in Niğbolu, Kula, Silistra, Rusçuk, and elsewhere. At the meeting the Janissaries swore allegiance to the sultan and declared that Osman had to be stripped of the privileges he enjoyed as a Janissary. Then the *ağa* sent a circular to all provincial *ocak*s (including the one in Vidin) informing them of the decisions and condemning those who had sided with the secessionist.[32] He appealed to the population of Vidin in particular to surrender Osman to the authorities and refrain from resistance.[33]

Finally, the diplomatic correspondence mentions some acts of despair undertaken by the Ottoman authorities. The head of Pazvantoğlu was priced ever higher. In December 1797 it already was worth 60,000 piastres, which according to the Austrians was still too low, considering his popularity. Because, the diplomat continued, "dans l'opinion publique il est le défenseur des anciennes lois de l'Empire, l'ennemi des innovations onéreuses, pret d'ailleurs ª devenir plus fidèle des sujets, si l'on réformoit les abus oppresifs."[34] Two weeks later, unable to stop the circulation of rumors about the rout of the sultan's army and the victory of the rebel, the authorities closed the cafés and forbade public discussion of the troubles around the revolt of Pazvantoğlu and even the mentioning of his name.[35] Despite the propaganda, Pazvantoğlu invariably emerged victorious in his conflicts with the sultan and the forces sent against him, and apparently enjoyed a very high reputation among Muslims to the end of his life.

Pazvantoğlu's views of the Ottoman government and "domestic" policy

Some of the accusations in the documents of the central authority find strong support in diplomatic correspondence. According to their evidence, Osman

Pazvantoğlu not only challenged the new sultan's policy of reforms and established an independent rule in one part of the empire like his powerful contemporaries in Albania, Yanya, Rusçuk, and elsewhere. He also planned to usurp the throne and replace the Ottoman dynasty. General J.-F. Carra-Saint-Cyr, French chargé d'affaires in the capital in 1797–98, writes in November 1798: "Il veut parvenir au Thrône, il réunit donc tous les mécontents de l'Empire."[36] In this case, the general refers to what one of Pazvantoğlu's closest associates, Dimitri Turnavity, had shared with him in a face-to-face discussion. Another, "milder" version envisioned the enthronement of one of the Ghiray *han*s who allied with him. This was closer to Ottoman reality, as the Ghirays were officially recognized dynastic heirs, in case the line of Ottoman rulers failed. In this version Pazvantoğlu reserved for himself the office of grand vezir.[37] Whatever his real intentions, no doubt his political and military successes and his popularity were considered extremely dangerous by the sultan, especially since the Vidin rebel was probably the first to challenge the Ottoman dynasty as such. Previous pretenders to the throne either belonged or claimed to belong to the family. As for the other contemporary secessionists, they were either too far from the capital or preferred independence within the borders of their possessions without openly threatening the dynasty's positions and the sultan's policy.

Indeed, Pazvantoğlu did other things to keep the Ottoman sultan on the alert. Thus, apart from the declared designs on the rule of the state, the diplomatic sources mention that he was minting his own currency. In January 1798 Russian diplomats relate that a Venetian, suspected of having earlier counterfeited Turkish money, had moved to Vidin and had started minting for Pazvantoğlu.[38] At the same time General Carra St. Cyr wrote that the Vidin rebel had started minting coins which bore the inscription "il n'y a qu'un seul Dieu" [there is only one God], on the one side, and "Liberté" [Liberty] on the other. The French diplomat was told that this currency already circulated in the capital.[39] Other sources say that his money was struck in Austrian mints.[40] There must have been something to these reports, however strange they sound, as a coin called "pazvantche" is mentioned in later Bulgarian sources. It appears in a letter of 1853, listed along with other currently circulating coins—*maccar, adliya, zwanziger, ikilik*, and others.[41] It is also defined in the *Dictionary of Bulgarian Language*, compiled by N. Gerov during the second half of the nineteenth century, as a "small copper coin minted by the independent *paşa* of Vidin Pazvantoğlu at the beginning of this [the nineteenth] century."[42] The rumors about this coin continued to circulate even after the liberation of Bulgaria. Thus in 1894 the director of the National Museum in Sofia was still trying to find at least one of these coins for the museum's collection. In a letter to one of the descendants of D. Hadzhitoshev he summarizes the existing information about the "pazvantc-he" as a coin minted by the *paşa* in 1803. It cost 30 *para*s and was covered by a thin layer of tin or probably silver.[43] Unfortunately, there is much to be clarified about the "pazvantche" yet. What might be considered certain is that Pazvantoğlu tried by all possible means to claim and show his independence.

It is difficult to imagine that a slogan for a change of the dynasty in itself would have earned Pazvantoğlu such wide popularity among the Muslims. It was openly articulated, through his non-Muslim agents, only in front of French politicians and diplomats, the only ones who would not have opposed such a change. But in these negotiations he also agreed to surrender all territories claimed by the French and even to accept French domination over the Ottoman state. In 1801, in front of Talleyrand, his emissaries offered the French Consulate the following:

> 1. De concourir de tous les moyens à tous les changements, que le Gouvernement français croiroit utiles dans le Gouvernement de l'Empire ottoman; 2. Si la Republique française se propose d'attaquer la Puissance Ottomane Pasvand-Oglou s'engage à la seconder de tous ses moyens et de Coopperer auvertement . . . à la Seule Condition qu'il lui laisserait une province où il pouroit vivre tranquillement sous la protection des Lois française, lui Pasvand-Oglou et son amis Gingis Métrémèt Gueray Sultan . . . .

In case France decided to conclude peace with the Ottoman empire, moreover, Pazvantoğlu was hoping to receive an amnesty with the help of France. He also declared himself protector of French trade in his *paşalık* and Wallachia and invited the French government to establish a trade commissioner in Vidin for the district and adjacent territories.[44] These designs may have been contemplated in reality or may have been gambits serving other projects: to learn the plans of France for the region or to establish contacts with the only power that at the moment was interested in changes to the status quo.

Pazvantoğlu seems to have had a story for each of the Great Powers, his Christian associates, and the Muslims, and it did not necessarily envisage a dynastic change. The very fact that, only a few months after swearing allegiance to Napoleon, his envoy N. Popovits visited the Russian ambassador in

Paris, requesting political asylum for his master in Russia, is quite revealing about the complicated situation, the flexibility it required, and the conflicting messages Pazvantoğlu was sending to the Great Powers in his attempt to survive and succeed. Russian and Austrian diplomats also heard of his designs as a persistent rumor or simply presented it in their reports as an undoubted truth. These sources, however, claim that he held very high esteem for the first Ottoman sultans, Süleyman the Magnificent in particular, and planned to restore their type of rule. According to the Austrian internuntius Rath Keal: "Sous le prétexte de réformer non seulement dans la ville de Widdin mais aussi dans les environs les défauts du nouveau Gouvernement en particulier les impôts nouveaux (Nizami Gedid) et de rétablir le système sur le pied de Sultan Suleïman II Kanouni, il a réussi sous main saturer la confiance des habitants voisins . . . ."[45]

What the sources seem to be unaninimous about, however, are the ideas reflected in his "proclamations." Russian, Austrian, and French diplomatic agents in the capital of the empire and in the Danube Principalities wrote similar reports of the contents of these documents. Thus, although we have not seen any copy of them, we may assume that they really were circulated and were the closest to the image Pazvantoğlu wanted to earn himself among the Muslim (and non-Muslim) population of the Ottoman state. The core of the information provided by the diplomats on other occasions confirms this. These ideas can be summarized as follows: he was against the "new order" (*nizam-i cedid*) introduced by Sultan Selim III. He declared his staunch support for the sultan himself but blamed evil advisers for the introduction of illegal (from an Islamic legal point of view) and onerous taxes, which laid a heavy burden on all Ottoman subjects, and for the establishment of the new military detachments at the expense of the Janissary corps. Russian diplomatic sources from Bucharest report in December 1797 that

> "Pazvandoglo published a manifesto compiled by himself, [containing] three articles: 1. That the sultan should be the only autocrat and ruler without any councils; 2. That the Janissaries should, according to the ancient usage, be the foremost army in the whole empire; and 3. That all new institutions must be destroyed in the entire empire and the ones of the olden times be restored in their place."[46]

Several months earlier, in March 1797, Chalgrin wrote to Louis XVIII (the report is included in the Austrian diplomatic correspondence) that the worrisome news of Pazvantoğlu's expansion toward Tărnovo, Nikopol, and Belgrade had arrived at the Porte together with a proclamation issued by the rebel. It announced that he was in command not of bandits or thieves but of true and pious Muslims who were inspired by the desire to preserve the Islamic faith and to maintain the purity and integrity of the old Ottoman customs against a corrupt government and the European "impiousness and perversions" it had introduced. Pazvantoğlu concluded that he would render himself in person in Constantinople at the head of a hundred thousand men to remove these fatal innovations that threatened the foundations of the Ottoman empire.[47] In January 1798, Rath Keal speaks of "his manifestos" and letters aimed at earning the favor of the Janissaries.[48] It is noteworthy that none of these anti-European appeals appear in the French diplomatic correspondence, as if the news of these program documents somehow bypassed the French diplomats. They are not mentioned in front of French politicians either. On the contrary, there we hear even "revolutionary" rhetoric and admiration for the ideas and the leaders of the French Revolution.

Thus, from the point of view of his contemporaries, Pazvantoğlu emerges primarily as a champion of the old militia (the Janissaries) against all the novelties inspired by Western influences.[49] All this, combined with his support for the Janissaries in Belgrade, explains why, as the observers of the time point out, all Janissaries expressed very high respect for Pazvantoğlu, refused to take part in the punitive campaigns against him, and were ready to side with him whenever possible.[50] He became a hero in their eyes, and they sang chants dedicated to him:

> After a hundred thousand bombs have been thrown against Widdin, I, Paswan Oğlu, the dog of the sultan, and the slave of the sultana Valide, have erected the standard of defence. I, Paswan Oğlu, the dog of the grand seignior, bark at his ministers. I wish to be submissive to my master, and I kiss the dust from his feet. I, Paswan Oğlu, &c.[51]

While it is not difficult to understand why he was so popular among the Janissaries, it remains to explore the reasons for such support in the wider circles of the Balkan Muslim population. Thus, one of the *dragoman*s at the Austrian embassy, Fleischackl, wrote in the spring of 1797 that on his way between Edirne and Istanbul everyone spoke of Pazvantoğlu, praised him and hoped that he would emerge victorious. According to the same observer the secessionist in Vidin had informants in all villages throughout the

European territories of the empire.[52] Maybe another fact, which appealed to the rank-and-file Muslims, was his obvious religiosity. Very often in publications dedicated to Pazvantoğlu, or just mentioning him, it is stated that he was a Bektashi.[53] This may be attributed to the resemblances between him and Ali Paşa of Yanya,[54] especially in that they both were surrounded by numerous Christian aides and showed some limited toleration for their Christian "subjects." However, unlike the case of Ali Paşa, none of the contemporaries ever qualified Pazvantoğlu as a Bektashi. Here we are unable to analyze all elements of his religious policy but shall only trace some aspects of his religiosity as revealed by documentary and material evidence.

Diplomatic sources, whatever their origins and prejudices, agree that he was in the first place a pious Muslim, who opposed the "dangerous" innovations introduced with the "new order" and regarded as "European" and "infidel" by the Muslim population. In 1797, for example, Chalgrin reported to Louis XVIII that "il est surtout musulman austère; il se fait appeller Sultan Osman, du nom de ce fameux Calife, qui successeur d'Omar l'an 644 se distingua par son attachement à la foi musulmane dont la conservation fut l'objet de toute son attention."[55] French Republican sources, too, stress his fidelity to Islam. General Carra St. Cyr, who had direct contacts with D. Turnavity, a close associate of Pazvantoğlu, described him to Talleyrand as "fidèle à l'Alcoran, il semble n'être inspiré que par Mahomet et n'avoit pour but que le bonheur du Peuple et la gloire du nom musulman."[56] Pazvantoğlu's envoys to the French Directory explicitly stated in front of Talleyrand that he was ready to make many concessions to the French and follow the orders of the French government, provided they were not contrary to the beliefs of the true Muslims.[57] Finally, a secret Russian report from Bucharest, referring to information originating from the Venetian physician of Pazvantoğlu, says that he regarded himself as ordained by God to exterminate all corruption rooted in the rule of Selim III and to restore the justice of the caliphs and the ancient Ottomans.[58] K. Kutsikos also adds to the romantic image of the pious and righteous "ruler": Pazvantoğlu was humane, compassionate, amiable, but just and punished severely all, even minor, crimes. He made many donations to poor widows and orphans and erected *han*s which supported travellers at no charge for two days.[59]

His construction projects satisfied primarily pragmatic needs, both military and urban. Here one should mention the Cross barracks, the repairs and renovation of the fortress walls where he followed European models, a palace as his residence, the repair of the four main roads going out of the city of Vidin, and the regulation of the city street network. Along with the secular buildings there were also several pious ones—a *külliye* (a compound of a mosque, *medrese*, and library), and a *hanegâh* dedicated to Salaheddin Baba, a local hero and saint, who perished defending Vidin from the Austrians in 1689. Again in line with the Islamic tradition he provided the town with *çeşme*s, a *mosluk*, and a *sebil* with an icehouse.[60]

According to one of the lists of the books, compiled in the 1830s, the so-called Pazvantoğlu Library contained over two thousand volumes. At its core were books bearing the seal of his father Ömer, or donor inscriptions of his mother Rukiye and several other outstanding citizens of Vidin. Pazvantoğlu is also the donor of a second, smaller library, at the *zaviye* of Salaheddin Baba. Unfortunately, the majority of the books belonging to these libraries are not in Bulgaria. Some were taken by the Russians as trophies after the Russo-Turkish War of 1877–78, others were submitted to the Ottoman authorities after 1878, and only some six hundred fifty manuscripts and old printed books remain in the National Library in Sofia. The books were listed under twenty-two headings in line with the traditional Islamic classification of sciences. The majority are books on Islamic law, including collections of Ottoman *fetva*s. Next come grammar studies. There are also a considerable number of historical and biographical works, Persian poetry, medical treatises, etc. The Library also possessed many of the titles published by İbrahim Müteferrika's press, exclusively secular books.[61] Nothing in the list of books, however, indicates any preference for Bektashi literature or Bektashi leanings of the donor; neither do any of the buildings constructed by the *paşa*. Nothings speaks of the attachment of Salaheddin Baba to the Bektashi dervish brotherhood. All this gives me grounds to support the recently voiced doubts concerning Pazvantoğlu's adherence to the Bektashi order.[62]

Perhaps his popularity will find further explanation if we add some more information from diplomatic sources. All diplomats are unanimous about one important fact: the new taxes providing financial means for the reforms and the new military detachments were abolished in the territories controlled by Pazvantoğlu. Instead of the heavy burden of the taxes on silk, grains, and wine, Pazvantoğlu seems to have levied one single tax, *harac*, paid by the *reaya* (by this time a term applied only to the taxpaying Christian population)[63] at the amount of 110 *para*s.[64] The Muslim population might have paid even less, but this factor for popular esteem is usually mentioned in the context of Christian taxpayers. Probably this is because, as mentioned above, Christians were the majority of the taxpayers in the region of Vidin, while Muslims were fewer and to a large extent included in the ranks of various military or paramilitary detachments. This, along with the relative security he could provide for the population of his mini-state where the robber bands were forbidden to pillage (at the expense of neighboring lands of hostile *ayans* or of Wallachia), attracted many people, Muslims and Christians alike, to settle in the Vidin region. Of course they could hardly protect themselves from the sultan's armies during the three sieges of Vidin which devastated the whole region. Besides, the "borders" of his possession shifted repeatedly over the years. Yet these events did not necessarily undercut his reputation as the lesser evil. It is clear that the news of his policy spread in and attracted various circles of Ottoman society.[65]

Pazvantoğlu and his Christian subjects

The above-listed elements of his policy can be regarded as some of the reasons why he would be supported by the rank-and-file Bulgarians and Serbs who lived in his territories. His possessions formed a small island where no new taxes were introduced. His policy brought to his side not only his own *reaya*, but also people living in the lands of other *ayans* in northern Bulgaria.

> Un grand nombre de Rayas de Sistow [Svishtov], de Tirnowa des environs de Widdin etc. surchargés d'impôts sur les soi, les blès et les vins abandonnèrent leurs cultures, et ayant reclamé la protection de Paswandoglou trouvèrent chez lui des terrains à faire valoir sous l'unique charge de 110 paras de haradsch. Les autres propriétaires voyant déserter leurs paysans, jetterent des hauts cris contre Paswandoglou, dont les possessions deviennent florissantes à leurs depens . . . .[66]

Not only that, at harvest and haymaking time he personally stayed with the peasants, defending them from the attacks of brigands.[67] Occasionally he punished those who pillaged territories belonging to his possessions.[68] According to Mériage, Bulgarian peasants said that Pazvantoğlu was an enemy only of the Turks, who feared him extremely and hid when he was in town.[69]

All diplomats reporting on the events in this Ottoman province also mention that Bulgarians comprised a good part of Pazvantoğlu's troops. In 1801, L. Kirico reported that a considerable part of the Vidin garrison consisted of Bulgarians.[70] The same year, according to that Russian diplomat, there was one detachment of *pandurs*, only Bulgarians, in Pazvantoğlu's military forces. Two of their commanders with ninety-six men changed sides, joined the *nazır* of Braila, and applied for amnesty to the central authorities.[71] In assessing this phenomenon one should take into account that such great social upheavals as the one witnessed during the "*kırcalı* time" can lead to relative blurring of earlier divisions. This made possible the participation of Muslims and Christians in the bands on (almost) equal footing, and the rise of Christians as leaders of some of them. Indeed, we see Christians among Pazvantoğlu's most famous commanders.[72]

It is strange that Bulgarians, who formed the majority of Pazvantoğlu's subjects and who must have benefited most from the above privileges, left no description of their *paşa*. It is even more surprising if we take into account that one of the best-educated and most intelligent Bulgarians of the time, the author of the first autobiography in modern Bulgarian literature, Bishop Sofronii, lived in Vidin between 1800 and 1803. Neither the autobiography nor any other work of his, including the two Vidin collections compiled by him during his stay in the city, contain any trace of his personal attitude to the *paşa*. The same applies to the inscriptions in the manuscript books that have survived to the present day. All one sees in them and in the autobiography are monotonous descriptions of the devastation of one or another town or village in the region, by one or another *kırcalı* band, by the troops of Pazvantoğlu, or by the troops sent by the central authorities to stamp out the revolt. Pazvantoğlu's troops are invariably called "Pazvandzhi's bandits." The bands came and went, did their job, and the peasants seem to have regarded them as part of their lives—comparable to the plague. The bandits, whom they obviously joined in an attempt to change their positions from objects to subjects, were their only link with the *paşa*, except for the tax collectors. Judging from Sofronii, being inside or outside the territory of the *paşa* seemed to make little difference. No mention of the lower taxes or the just treatment appears.

Soon after the First Serbian Uprising began (1804), most of Pazvantoğlu's Christian commanders and soldiers joined the ranks of the rebels. It should be pointed out that at the beginning Pazvantoğlu refrained from open conflict with the Serbs, but his (armed) neutrality gradually turned into a total divergence between the *paşa* and his Christian subjects, to the extent that they became open enemies. The Serbian Uprising posed a serious dilemma to the Vidin rebel. On the one hand, the Belgrade Janissaries had been among his allies from the beginning of his revolt in the early 1790s, and ever since then he had never missed the opportunity to defend their demands and interests before the central authority. That is why he immediately sent one of his "generals," Guşançalı Halil, with one thousand *kırcalı*s in aid of the four *dahi*s. On the other hand, he had to reckon with the situation in his own possessions, particularly with the fact that the Christians—Bulgarians and Serbs—were the vast majority of his subjects. To prevent their siding with the Serbian insurrectionists, the Vidin *paşa* satisfied all the demands of his Christian subjects. This included further reduction of the tax and prohibition of any additional claims of his representatives in these regions; replacement of his *subaşı*s with the *kneze*s of the Christians as his administrative officers; and permission and even assistance for the construction of churches. All this, according to Russian diplomatic sources, he did in order to keep the Bulgarians on his side.[73] The complex situation is reflected in Russian diplomatic correspondence, which followed the events in the region very closely and is in many ways the most reliable source about them. In 1805, the Russian diplomats reported that Pazvantoğlu's forces, led by Guşançalı Halil, acted in alliance with Kara George[74] against the troops of the central authorities, and that Pazvantoğlu congratulated the Serbs on their victories with special letters. This, according to the Russians, he did "in order to reduce the influence of Serbs over Bulgarians."[75]

Despite all efforts to preserve the status quo, however, he was quickly losing his Bulgarian soldiers, who chose to fight under the command of Christians and were deserting the Vidin rebel in masses. The period 1805–1806 marked a threshold in the relations between Christians and Pazvantoğlu. In November 1805, when the town of Smederevo was taken by the Serbian insurrectionists, the Janissary garrison was allowed to retire to Vidin.[76] By that time the Serbian Uprising had already acquired the features of a national liberation struggle not only against the four *dahi*s but against Ottoman rule in general. Bulgarians under Pazvantoğlu obviously understood the turn in the events because despite the concessions, not only did they join the Serbs, but many villages rose against his rule.[77] In 1805, one of the administrators of Pazvantoğlu, Pintso, a Christian who ruled the westernmost territories of the *paşalık*, sided with the Serbs. He was routed by Pazvantoğlu's troops and managed to escape with the Serbs, but the inhabitants of four of the villages that supported him were massacred.[78] A year later Pazvantoğlu ordered the slaughter of the bishop of Vidin and many Bulgarian notables and priests on the accusation of secret relations with the Serbs.[79] This seems to have put an end to the "marriage of convenience" between the *paşa* and his Orthodox Christian subjects. The available "domestic" Bulgarian sources imply that there was no love from the very beginning.

Pazvantoğlu's Christian allies and aides

While Pazvantoğlu's military commanders were majority Muslims and minority Christians, probably Bulgarians, his diplomats were mainly "Greeks."[80] It is not always clear whose agent a particular person was, however. Lambo Dzhanoğlu, one of Pazvantoğlu's doctors, acted as his adviser but seems to have been also an informant for the Russians.[81] This is also valid of Bishop Kalinikos[82] and others. Very often it is difficult to understand the "division of labor" among his assistants and associates, as well as their professional specialization—one combined the functions of a merchant, *bazirgânbaşı*, and doctor; another doctor was also a "diplomat"; and a merchant-revolutionary was also his messenger to the French in the capital, to the Russian consuls in Moldavia and Wallachia, and his negotiator with the Ottomans. Indeed, one of the most influential groups of non-Muslims around Pazvantoğlu was that of his physicians—Greeks, Venetians, Jews—all of them being involved in various political-diplomatic schemes.[83]

And here we touch further upon the subject of the broader relations between Pazvantoğlu and non-Muslims, beyond the simple relaxation of taxes and the relative security. To a large extent the situation and the atmosphere in the region of Vidin resembled those of the earliest Ottoman period, when many Christians joined the conquerors in a similar urge for plunder. Yet, despite the resemblance, there were also many differences. These, of course, derived from the different times: the changed balance of power between the Ottomans and their neighbors, but most of all from the age of nationalism that had stepped into the Balkans. The French revolution, the chaos in political alignments at the time, and the wars gave additional impetus to processes that had already started in Balkan societies.

Pazvantoğlu, Rhigas and his organization

It is not surprising that Pazvantoğlu was assisted by "Greeks" in many of his undertakings, and particularly in his diplomatic relations with the Christian powers. According to G. Olivier, Pazvantoğlu was aware that he needed the

support of the "Greeks" (i.e., Orthodox Christians) in the first place because
they comprised the larger part of the population in European Turkey. For
that reason he tried to win them over to his cause by introducing the ancient
laws of Sultan Süleyman I in the hope of improving their situation. According to the same author, he promised the Orthodox freedom of religion and
the removal of the humiliating position of the *reaya*, employing the slogan
of "freedom and justice," words which had a magic effect on the Greeks.
That was why they regarded him as their future liberator.[84]

During the French Revolution Greek society gradually began to split
around the subject of liberation and the power from which this could be
expected. The wars of the Republic, which brought the revolutionary armies
very close to Greek lands, combined with the growing disappointment of
some Greeks after Russian foreign policy turned toward preservation of the
status quo, made some Greek intellectuals, especially among those living
in western Europe, look for another protector in the French Republic. The
time was also considered convenient for a general uprising because of the
increasing disintegration of the Ottoman empire under the pressure of its
neighbors without and rebellious *paşa*s within. One of those who greeted
the outbreak of the French Revolution was Rhigas Velestinlis.[85] He established contacts with French emissaries in the Danube Principalities and with
many of his co-nationals who served the Republic. Under the influence of
the ideas of the French Revolution Rhigas became a staunch republican. He
started preparing the program documents of a future all-Balkan revolution
and a plan for an uprising whose success depended on the decisive assistance of France.[86] Among these documents was also his *Battle-song (Thourios)*,
written probably in 1796 or in the beginning of 1797 under the impact of
the *Marseillaise*, an exultant hymn of the anti-Ottoman revolution in which
he appealed to Balkan peoples and some of the secessionists in the Ottoman
state to rise against the sultan. It was in this context that I first regarded the
evidence of Chr. Perraivos about Rhigas's close relations with Pazvantoğlu,
as well as the text of the often-discussed verses in Rhigas's *Thourios*:

> Passavanoglou, why dost thou so long remain impassive?
> Rush towards the Balkans, it is there that thou should like
>   the eagle build thy nest.
> Let not owls nor crows worry thee.
> Join the rayas if thou wish to conquer.
> Silistrie, Braila, Ismaila and Chilie,

Bensderi and Chotzin stretch out their arms to thee.
Send reinforcements and they will fall at thy feet
as they no longer bear to live under tyranny.
Georgian! Sleep no longer, jump up,
Here is the occasion to do like the one from Broussa.
And thou who in Aleppo dreams of liberty, rise.
Pasha! Appear forthwith on the battlefields.
Rise at the head of thy armies,
Otherwise thou will remain under the orders of Stamboul.
Lions of Egypt, above all elect a king from among your
    beys.
Let not the kharatch from Egypt appear in Stamboul
So that perishes the wolf that tyrannizes you.[87]

In fact, the mere list of the *paşa*s addressed by Rhigas hardly suggests anything beyond the desires of an ardent revolutionary seeking help for the liberation of his co-nationals wherever possible. Its closer analysis reveals that although it may look like some sort of an alliance of all oppositional elements in the empire at the time—if not real, at least in the imagination of the Greek revolutionary—it is clear that it is far from being so. In fact, two of the major power centers in Rumeli were obviously consciously left out: Ali Paşa Tepedelenli and the Buşatlıs. Despite their successes against the central authority they were not considered allies, the main reason probably being that both of them ruled over Greeks, and waged wars on groups among their Orthodox Christian populations: Ali Paşa on the Suliots, and the Buşatlıs on the Montenegrin tribes.[88] The death of Kara Mahmut Buşatlı in Montenegro at about this time may well also have been a factor.

Judging also from the fact that in later versions of the song the whole passage about Pazvantoğlu and the other Ottoman separatists is missing, we may conclude that the original text of the *Thourios* reflects to a great extent what Rhigas was hoping for rather than any reality. And I would have maintained this rather skeptical view about any direct relations between the Greek revolutionary and the Vidin rebel had I not come across two documents related to the mission, sent to Paris by Pazvantoğlu in the hope of establishing direct contact with Napoleon and the Directory in 1801.[89]

The two envoys, Nedelko Popovits and Polisoi Kondon, related in front of Talleyrand the story of Pazvantoğlu and his attempts to establish contacts with France. Among other interesting details, the two said that:

Il [Pazvantoğlu] n'est dans aucune relation avec l'Autriche et la Russie. Il fait seulement que cette dernière Puissance n'entreprendra rien contre lui, si elle a l'assurance qu'il ménagera la Moldavie. Quant à l'Autriche, elle se borne jusqu'à présent à servir les inquiétudes de la Porte en lui envoyant de tems en tems des Grecs résidens en Allemagne, et dont on découvre les intelligences avec le Pacha de Vidin.

Il y a quelques années, on découvrit à Vienne une vaste conspiration contre la Turquie dont les agens de Passavan-Oglou conduisoient les ressorts. Polisoi Condon en étois, huit Grecs furent livrés au Pacha de Belgrade qui les fut étrangler. Polisoi assure qu'ils étoient les plus grands hommes de sa nation. Quinze ou vingt furent exilés dans différentes provinces de la maison d'Autriche. Lui, Polisoi ne fut que soupconne et il fut seulement privé de sa chaire de Literature grecque à Vienne.

La découverte de Cette Conspiration fut l'effet de la mission d'un homme que Passavan-Oglou envoyoit au Premier Consul et qui fut arreté. Les papiers dont il étoit porteur conduisirent l'inquisition Autrichienne à rechercher les Agens du Pacha et leurs Correspondances. Depuis cette echec Passavan-Oglou a sans cesse envoyé des deputés, mais sans munir de papiers. Ils ont tous été arrètés ou assassinés. Nedelko est le seul qui soit parvenu à éxécuter les ordres de Son Maitre . . . .[90]

The exposé of Pazvantoğlu's envoys may be regarded as some corroboration of the more "physical" contacts between Pazvantoğlu and Rhigas as it gives the story of Rhigas's *hetairia*. Indeed, in 1796, when the armies of the Directory invaded Italy and then took the Ionian islands, reaching the Ottoman border, Rhigas decided that the time had come to prepare the uprising in Greece. He left Bucharest and went to Vienna, where he published his *Battle-song*, the *Declaration of the Rights of Man*, and the constitution of the future republic. His plans were to move to the Morea with his followers and proclaim the uprising. In Vienna he worked on the organization of his revolutionary network in the Danube Principalities, Austria, and Greece. Toward the end of 1797, however, he was betrayed to the Austrian police and arrested. He was interrogated in Trieste and Vienna and then surrendered with seven associates to the Ottoman authorities. In June 1798 Rhigas and his friends were strangled at the order of the *muhafiz* of the Belgrade fortress.

On the other hand, the story told by the emissaries may have been merely a ploy on the part of Pazvantoğlu. He could easily have been informed about the events and used the story for his own purposes. Judging from the diplomatic correspondence, the news of the tragic death and the fate of Rhigas's *hetairia* had spread immediately throughout the Balkans. Russian diplomatic sources in Bucharest and Jassy reported almost immediately the news of the arrest and further fate of Rhigas and his companions.[91]

In his memoirs Chr. Perraivos, one of the closest friends of Rhigas, refers to a romantic meeting between the two in 1788 when Rhigas, "eparhos"[92] of Craiova at that time, saved the life of Pazvantoğlu, who was being prosecuted on the Wallachian prince's order.[93] However fabulous it may sound, it seems that at some point Pazvantoğlu had indeed crossed the border, persecuted by the enemies of his father in Vidin, and had found asylum in Austria where "il fut fort bien traité" [he was very well treated].[94] Other evidence may place this event a little bit earlier, at the time of the execution of his father or shortly afterwards, that is, around 1788, but this has yet to be researched. Taking into account Pazvantoğlu's family and friendship ties across the Danube, it is likely. It is also known that in 1790 Rhigas accompanied his patron Baron de Langerfeld to Vienna, where he stayed more than six months. No doubt he not only visited Vienna and other Austrian towns but also stayed in contact with the Greek communities there.[95]

Pazvantoğlu did indeed have problems with the Wallachian prince and took part in the war with the Austrians in 1787–91. Thus, there are many chances that the story of the personal acquaintance of Rhigas and Pazvantoğlu be at least partly true. In any case the conditions on both sides of the river and the border make such an encounter quite probable. The contacts between the Greek communities in Vidin and Bucharest are also well documented. Finally, we know of at least one person who not only knew both men but was very close to Pazvantoğlu and a member of Rhigas's movement, and could have served as a link between them.

Dimitri Turnavity was well known to contemporary diplomats and politicians in the Ottoman capital, the Danube Principalities, and to Pazvantoğlu. A Greek merchant, "*barataire*"[96] of France, he was a favorite of Wallachian princes and served as their envoy to Vidin. He was also one of the merchants who supplied provisions to the Wallachian army and Pazvantoğlu's troops. On the other hand, he communicated with Russian and French diplomats as a representative of Pazvantoğlu.[97] As summarized by the Austrian internuntius on the occasion of Turnavity's murder, "ever since the Svishtov peace treaty he was playing a dangerous role in Wallachia, dedicated to the French, employed by the princes, and making frequent trips to Vidin."[98] It is also significant that Turnavity was arrested and murdered in Istanbul shortly after the detention of Rhigas.

If we accept that there existed some connection and even collaboration between Rhigas and Osman Pazvantoğlu, we have to deal with at least one disputable issue, that of precedence. The *paşa*'s envoys claimed in front of Talleyrand that Rhigas and the other Greeks were members of Pazvantoğlu's conspiracy, while all Greek sources, Perraivos in particular, insist that Rhigas exerted powerful influence on the *paşa*. It seems to me that it is not very difficult to reconcile these contradictory opinions. It is quite probable that both parties were interested in the other's participation and collaboration and tried to use it for their own purposes. Pazvantoğlu, though aiming at the preservation of the Ottoman empire and strengthening it on the basis of the principles of ancient times, or at his own ascension to the throne (or at least as grand vezir), relied on the services of "Greeks" to carry out his foreign policy and in his relations with Wallachia and the central authorities. In the short run, he might even have regarded an uprising of the Christian population in the Balkans as another destabilizing factor that would eventually shatter the sultan's position and bring him the throne. Rhigas, too, may have seen in this cooperation a useful thing, but only for the purposes of Greek revolution. No wonder that after Rhigas's death and after his own fall from the political scene Pazvantoğlu disappeared from the later versions of the *Thourios*.

The above-discussed contacts between Pazvantoğlu and the French Directory of 1801 take us to at least two other important groups among the Orthodox Christians who supported the rebel. Both, although not numerous, were very influential among the local population, for they were wealthy and enjoyed a monopoly over spiritual life: they were the merchants and the high Orthodox clergy.

Pazvantoğlu and local merchants

Merchants apparently enjoyed specific privileges and freedoms under his rule, including the care he showed for their caravans and security. In 1798, diplomatic sources reported: "il traite avec douceur les habitants, contient par une discipline sévère sa Soldatesque, abolit partout les nouveau impôts, protége les voyageurs et les Caravanes."[99] The offers which Pazvantoğlu sent to Napoleon in 1801, listed above, also speak of the special attention paid to the development of trade in his possessions, and of the importance he attributed to international trade in particular, inviting a French trade consul to Vidin.

I shall discuss Pazvantoğlu's relations with two men in particular. Nedelko Popovits, Pazvantoğlu's envoy to Napoleon, was, like Turnavity, a well-to-do merchant. According to what he himself declared, he was living in Vidin, near Pazvantoğlu, as the *bazirgânbaşı* of the governor, but his official title was "doctor of the *paşa*." His main obligations in the *paşa*'s government were to direct his finances and international correspondence. Nedelko explained that he managed to obtain a passport as a merchant from an Imperial (Austrian) vice-consul in Galați, in the Danube Principalities, who was "devoted to the association of the Greeks in Germany." The merchant went there from Vidin on a boat belonging to a Jew. Then he moved to Vienna, where he was already expected by his companion Polisoi. Both managed to get passports to attend the trade fair in Leipzig, Nedelko as an "Armenian merchant," Polisoi as a professor who wanted to re-publish his works in Greek literature. Their next stop was Dresden, whence, with the help of representatives of the French Consulate, they finally reached Paris. All this he told Talleyrand, who remarked that the merchant spoke German. The foreign minister also remarked that the "physician" had an exuberance of spirit which he had obviously learnt to suppress in the court of the Turkish governor. This is what the merchant himself decided to reveal.

More information about him, however, is contained in other sources, and it makes him an even more interesting personality. First, we have to explain that there is no chance that he was an ethnic "Armenian." The name suggests either Bulgarian or Serbian nationality. It is quite probable, though, that he did not mean an ethnic affiliation but rather an institution. Armenian merchants from Asia Minor and even Iran started settling in the Balkan provinces of the empire during the seventeenth century and gradually became some of the main agents in the international and inter-regional trade, enjoying also a specific tax and communal regime.[100] While this is a plausible explanation, there are other disputable issues. For example, why did he need to be "doctor of the *paşa*" if he already had other important positions, and it is certain that Pazvantoğlu had several other physicians? It should also be pointed out that Nedelko withheld some information from Talleyrand. Apparently he was a well-known merchant, with important deals in Vienna amounting to tens of thousands of piastres, and a name known to Russian and Austrian diplomats in the Ottoman capital and in the Danube Principalities. He also did not mention that he was a "Russian subject" (probably "*barataire*"). His importance is made clear by the documents issued by both Russian and Austrian chancelleries concerning his deals and trips, which confirm that he had special relations with Pazvantoğlu but also enjoyed the protection of Ipsilanti, "prince and *dragoman* at the Porte." Like Turnavity, Popovits was involved in supplying provisions for the troops of Pazvantoğlu. His deals in Vienna, we learn from the reference to two judicial processes (of 1796) taking place there, were within the framework of the company of "Alexis son of George and Nedelko Popovits and Co.," called "Greek merchants" by the Austrian ambassador in Istanbul, Rath Keal, who issued to them a letter of recommendation at the express request of Ipsilanti. In 1802, Popovits, who obviously stayed in Paris after his audience with Talleyrand, visited the Russian ambassador in the French capital, Count Markov. This time the main purpose of Pazvantoğlu's envoy was to seek the benevolence and protection of the Russian tsar for his master. In 1803 in a letter to the Wallachian prince Kalinikos, the bishop of Vidin, insisted that Popovits's only purpose in Paris was to meet Count Markov and submit Pazvantoğlu's application for Russian protection and citizenship.[101] Unfortunately, for the time being, I have been unable to retrieve more consistent evidence about Popovits, except for the fact that he stayed in Vidin after the death of Pazvantoğlu and in 1807 served as an envoy of the Ottoman government to Kara George.[102] After this decade of active participation in politics and in the economy of the region he disappears from the available documentation.

Popular memory and some material objects relate to Pazvantoğlu yet another interesting personality of the time, Dimitraki Hadzhitoshev. According to local tradition in Vratsa, one of the few towns in northwestern Bulgaria which managed to repulse Pazvantoğlu's troops twice, Bulgarian notables there were divided into two "parties" in their feelings for the ruler of Vidin. After the second siege of Vidin in 1798, Pazvantoğlu bribed the richest and most influential *çorbacı* in the town, Dimitraki, sending him many precious objects. However, in the attempt to submit the town to the *paşa*, Dimitraki encountered the opposition of other powerful Bulgarian families.[103] Dimitraki preserved his good relations with Pazvantoğlu and his successor in Vidin and on several occasions served as a mediator between them and other Christians.[104] In another version, mainly of his descendants, Dimitraki received the said objects in 1806 again from Pazvantoğlu—but as a show of respect.[105] Dimitraki's later life is much better known, since he was among the earliest active fighters for a Bulgarian clerical hierarchy and against the Greek bishops in Bulgaria. This struggle brought about his sentencing to death in 1827 on the accusation of political relations with Russia and with the Serbian prince Miloš, and of incitement of the local population to rebellion and disobedience.[106]

In 1805, two Jews, Abraham and Isaac, served Pazvantoğlu in Vienna, where Abraham was also established as a merchant. The main purpose of the latter's stay in the Austrian capital city was to provide information about political events in Europe.[107] There were probably others who contributed information and maintained the international relations of the Vidin *paşa* whose names have remained unknown to us. It seems, however, that Pazvantoğlu indeed had had a special attitude to the merchants and had somehow won their support. "Il peut puiser dans la bourse de tous les negocians de ses Gouvernemens, qui se sont engagés par écrit à lui devouer leurs fortunes," Popovits proudly told Talleyrand.[108] This may or may not have been true. It may also have been forced upon them. Yet all this scattered evidence really speaks of a special attitude on the part of the merchants as well.[109]

Pazvantoğlu and the Orthodox clergy

The other envoy to Paris who claimed to have been member of Rhigas's organization, Polisoi Condon, in his own words a priest and professor in Greek and Latin literature in Vienna, presents us with no fewer surprises than Nedelko. In all probability, this was Polyzois Kontos.[110] Here we shall not dwell on details of his biography, as he was a well-known Greek intellectual of the end of the eighteenth and beginning of the nineteenth century. Of importance here are the coincidences in his biography with the fact of the above-mentioned mission in Paris. Polyzois Kontos had been a teacher, in Vienna, of the sons of Prince Adam Czartoryski, the future Russian minister of foreign affairs. In 1795 he was invited by the Orthodox community in Pest, where he served as a priest and teacher in the Greek school, then moved again, to Tokay and Vienna. In 1801–1802 he was in Paris, where we see him probably in the capacity of Pazvantoğlu's envoy. There he wrote an ode dedicated to Napoleon, which he read in the presence of Napoleon himself and the academicians. Then Polyzois went to London and back to Vienna, where he stayed until he moved to Wallachia in 1805. He was one of the leading specialists in Hellenic Studies and knew French and Italian (Talleyrand only mentions Italian). He was also one of the most outstanding representatives of the "reaction" against the ideas of the Enlightenment and the French Revolution in Greek society. One of his most famous works in this vein is the *Dialogues of the Dead*, published in 1793 and regarded as an open indictment of Voltaire, who is held responsible for many evils. In 1802, he informed the Austrian authorities about A. Korais's intention to disseminate in Turkish-occupied lands his own translation of Cesare Beccaria's *Crimes and Punishments*, published during the same year. The Austrian government reacted immediately, ordering the police in Vienna to prevent the dispatch of the books. All these facts make it implausible that Polyzois Kontos could have been in any way associated with the conspiracy of the ardent admirer of the ideas of the Enlightenment and the French Republic and of the slogan of Equality-Fraternity-Liberty, Rhigas. Yet, if we set apart the ideas, all other facts fit perfectly with the information about Pazvantoğlu's envoy.

There is, however, another, though less probable, possibility for the identification of Polisoi. Russian diplomatic correspondence mentions a different name as Nedelko Popovits's companion in Paris—a certain Hazo. In a letter to C. Ipsilanti in Bucharest, the bishop of Vidin, too, spoke of a "Hazo" who "n'avait ni mission, ni même connaissance de celle dont Popowitch était chargé." (This probably meant that the said Hazo was not aware of the fact that Popovits had to meet Count Markov rather than anybody else.) If we take into account the name of the envoy as rendered to Talleyrand and the "Russian" version, this may take us to Dimitrios Chatzi Polyzou (Polyzos). He too moved in Greek educational circles, being a teacher in Pest, in Hungro-Wallachia, in Leipzig and Vienna. In 1791, he published *Vengeance Most Just . . . on Ignorance, and Errors made in Ignorance by the Printer*, and in 1800, an *Essay on Orthography* from [the Grammar of] Theodoros Gazis.[111]

Another group of interesting characters among the Orthodox clergy who cooperated with Pazvantoğlu are the Orthodox metropolitans who resided in Vidin. Officially Gregory was metropolitan in Vidin between 1791 and 1801, but he managed to escape from Vidin in 1798. Interestingly, we see him also in business relations with Nedelko Popovits. Between 1798 and 1801 there was no metropolitan of Vidin residing in the city, and Pazvantoğlu tried to secure the appointment of one of his closest associates, the monk Kalinikos. For that reason he and Kalinikos invited Sofronii, the Bulgarian bishop of Vratsa, to Vidin in 1800 and kept him there until 1803.[112] The latter was among those who helped Kalinikos receive the Vidin see in 1803. In 1803, Sofronii moved to Wallachia. For a short while, in 1804, another metropolitan, Benedict, was appointed by the patriarch. However, he was beheaded soon after his appointment, during the same year, and Kalinikos was restored to the position. In 1806, Kalinikos too lost his head. His successor Dionysius managed to survive.

While Benedict was executed for failing to pay the sum of money promised to the *paşa*, Kalinikos and Sofronii are much more interesting for our purpose here. Kalinikos was a faithful assistant to the *paşa* in his relations with the Christian *reaya* and with the Orthodox political factors in the region. It was mainly through him that Pazvantoğlu maintained his relations with Russia. He also wrote the letter expressing the wish of his master to become a subject of the tsar. It is not quite clear how much he knew about all the schemes of Pazvantoğlu. In any case, some of the Russian correspondence mentions him as one of the very few people, if not the only one, in whom the *paşa* trusted entirely. However, when the Serbian uprising began, he apparently finally changed sides—and was murdered with several Bulgarian priests and other notables, on accusation of being in secret contact with the Serbs.

Sofronii is even more enigmatic. Despite the three years spent in Vidin, he does not say a word about the *paşa* in his autobiography and on several occasions complained of having been kept in prison and being unable to visit his flock. However, recently it became clear that during his "three years of imprisonment" in Vidin he had visited Wallachia several times in 1802 and had even ordained priests before finally settling there in 1803. It was during these visits that he intervened in front of the Wallachian metropolitan in favor of the appointment of Kalinikos to the Vidin see.[113] The silence of Sofronii and his subsequent engagement in a political initiative aimed at gaining some autonomy for Bulgarians has led V. Mutafchieva to the thought that during his stay in Vidin he participated in a vast political conspiracy, which made him silent about these years in his autobiography.[114] I tend instead to agree with another, recently voiced, interpretation.[115] Taking into account Sofronii's rather reluctant participation in the political action in question, I think it most probable that his close contacts with the Phanariot princes and boyars of Wallachia, and his boundless respect and admiration for Russia, contributed much to his aversion from the rebel. We should not also forget that at the time he wrote his *Autobiography*, his grandson Stefan Bogoridi, the future prince of the island of Samos, had already entered the ranks of the high Ottoman bureaucracy as a *dragoman*. No wonder he would try to be careful in expressing views that could harm his grandson's career.

It is also possible to draw a parallel between the attitude of Rhigas to Ali Paşa Tepedelenli and that of Sofronii to Pazvantoğlu. The two *paşa*s, as mentioned above, were among the most important opponents of the Ottoman sultan, and rose in open revolt against the central authority. At the time of the writing of the *Thourios*, however, Ali Paşa was also at war with the Suliots, and this could hardly make him a potential ally of the Greek revolutionaries in their struggle for liberation from Ottoman rule. The same is also true for the attitude of Sofronii to Pazvantoğlu. It is not clear whether Sofronii was planning to publish his autobiography and what audience he addressed in it. The date of its writing is also unknown, but it is certain that it was finished after he left Vidin (it ends with his stay there) in 1803, most probably after 1805 (it is included in a manuscript with another work of his dated 1805). By that time, however, the paths of the Vidin *paşa* and his Christian subjects had already separated. Not only that, Pazvantoğlu had ordered the slaughter of the metropolitan and of many Bulgarian elders and priests on suspicion of being supporters of the Serbian Uprising in January 1806. In this situation it is understandable that Sofronii would avoid emphasizing his relations with Pazvantoğlu and any services he might have done for the latter, and would include no praise of his "just" rule.

Despite ups and downs in his contacts with his Christian subjects and other groups in Balkan Christian societies, in his relations with the Great Powers, with the Danube Principalities, and even with the Porte, Pazvantoğlu relied almost exclusively on the assistance of his Orthodox Christian merchants, clerics, and physicians. It was with their help that Osman Pazvantoğlu successfully found his way in the complex labyrinth of contemporary international relations and managed to keep the Great Powers interested in his personality and actions. Apparently he carefully followed developments in international relations and in the European states. He had developed a network of spies, Christians and Jews, who kept him informed to a surprising degree. He knew of changes in the French political structure, information he owed primarily to his "Greek" spies, but what was more important, he was well aware of the complex interests of each of the European states in the region and managed to play his game with each of them, making them compete for his attention.

Conclusion

When considering the figure of Osman Pazvantoğlu, one should take into account all aspects of his activities and relations with various strata of Ottoman society and abroad. One should also not forget the features of the time and place in which he lived, and the nature of the border area, which imposed its own rules for those who wanted to administer it. The border life probably contributed to the emergence (or rather to the preservation) of a border spirit close to that of the early Ottoman *uc* and its atmosphere. Yet in many ways it differed considerably, because this was also the beginning of the age of nationalism for Balkan peoples. In fact, Vidin brought together many of the outstanding leaders of the Awakening of Balkan peoples—Greeks, Bulgarians, Serbs. In a way Osman Pazvantoğlu was a man of his time, and he too was aiming at a revival.

Despite all variations in his policy, despite all expectations and worries of the foreign powers and the promises he gave to each of these powers, throughout his life Pazvantoğlu followed one policy, aiming at the restoration of the former glory of the Ottoman empire and of the Janissary corps as the embodiment of its power in the classical age. Sources vary in their interpretations of Pazvantoğlu's aim—whether he planned to establish independent rule in northern Bulgaria with Vidin as his capital, or to overthrow the reigning dynasty and take the throne in Constantinople, or, again in a change of the dynasty, to become the grand vezir. The important thing for him was to restore the principles of government from the time of Sultan Süleyman I and block the introduction of novelties, especially ones influenced by Europe. In fact, no matter what he said to French diplomats, or what suspicions Austrian diplomats held regarding him, Pazvantoğlu invariably remained a staunch supporter of Islam and its principles in both his public and his private life. He was an intelligent man with a wide network of spies who kept him well informed of the priorities of his adversaries and partners. Thus, in 1801 the French learned that he admired their revolution and their consul. He declared he was ready to serve them—but only if they did not in any way infringe on the pious feelings of Muslims. At the same time and through the same envoy he started negotiations with the Russians, requesting Russian citizenship and expressing admiration for the tsar. Only a few years earlier the Austrians had discussed quite seriously with the Porte what to do if Pazvantoğlu asked for political asylum in Austria.

One may suspect that his relations with the leaders of the Balkan nations had the same entirely pragmatic basis, each expecting profits from the other. He may have used the rhetoric he applied in his contacts with the Great Powers also to the corresponding groups of the Balkan peoples—the "democratic" and "revolutionary" for France and Rhigas, but mere submission to the orders of the tsar for Russia and the Orthodox hierarchs.

It is my deep belief, however, that his true self appeared in his contacts with the Muslims and in his opposition to the innovations that, in his opinion, undermined the bases of the empire. What he was aiming at was not a republic after the French model, and he was far from introducing equality and freedom in his mini-state. Yet he also had to reckon with the situation in his territories. Despite the great number of Janissaries, the majority of the population were Christians, Bulgarian and Serbian peasants. He had to make their situation bearable by introducing measures that improved the situation of the *reaya* while complying with Islamic principles. His political aims also forced him to rely on "his" Christians for his military expansion and for his diplomatic contacts. His policy earned him recognition—but mainly from outside rather than within his territories. The relations with the *reaya* were based primarily on cold calculation on both sides. Pazvantoğlu never intended to reform the empire in favor of the Christians. What he probably planned was some improvement of the situation of the *reaya* in line with Islamic tradition and the principles of the Ottoman government from the "golden age" of Süleyman the Magnificent. Christians living on his territory replied with the same level of trust, which did not imply sincere loyalty. Once the Serbian uprising began, the *reaya* sided with their co-religionists. Pazvantoğlu was also deserted by his associates from the Rhigas circle. For them he had been an opportunity for further pressure on the empire, and for a short while their paths went in parallel. With the destruction of Rhigas's *hetairia* their paths diverged, and when the Greek War of Independence began, Pazvantoğlu was no longer alive and no longer interesting to them, living only in the memory of the companions of Rhigas. The same applied to those who regarded Russia as the liberator of Orthodox Christians, mainly in the circles of the high Christian hierarchy but also among the merchants. Even Kalinikos, who had stayed with Pazvantoğlu for nearly a decade, seems to have deserted him at the end. There was probably only one exception, Nedelko Popovits, but this exception only underscores the rule. By that time the Vidin *paşa* had lost his struggles for independence and for the revival of the Ottoman state. Pressed in his corner by the Russians, the Serbs, and the Austrians, betrayed by his Christian subjects and allies, all he could hope for was to preserve his rule. It was among the Janissaries and the rank-and-file Muslims that Pazvantoğlu earned his real and lasting fame. They created and circulated songs for him in which he emerges as a true hero. The age of nationalism had set in in the Balkans.

Notes

1. Here I refer to the title of a book devoted to the reign of Sultan Selim III. Stanford J. Shaw, *Between Old and New: The Ottoman Empire under Sultan Selim III (1789–1807)* (Cambridge, Mass.: Harvard University Press, 1971).

2. A document of 1785 speaks of the "*kırcalı eşkiyası*," that is, *kırcalı* bandits. Soon this term seems to have been replaced in Ottoman documentation by "*dağlı eşkiyası*." In Bulgarian folklore and literature, however, *kırcalı* was preserved as the only term for this phenomenon. See a definition of the term and the phenomenon in Vera Mutafchieva, *Kărdzhaliisko vreme* (Sofia: Nauka i izkustvo, 1977), 59–63.

3. On the secession in central Rumeli see the above-cited monographs of Mutafchieva and Shaw, passim.

4. According to M. Glenny these acted as a bridge between the Ottoman empire and the nation-states that eventually emerged on the peninsula, a statement which is of course anachronistic. Misha Glenny, *Balkans, 1804–1999: Nationalism, War and the Great Powers* (London: Granta Books, 2000), 5.

5. Maria Theophilowa, *Die Rebellion des Paschas Paswan-Ogllou und ihre Bedeutung für die bulgarische Befreiungsbewegung im XIX Jahrhundert* (Zürich: Gebr. Leeman, 1914). Later translated into Bulgarian: Maria Teofilova, *Buntăt na Pazvanoglu i negovoto znachenie za Bălgarskoto osvoboditelno dvizhenie v XIX vek. Prinos kăm predistoriiata na bălgarskoto osvoboditelno dvizhenie* (Sofia: Hemus, 1932); Simeon Vankov, *Osman Paspanoglu, Vidinski pasha. Stranitsi ot istoriiata na Iztochniia văpros, Voennoistoricheski sbornik* 62 (Sofia, 1947). The following titles, though touching upon many of the problems I discuss treat Osman Pazvantoğlu as an element of the broader picture of the situation in the Balkans at the end of the eighteenth–beginning of the nineteenth centuries. Mutafchieva, *Kărdzhaliisko vreme,* passim; Viktor Grachev, *Balkanskie vladeniia Osmanskoi imperii na rubezhe XVIII–XIX vv.* (Moscow: Nauka, 1990), 43–50 and passim. The pages on Pazvantoğlu in Shaw's, *Between Old and New*, consider him mainly as one of the obstacles to the reforms of Selim III rather than as an independent political factor. Finally, there is an article dedicated to Pazvantoğlu as an example of the merger of artisanship, Janissaries (*yamak*s), and Bektashism in the Ottoman state, which despite some very interesting points actually rests on some incorrect assumptions: Deena Sadat, "Ayan and Aga: The Transformation of the Bektashi Corps in the Eighteenth Century," *The Muslim World* 63, no. 3 (July 1973): 206–19. Of course here should also be cited the articles of Fehim Bajraktarević, "Paswan-Oghlu," in *EI 2*, vol. 8 (Leiden, 1995), 284–85, and A. Cevat Eren, "Pazvand-oğlu," in *İslam Ansiklopedisi*, vol. 9 (Istanbul, 1964), 532–35. After this study was submitted for publication one more article had appeared dedicated to Pazvantoğlu, Robert Zens, "Pasvanoğlu Osman Paşa and the Paşalık

of Belgrade, 1791–1807," *International Journal of Turkish Studies* 8 (Spring 2002): 88–104.

6. To my knowledge the latest study on him is that of Katherine E. Fleming, *The Muslim Bonaparte: Diplomacy and Orientalism in Ali Pasha's Greece* (Princeton, N.J.: Princeton University Press, 1999).

7. A large number of these documents have been published, though with some inaccuracies in the translation by D. Ihchiev. See Diamandi Ihchiev, "Turski dărzhavni dokumenti za kărdzhaliite," *Sbornik za narodni umotvoreniia, nauka i knizhnina* (hereafter *SbNUNK*) 22–23 (Sofia, 1906–1907): 1–71, providing the general background of the *kırcalı/ dağlı* unrest; idem, "Turski dărzhavni dokumenti za Osman Pazvantoglu Vidinski" (hereafter TDDOPV), *SbNUNK* 24, no. 1 (Sofia, 1908): 1–126. Both publications contain documents from the *kadı* registers of Sofia and Vidin.

8. L. Popov, "Prinos za izuchavane minaloto na bălgarskoto otechestvo," *Sb-NUNK* 24, no. 1 (Sofia, 1908): 1–157 (Austrian, Prussian and French diplomatic correspondence); Ivan Pavlović, "Ispisi iz frantsuskih arhiva o Pazvantoglu (od 1795 do 1807 godina)," *Spomenik Srpske kralyevske akademiye*, Pt. 3 (Belgrade, 1890): 105–28 (French documents); Pavel Oreshkov, "Niakolko dokumenta za Pazvantoglu i Sofroniia Vrachanski (1800–1812)," *Sbornik na BAN* 3 (Sofia, 1914): 1–54 (Russian diplomatic documents); Dimităr Yotsov, "Materiali za Pazvant-oglu, izvlecheni iz ruskite arhivi," *Periodichesko spisanie na BKD v Sofiia* 68 (Sofia, 1908): 749–55 (Russian documents); *Documente privind Istoria Românici* (hereafter *DPIR*), Collectia Eudoxiu Hurmuzaki (seria noua), vol. 4, Rapoarte diplomatiçe Ruse (1797–1806) (Bucharest: Ed. Ştinţifica, 1974). See also the notes of Colonel A. Mériage, who came to Vidin a couple of months after the death of Pazvantoğlu and stayed there more than a year. Grégoire Iakichitch, "Notes sur Passvan Oglou par l'adjutant-commandant Mériage," *Revue slave* 1 (1906) : 261–79; 418–29; 2 (1907): 139–44, 436–48; 3 (1907): 138–44, 278–88. Although his information was collected some months after the death of Pazvantoğlu, Mériage provides very interesting and mostly reliable data that is at least to some extent corroborated by our other sources.

9. François C. H. I. Pouqueville, *Travels through Morea, Albania, and several other parts of the Ottoman Empire to Constantinople during the years 1798, 1799, 1800, and 1801* (London, 1806), 100; Guillaume-Antoine Olivier, *Voyage dans l'Empire ottomane, l'Egypte et la Perse, fait par ordre du gouvernement pendant les six premières années de la République*, vol. 1 (Paris, an 9/1801), 192–222. I have used the latter in Bulgarian translation in: Bistra Tsvetkova, ed., *Frenski pătepisi za Balkanite, XV–XVIII v.* (Sofia: Nauka i izkustvo, 1975), 458–502.

10. See Rhigas's selected works published in Bulgarian and Greek, in Rigas Velestinlis, *Revolyutsionno* (Sofia: Izdatelska kăshta Ivan Vazov, 1998). An in-

teresting biography of Pazvantoğlu was written and published in 1800 by a contemporary Greek author, Konstantinos Gueorguiades Kutsikos. See Vărban Todorov, "Malko izvestno izdanie za Osman Pazvantoglu," *Istoricheski pregled*, no. 3 (Sofia, 1990): 84–91.

11. Sofronii Vrachanski, *Zhitie i stradanie greshnago Sofroniia*, ed. N. Dyilevskii (Sofia: Nauka i izkustvo, 1989).

12. V. Nachev and N. Fermandzhiev, eds., *Pisahme da se znae. Pripiski i letopisi* (Sofia: OF, 1984).

13. See for example *DPIR*, doc. 28, Anexa IV, p. 107, of 11 December 1797, Russian diplomatic information from Bucharest: "Pazvandoglo published a manifesto compiled by himself, [containing] three articles" or Popov, "Prinos za izuchavane minaloto," report of M-r Chalgrin to Louis XVIII, of March 1797, doc. 9, 4; and a dispatch of the Austrian internuntius Rath Keal of 25 January 1798, in ibid., doc. 5, 23–24.

14. This short exposé on agrarian relations in the region is based on Strashimir Dimitrov, *Văstanieto ot 1850 g. v Bălgariia* (Sofia: BAN, 1972), 13–34. There is useful information on the subject also in Hristo Gandev, "Zarazhdane na kapitalisticheski otnosheniia v chiflishkoto stopanstvo na Severozapadna Bălgariia prez XVIII vek,"in idem, *Problemi na Bălgarskoto Văzrazhdane* (Sofia: Nauka i izkustvo, 1976), 271–394.

15. NBKM (St. St. Cyril and Methodius National Library), Or. Dept., S 38 (Vidin *kadı* register, of 1705–13), passim.

16. NBKM, Or. Dept., Vidin, *muhafız*, a.u. 2534. For more detail on these events Svetlana Ivanova, "Widdin," in *EI 2*, vol. 11, 205–208.

17. Dimitrov, *Văstanieto ot 1850*, 32.

18. See Rossitsa Gradeva, "War and Peace along the Danube: Vidin at the End of the 17th Century," in *The Ottomans and the Sea*, K. Fleet, ed., *Oriente moderno* 20 (81), no. 1 (2001): 149–75.

19. Iakichitch, "Notes sur Passvan Oglou," 265–69. See also Stojan Novaković, *Tursko tsarstvo pred srbski ustanak* (Belgrade, 1906), 330ff.; Ciprien Robert, *Les Slaves de Turquie*, vol. 2 (Paris: Passard, 1852), 294, who might be considered an independent source, based on stories circulated in the area when he visited it. It is repeated in several later works dedicated to that period. See for example Konstantin Irechek, *Istoriia na bălgarite* (Sofia: Nauka i izkustvo, 1978), 529. There are also variations of the family history, for example, in Todorov, "Malko izvestno izdanie," 87.

20. Ihchiev, "TDDOPV," 9–12; NBKM, Or. Dept., S 59, p. 86.

21. See Mutafchieva, *Kărdzhaliisko vreme*, 69–76.

22. There are no significant differences between the contemporary sources concerning the political events in which he was involved. Here I follow Mutafchieva *Kărdzhaliisko vreme*, passim; Grachev, *Balkanskie vladeniia,* passim; Ihchiev, "TDDOPV," passim; Shaw, *Between Old and New,* passim.

23. Mutafchieva, *Kărdzhaliisko vreme*, 101. Similar acts were undertaken by the central authorities. As early as 1785 the Porte started appealing to the *reaya* to organize, resist, repulse, and even attack the bandits. Soon these appeals were addressed not only to the local Muslims, but also to the entire population of these regions. Thus in 1793 the authority began to arm all, including the Christians, which came in direct contradiction with age-old traditions forbidding Christians to bear arms. Ibid., 103–104. Shaw places this event in 1799, when the governor of the Belgrade *Paşalık* allowed the local *knez*es to organize and arm native Serbian troops as auxiliaries. They were to be supported directly by the local population without the necessity of new Ottoman taxes, Shaw, *Between Old and New*, 306. See also Glenny (*Balkans*, 6), who says that in 1799 Selim III issued a *ferman* permitting the Christians to carry weapons—a rifle, two pistols, and a yatagan. This allowed the peasants to form armed units in aid of the *sipahi*s and the supporters of Selim's reforms against the Janissaries.

24. Ihchiev, "TDDOPV," docs. VI–VIII, 15–16, concerning his appointment to collect the *cizye* of Gypsies in the *vilayet*s of Vidin and Nikopol.

25. Oreshkov, "Niakolko dokumenta za Pazvantoglu," 25.

26. Popov, "Prinos za izuchavane minaloto," 6.

27. The last news of Pazvantoğlu's son comes in 1811, when an English traveller, John Galt, passed through Vidin. He heard of the marriage of the widow and tells a curious story about the son of Osman, Ali, who must have been a spoilt young man. John Galt, *Voyages and Travels, in the Years 1809, 1810, and 1811; Containing Statistical, Commercial, and Miscellaneous Observations on Gibraltar, Sardinia, Sicily, Malta, Serigo, and Turkey* (London, 1812). I have used the Bulgarian translation in Maria Todorova, ed., *Angliiski pātepisi za Balkanite, kraia na XVI v.–30te godini na XIX v.* (Sofia: Nauka i izkustvo, 1987), 535, 539.

28. See the *ferman* ordering confiscation in Ihchiev, "TDDOPV," doc. CVI, 125–28.

29. The date is not indicated in the *fetva*s but they were recorded with other documents from 1797. Besides, in December 1797 the Austrian ambassador informed his government that "cet homme remuant et coupable venoit d'être dépouillé de tous ses droits, maudit et proscrit" [this restless and reprehensible man has just been stripped of all his rights, accursed and outlawed]. Popov, "Prinos za izuchavane minaloto," doc. 39, 18. The French texts are rendered in their original spelling.

30. Ihchiev, "TDDOPV," doc. XXVII, 35–37.

31. Ibid., doc. XXX, 41–42; doc. XXXIII, 45–46; doc. XXXIV, 50; doc. XXXV, 51, all of November 1797; doc. XXXVIII, 53–54, of December 1797, and others.

32. Quoted from Mutafchieva, *Kărdzhaliisko vreme*, 159–60.

33. Ihchiev, "TDDOPV," 40–43.
34. Popov, "Prinos za izuchavane minaloto," doc. 40, 20 [in public opinion he is the defender of the ancient laws of the empire, an enemy of the onerous innovations, moreover, ready to become the most faithful of the subjects if the oppressive abuses were to be corrected].
35. Ibid., doc. 43, 20–21. The prohibition against mentioning the name of Pazvantoğlu is also reported on two occasions by Ruffin, the French chargé d'affaires in 1798. Ibid., doc. 6, 134; doc. 10, 140.
36. Ibid., doc. 11, 136 [He wants to get to the throne, therefore he has united all the discontented in the empire].
37. Oreshkov, "Niakolko dokumenta za Pazvantoglu," 13, doc. 7, 37–38, of 23.02.1802; Pavlović, "Ispisi iz frantsuskih arhiva," doc. XX, 122–23; doc. XXI, 124, of 22.09. –22.10.1801; Popov, "Prinos za izuchavane minaloto," 116, of March 1800; Mutafchieva, *Kārdzhaliisko vreme*, 210. The rumor is also reported by Bishop Sofronii. Sofronii Vrachanski, *Zhitie i stradanie greshnago Sofroniia*, 75, n. 298, 109.
38. *DPIR*, doc. 37, Anexa III, 125.
39. Popov, "Prinos za izuchavane minaloto," doc. 7, 135.
40. Irechek, *Istoriia na bălgarite*, 531.
41. Rumiana Radkova, *Văzrozhdenetsăt Hristo Dupnichanin* (Sofia: BAN, 1997), 88–89.
42. Naiden Gerov, compiler, *Rechnik na bălgarskiia ezik*, vol. 4, pt. 2, ed. T. Panchev (Plovdiv, 1901), 5.
43. Valeria Tarashoeva and others, eds., *Semeen arhiv na Hadzhitoshevi*, vol. 2 (1827–1878) (Sofia: BG Print, 2002), doc. 496, 454.
44. Pavlović, "Ispisi iz frantsuskih arhiva," doc. XX, 121–22 [1. To work with all means towards all the changes that the French Government will deem useful in the government of the Ottoman empire; 2. If the French Republic contemplates attacking the Ottoman Power, Pasvand-Oglou undertakes to assist it with all his means and to openly cooperate . . . with the single condition that a province be left to him where he and his friend Gingis Metremet Gueray Sultan could live peacefully under the protection of French laws].
45. Popov, "Prinos za izuchavane minaloto," doc. 39, 17, of 1797 [Under the pretext of reforming not only in the city of Widdin but also in its neighborhood the faults of the new Government, in particular with regards to the new taxes (Nizami Gedid) and to reestablish the system on the footing of Sultan Süleyman I Kanouni, he has succeeded underhand to swamp the trust of the neighboring inhabitants]. The diplomat goes on to say that Pazvantoğlu's projects were to "push things till he gets the throne."
46. *DPIR*, doc. 28, Anexa IV, p. 107, of 11 December 1797. At the end of November the Prussian diplomatic agent in the capital, Knobelsdorff, speaks of probably the same document: "He says he is faithful to his master but has risen

against those who surround him and who, by their evil advice, have encouraged him to institute the *Nizam-i cedid*, the name of the regulation for the new taxes." Popov, "Prinos za izuchavane minaloto," 120.

47. Ibid., doc. 9, 4–5. The information about the demands of Pazvantoğlu sent by Rath Keal at the beginning of April 1797 may also have been drawn from one of these documents: "Tout en vantant sa fidélité au Sultan ce chef s'éleve contre les nouveautés militaires, flatte le corps si redoutable et si mécontent des Janissaires, blame la docilité des Toptchis à adopter la discipline des Infidèles, et offre sa protection aux Rayas contre le Nizami-gedid, proscrit par la loi Mahométan" [While boasting of his loyalty to the Sultan, this chief rises against the military novelties, flatters the so formidable and so dissatisfied corps of Jannisaires, criticizes the docility with which the Toptchis adopt the discipline of the Unbelivers, and offers his protection to the Rayas, against the Nizami-gedid prohibited by the Moslem law]. Ibid., doc. 10, 5.

48. Ibid., doc. 3, 22: Pazvantoğlu sent a letter to the *bazirgânbaşı* of the Janissaries in which he demanded the seven-year arrears of the salaries of the Janissaries in Vidin and nine-year ones of those in Belgrade.

49. Ibid., doc. 38, 17, of November 1797, Rath Keal.

50. Olivier, *Voyage dans l' Empire ottomane*, 473. This popularity and high esteem, as well as the main reasons for the Janissaries' support are also confirmed by G. Kutsikos (Todorov, "Malko izvestno izdanie," 89): "The Janissaries regard him as their God"; Robert, *Les Slaves de Turquie*, 298: "Plus le sultan s'éloignait des janissaires et favorisait les institutions des ghiaours, plus des janissaires s'agrissaient contre le sultan et contre les frères des ghiaours" [The more the sultan estranges from the Janissaries and favors the ghiaours' institutions, the more the Janissaries are getting embittered against the sultan and the brothers of the ghiaours].

51. Pouqueville, *Travels through Morea*, 100. See also the *Pazvandoğlu Destanı*, in Osman Keskioğlu, *Bulgaristan'da Müslümanlar ve İslam Eserleri* (n. p. and n. d.), 99–101; Vankov, *Osman Paspanoglu*, 87–88.

52. Popov, "Prinos za izuchavane minaloto," doc. 14, 8.

53. See for example Sadat, "Ayan and Aga," passim.

54. F. W. Hasluck, *Christianity and Islam under the Sultans*, vol. 2 (New York: Octagon Books, 1973), 593. This author makes the direct connection: "He (Osman Pazvantoğlu) seems to have been a strong partisan of the Janissaries . . . and of the *ancien régime*, and his fief of Kirja or Kirja Ali . . . has been in its time an important Bektashi centre as containing the tomb of the saint Said Ali." Recently Ali Paşa's Bektashism was also subjected to critical investigation. See Nathalie Clayer, "The Myth of Ali Pasha and the Bektashis. The Construction of an 'Albanian Bektashi National History'," in Stephanie Schwandner-Sievers and Bernd J. Fischer, eds., *Albanian Identities. Myth and History* (London: Hurst & Company, 2002), 127–133.

55. Popov, "Prinos za izuchavane minaloto," doc. 9, 5 [He is above all an austere Muslim; he is called Sultan Osman after the name of that famous caliph, who, a successor to Omar, in 644 distinguished himself by his attachment to the Islamic faith to whose preservation he devotes all his attention].

56. Ibid., doc. 11, 135 [faithful to the Alcoran he seems to be inspired by Mahomet only and to have as his one aim the good fortune of the people and the glory of the name of the Muslims].

57. Pavlović, "Ispisi iz frantsuskih arhiva," doc. XX, 122, of 22.09. –22.10.1801: "Pasvand-Oglou promet d'entreprendre avec son audace ordinaire l'Exécution des ordres du Gouvernement françai [sic] de telle nature qu'ils soient en supposant toujours qu'ils ne seront points dirigés contre la Croyance des vrais Musulmans" [Pasvand-Oglou promises to undertake with his usual audacity to carry out the orders of the French government, of whatever nature they may be, taking for granted that they will not be in contradiction with the beliefs of the true Moslems.]

58. *DPIR*, doc. 27, 102, of November 1797.

59. Todorov, "Malko izvestno izdanie," 90.

60. On his construction work in Vidin, see: Ivanova, "Widdin"; Machiel Kiel, "Urban Development in Bulgaria in the Turkish Period," *International Journal of Turkish Studies* 4, no. 2 (1989): 101–102, Plates 20 and 21; Mihaila Staynova, "Ottoman Libraries in Vidin," *Etudes balkaniques*, no. 2 (Sofia, 1979); idem, "Za vakăfskata deinost na Osman Pazvantoglu văv Vidin i Vidinskiia krai," *Vekove*, no. 6 (Sofia, 1982); idem, *Osmanskite biblioteki v bălgarskite zemi, XV–XIX v.* (Sofia: NBKM, 1982); Todor Zlatev, *Bălgarskite gradove po r. Dunav prez epohata na Văzrazhdaneto* (Sofia: Nauka i Izkustvo, 1962), 11–58.

61. On the books and the libraries founded by Osman Paşa see the works of Ivanova and Staynova cited in n. 64, as well as Svetlana Ivanova, "The Sicills of the Ottoman Kadis. Observations on the Sicill Collection of the National Library in Sofia, Bulgaria," in Kemal. Çiçek, ed., *Pax Ottomana. Studies in Memoriam Prof. Dr. Nejat Göyünç* (Ankara: Yeni Türkiye, 2001), 70; Stoyanka Kenderova and Zorka Ivanova, compilers, *From the Collections of Ottoman Libraries in Bulgaria during the 18th–19th centuries: Catalogue of the Exhibition of Manuscripts and Old Printed Books, Sofia, May 1998* (Sofia: NBKM, 1999), 20–25; M. L. Maleev, "Opis na neduhovnite knigi ot vidinskata biblioteka na Pazvantoglu Osman aga," *SbNUNK* 3 (1890): 405–409.

62. Liubomir Mikov, "Dva kăsni osmanski pametnika v Severozapadna Bălgariia," in Evgenia Mitseva, ed., *Prostranstva na drugostta* (forthcoming). I wish to thank the author for allowing me to use the unpublished paper. The author correctly points out that there is no explicit evidence about Salaheddin's belonging to the Bektashi order; that not all Janissaries professed Bektashism; that Bektashis showed a rather formal attitude to the mosque as a cult building.

He also turns our attention to the names of the members of the Pazvantoğlu family, Ömer and Osman, the names of two of the righteous caliphs, in respect to which there was a religious taboo among the Bektashis. Here one may also add the association in name with the third caliph, association which according to the diplomatic correspondence was particularly prized by Pazvantoğlu. The names, however, may be misleading as an indicator in this respect, as Osman's son's name is Ali, the name of the fourth righteous caliph, who was particularly revered by Bektashis. Here I am more inclined to see an association with the caliphs consciously sought by Osman, rather than anything else.

63. On the evolution of the meaning of the term in Ottoman documentation see Joseph Kabrda, "Raia," *Izvestiia na Istoricheskoto druzhestvo v Sofiia* 14–15 (1937): 176–85.

64. Popov, " Prinos za izuchavane minaloto," doc. 10, 6. This meant about two *kuruş*. See Şevket Pamuk, "Appendix," in *An Economic and Social History of the Ottoman Empire, 1300–1914*, eds. Halil İnalcık and Donald Quatert (Cambridge: Cambridge University Press, 1994), 967. Unfortunately, I am not aware of studies where the tax burden of peasants in "ordinary" Ottoman provinces is estimated.

65. See a report of a police informant about moods in Istanbul cafés. One trader for example said: "earlier people spoke of the great equity shown by this man. There were even cases when he treated with care the people in the conquered territories while from the *reaya* he collected one golden piece as *harac*," NBKM, Or. Dept., 9/32. Quoted from Mutafchieva, *Kărdzhaliisko vreme*, 172.

66. Popov, "Prinos za izuchavane minaloto," doc. 10, 6 [A large number of Rayas from Sistow, Tirnowa in the surroundings of Widdin etc. overloaded with the taxes on silk, grains, and wine leave their arable lands, and having begged Paswandoglou's protection they find with him plots to cultivate with one single burden of 110 paras of haradsch. The other landlords having seen their peasants desert them, cry out against Paswandoglou whose possessions flourish at their expense]. Compare also with n. 65. On the other hand, Shaw writes that when Pazvantoğlu invaded Kraina which previously enjoyed specific tax and administrative status, all privileges of local Christians were curbed and the taxes were increased, while *yamaks* fleeing from Belgrade introduced a ferocious regime in the area. Shaw, *Between Old and New*, 240–41.

67. Report of the Russian diplomat Kirico, based in Wallachia, *DPIR*, 322.

68. Again evidence of Kirico from 1804, who says that this was how Pazvantoğlu tried to keep his credit high with local Christians. Quoted from Grachev, *Balkanskie vladeniia*, 101.

69. Iakichitch, "Notes sur Passvan Oglou," 284.

70. *DPIR*, 319.

71. Grachev, *Balkanskie vladeniia*, 87.

72. *DPIR*, doc. 8, 74, of 22.04.1797, from Bucharest: "il [Pazvantoğlu] compte en tout sur la fidélité des Grecs qu'il a à sa solde" [he [Pazvantoğlu] relies in everything on the fidelity of the Greeks whom he has in his payroll]; Irechek, *Istoriia na bălgarite*, 538; Mutafchieva, *Kărdzhaliisko vreme*, 339–57, etc. Mutafchieva in particular claims that this period was decisive in the accumulation of political and military experience by Bulgarians, taking part in the bands of many *ayan*s and defending their places from these bands. This was the time when arms entered the houses of many local people who were sometimes forced to use them by the local or the central authority.

73. Shteriu Atanasov, *Selskite văstaniia v Bălgariia kăm kraia na XVIII i nachaloto na XIX v i săzdavaneto na Bălgarskata zemska voiska* (Sofia: Dărzhavno voenno izdatelstvo, 1958), 142, 151.

74. On Kara George, see, for example, M. Vukičević, *Karadjordje*, vols. 1–2 (Belgrade, 1907–12). It was probably then that emerged the legend told in Robert, *Les Slaves de Turquie*, 295: "En 1791, il se lia, dit-on, d'amitié avec le héros de la Serbie, Tserni George. Les Grecs, amis de merveilleux, racontent que ces deux grands haïdouks, après avoir communié ensemble, s'unirent dans une église par le *vlam* ou *pobratstvo* (serment de fraternité)" [In 1791, he struck, it is said, a friendship with the hero of Serbia, Tserni George. Greeks, with their fondness for the marvellous, tell how these two great haïdouks, after having partaken of communion, were united in a church by the vlam or pobratstvo (oath of brotherhood)].

75. Atanasov, *Selskite văstaniia*, 152.

76. Shaw, *Between Old and New*, 327.

77. Dimităr Kosev and others, eds., *Istoriia na Bălgariia*, vol. 5 (Sofia: BAN, 1985), 176.

78. Oreshkov, "Niakolko dokumenta za Pazvantoglu," 25; Iakichitch, "Notes sur Passvan Oglou," 446.

79. Oreshkov, "Niakolko dokumenta za Pazvantoglu," 24, 48; Popov, "Prinos za izuchavane minaloto," 101.

80. In the pre-nationalist age, "Greek" or "Rum" was a generic name for all Orthodox Christians in the Ottoman empire, and especially for those who belonged to the Constantinople Patriarchate.

81. Oreshkov, "Niakolko dokumenta za Pazvantoglu," doc. 3, 35, of 1801, a letter from L. Dzhanoğlu to L. Kirico which reveals him as an intermediary between the Russians and Pazvantoğlu; *DPIR*, docs. 466–68, 567–69, of October–December 1804, discussing the reasons why L. Dzhanoğlu was put to death by Pazvantoğlu.

82. Oreshkov, "Niakolko dokumenta za Pazvantoglu," doc. 2, 34, of December 1800, doc. 4, 35, of January 1801; *DPIR*, doc. 253, 384, of June 1802, doc. 11, 414–16, July–August 1802, doc. 327, 445–46, of November 1802.

83. There must have been some truth in all the stories circulating about

Pazvantoğlu's special relations with this profession. See for example the stories told by Mériage in Iakichitch, "Notes sur Passvan Oglou," 285, but also many documents relating to him "importing" doctors.

84. Olivier, *Voyage dans l' Empire ottomane*, 473.

85. We are unable to list here the complete bibliography on Rhigas, but see, for example, Notis Botzaris, *Visions balkaniques dans la préparation de la révolution greque (1789–1821)* (Genève-Paris, 1962); Apostolos Daskalakis, "'Thourios Hymnos' le chant de la liberté de Rhigas Velestinlis," *Balkan Studies* 4, no. 2 (1963) : 315–46; A. J. Manessis, "L'activité et les projets politiques d'un patriote Grec dans les Balkans vers la fin du XVIIIe siècle," *Balkan Studies* 3, no. 1 (1962): 75–118; Georgios Zoidis, *Rigas Velestinlis* (Sofia: OF, 1973, also published in Greek), and many others, especially after 1998, when the 200th anniversary of Rhigas's tragic end was commemorated.

86. These documents included *New Political Administration of the Inhabitants of Rumeli, Asia Minor, the Mediterranean Islands and Wallachia-Bogdania*, which contained a *Declaration of the Rights of Man* and the *Constitution of the Free State*, based on the *Déclaration des droits de l'homme et du citoyen* and the Jacobin constitution of 1793, and adapted to the conditions prevailing in the Ottoman state.

87. I would like to thank the anonymous translator of the *Thourios* into English. He will recognize his piece of work. Cf. Daskalakis, "'Thourios Hymnos'," 347.

88. See for example Dennis Skiotis, "From Bandit to Pasha: First Steps in the Rise to Power of Ali of Tepelen, 1750–1784," *IJMES* 2 (1971): 219–44; Grachev, *Balkanskie vladeniia*, 36–42.

89. Pavlović, "Ispisi iz frantsuskih arhiva," docs. XX and XXI, 121–26, of 22.09. –22.10. 1801.

90. Ibid., p. 125 [He [P.] has no relations with Austria or Russia. He only acts so that the latter Power does not undertake anything against him if she is convinced that he will be careful with Moldavia. As for Austria, she limits herself for the time being to attend to the worries of the Porte by sending her from time to time Greek residents in Germany who are known to be in contact with the Pasha of Vidin. A few years back, a wide conspiracy against Turkey was discovered in Vienna led by agents of Passavan-oglou. Polisoi Condon was involved in it, eight Greeks were handed over to the Pasha of Belgrade who had them strangled. Polisoi claims that they were the greatest men of his nation. Fifteen to twenty were sent in exile to various Habsburg provinces. Polisoi himself, was only suspected and managed to get away by being deprived from his chair of Greek literature in Vienna. The conspiracy was given away by the arrest of a man that Passavan-oglou had sent to the First Consul. The papers he was carrying led the Austrian Inquisition to look for the agents of the Pasha and their letters. After this failure, Passavan-Oglou went on ceaselessly sen-

ding agents but without providing them with any papers. They all have been arrested or murdered. Nedelko is the only one who has been able to carry out His Master's orders]. Although this document is well known in Serbian and Bulgarian historiography, it has never been analyzed in the context of eventual relations between Pazvantoğlu and Rhigas.

91. *DPIR*, doc. 33, 115, of 8.01.1798; doc. 34, 117, 10.01.1798.

92. It is not quite clear what "eparhos" meant in this case, and this period of Rhigas's life is also unclear, but generally the term means administrator, governor.

93. L. Vranousis, *Rhigas Velestinlis* (Athens, 1954), p. 24, tells the story on the basis of the narration of Chr. Perraivos, *Apomnemonevmata polemika* (Athens, 1836).

94. Austrian sources say this happened in 1792, when he was about twenty-years old. Popov, "Prinos za izuchavane minaloto," doc. 10, 6, of April 1797.

95. Daskalakis, "'Thourios Hymnos'," passim; Zoidis, *Rigas Velestinlis*, 48.

96. "Barataire"/"baratais" comes from the Turkish *beratlı*, holder of a *berat*, a patent. See a detailed explanation of the term in Alexander de Groot, "Protection and Nationality. The Decline of the Drogmans," in *Istanbul et les langues orientales: Actes du colloque organise par l'IFEA et l'INALCO. Istanbul, 29–31 mai 1995*, ed. Frederick Hitzel, *Varia Turcica*, 31 (Paris-Montreal: l'Harmattan, 1997), 235–55.

97. See, for example, *DPIR*, doc. 28, Anexa IV, 107, December 1797, messenger of the Wallachian prince and the Ottoman authorities to Pazvantoğlu; doc. 30, Anexa 1, December 1797, bringing a letter in Turkish from Pazvantoğlu to Kirico, the Russian diplomatic representative in Bucharest; Popov, "Prinos za izuchavane minaloto," 133, October 1797, bringing a letter from Pazvantoğlu to the French ambassador; doc. 16, 138, February 1798, about his coming to the capital to negotiate with the Ottoman authorities, but also with the French, sent by Pazvantoğlu.

98. Popov, "Prinos za izuchavane minaloto," doc. 6, 26, 24 February 1798.

99. Popov, "Prinos za izuchavane minaloto," doc. 3, 22, of January 1798" [he treats with mildness the inhabitants, controls with a harsh discipline his Warriors, abolishes everywhere the new taxes, protects the travellers and the Caravans]. This fact is also confirmed by the envoys of Osman to Napoleon. Pavlović, "Ispisi iz frantsuskih arhiva," doc. XXI, 125, of 1801.

100. See Svetlana Ivanova, "The 'own' foreigners of the Empire. Armenians and Acem Tüccars, 17th–18th centuries," *Oriente moderno* (forthcoming). I wish to thank the author for allowing me to use her unpublished work.

101. See Popov, "Prinos za izuchavane minaloto," doc. 27, 34, of 1798; Oreshkov, "Niakolko dokumenta za Pazvantoglu," doc. 2, 34, doc. 7, 37–38; *DPIR*, doc. 297, 507, of 1803; Vankov, *Osman Paspanoglu*, 115.

102. Vankov, *Osman Paspanoglu*, 114.

103. Yordan Gueorguiev, "Grad Vratsa," *SbNUNK* 20 (1904), 11.

104. Andrei Tsvetkov, "Politichesko dvizhenie văv Vratsa ot kraia na XVIII i na-chaloto na XIX vek," in *Istoriia na grad Vratsa*, vol. 1, *Ot drevnostta do Osvobozhdenieto* (Sofia: OF, 1976), 177.

105. The issue of the bribe/gift given by Pazvantoğlu to this powerful Bulgarian remains open. A list of books, documents, and precious objects purchased by the National Library and the National Museum from the descendants of Dimitraki (in 1894) mentions among them the following: a tobacco-pouch of Persian silk, a spoon of tortoise shell decorated with corals, but also a purse lavishly embroidered with gold presented to Dimitraki by a Serbian girl ensla-ved by the *paşa* who escaped with the help of the Bulgarian notable. Several years later one of Dimitraki's grandsons included in a list of the so-called gift from Pazvantoğlu, which were still with the family, *çubuk*s (long tobacco pipe), a white *kalpak* (fur hat) around which he used to wind a nice silk cloth, two *enteri*s (loose robe), an outer *çuha* (broadcloth) garment, a beautiful *fer-mene* (short braided waistcoat) of green plush and embroidered with gold, the above-mentioned tortoise-shell spoon with corals, a silver cartridge-box and a pouch for gunpowder. Valeria Tarashoeva and others, eds., *Semeen arhiv*, doc. 493, 450; doc. 503, 464.

106. Dimitraki's father, Hadzhi Tosho, the founder of this powerful clan, and the early history of the Hadzhitoshevs still await historical research, especially given the fact that in their case we have one of the earliest family archives in Bulgarian history. See Kirila Văzvăzova-Teodorova and others, eds., *Semeen arhiv na Hadzhitoshevi (1754–1827)*, vol. 1 (Sofia: BAN, 1984) and the abo-ve-cited vol. 2. On Dimitraki see details in Svetla Ianeva "Dimitraki Tsenov HADZHITOSHEV," in *Koi koi e sred bălgarite, XV–XIX v.*, ed. Iliia Todev (Sofia: Anubis, 2000), 281–83, and the bibliography cited there.

107. Iakichitch, "Notes sur Passvan Oglou," 444–46. Mériage also mentions ano-ther Christian envoy, the "Greek" Atanas, who was earlier sent to Archduke Charles.

108. Pavlović, "Ispisi iz frantsuskih arhiva," 125 [he can dip into the purses of all the merchants in the territory under his rule who have undertaken by writing to devote their fortunes to him].

109. Mériage tells a sentimental story. A Bulgarian merchant Gallo had lent money to many Turks who avoided paying their debts to him, which brought the man to such despair that he attempted suicide. He was saved, the *paşa* heard of the case, summoned all involved, and ordered their punishment (beating with a stick) and the payment of all debts within 24 hours. Pavlović, "Ispisi iz frant-suskih arhiva," 283–84.

110. About him see C. Sathas, *Neohellenic Literature* (Athens, 1868), p. 652 (in Greek); Konstantinos Staikos, *Greek editions from the time of the Neohelle-nic Enlightenment* (Athens: Europaiko Politiko Kentro-Delfon, 1998), 62, 92,

125, 130, 170, 175 (in Greek and English). I wish to thank Prof. N. Danova for helping me identify Polisoi with Polyzois.

111. (W)ho "had neither a mission nor was knowledgeable about the one with which Popowitch was entrusted."About him see *DPIR*, doc. 297, 507; Staikos, *Greek editions*, 140, 142, 160. For the time being I am more inclined to identify Polisoi Condon with Polyzois Kontòs.

112. There is extensive literature in Bulgarian on Sofronii of Vratsa, devoted both to his political and literary activities. See Nina Vutova, ed., *Sofronii Vrachanski, 1739–1813: Bio-bibliografski ukazatel* (Sofia: NBKM, 1989). See also Jacque Feuillet, *Sofroni Vračanski: Vie et tribulations du pecheur Sofroni* (Sofia: Sofia-Press, 1986); Louis Leger, "La Bulgarie sous Pasvan Oglou. Memoires de l'évêque Sofroni," in his *La Bulgarie* (Paris, 1885), 81–141. Sofronii is also the founder of the first Phanariot family of Bulgarian background, that of the Bogoridi/Bogorides.

113. Nicolae Dură, "New Discoveries—on the Basis of Original Documentary Materials—on the Life and Activity of Bishop Sofronij Vračanski (1739–1813) in Wallachia, His Adoptive Country (1802–1813)," *Bulgarian Historical Review*, no. 1 (1991): 30–31.

114. Vera Mutafchieva, *Kniga za Sofronii* (Sofia: Voenno Izdatelstvo, 1978), 161–62ff.

115. Valentina Racheva, "Văprositelni okolo politicheskata deinost na Sofronii Vrachanski," *Istoriia*, no. 1 (Sofia, 1995): 31–40.

Bibliography

Abou El Haj, Rifaat Ali. "Ottoman Attitudes Towards Peace Making: The Karlowitz Case." *Der Islam* 51 (1974): 131–37.

———. *Formation of the Modern State: The Ottoman Empire Sixteenth to Eighteenth Centuries*. Binghamton: SUNY Press, 1992.

Abu-Manneh, Butrus. "The Naqshbandiyya-Mujaddidiyya in the Ottoman Lands in the Early 19th Century." *Die Welt des Islams* 22 (1982): 1–36.

Adanır, Fikret, and Suraiya Faroqhi, eds. *The Ottomans and the Balkans: A Discussion of the Historiography*. Leiden: Brill, 2002.

Adanır, Fikret. "Balkan Historiography Related to the Ottoman Empire Since 1945." In *Ottoman Past and Today's Turkey*, ed. Kemal H. Karpat. Leiden: Brill, 2000.

———. "Heiduckentum und Osmanische Herrschaft." *Südost-Forschungen* 41 (1982): 43–116.

Aksan, Virginia. "Feeding the Ottoman Troops on the Danube." *War and Society* 13 (1995): 1–14.

———. "Locating the Ottomans Among Early Modern Empires." *Journal of Early Modern History* 3 (1999): 103–34.

———. "Ottoman Military Recruitment Strategies in the Late Eighteenth Century." In *Arming the State*, ed. Erik Zurcher, 21–39. London: I. B. Tauris, 1999.

———. "Ottoman War and Warfare 1453–1812." In *War in the Early Modern World, 1450–1815*, ed. Jeremy Black, 147–76. London: UCL Press, 1999.

———. "Whatever Happened to the Janissaries?" *War in History* 5 (1998): 23–36.

———. *An Ottoman Statesman in War and Peace: Ahmed Resmi Efendi, 1700–1783*. Leiden: Brill 1995.

Alexandrescu-Dersca Bulgaru, M. M. "L'Approvisionnement d'Istanbul par les Principautés roumaines aux XIIIe Siècle." *Revue de l'Occident Musulman et de la Méditerranée*, 1992–94: 73–78.

Anastasopoulos, Antonis. "Imperial Institutions and Local Communities: Ottoman Karaferye, 1758–1774." Ph.D. diss., University of Cambridge, 1999.

———. "Lighting the Flame of Disorder: *Ayan* Infighting and State Intervention in Ottoman Karaferye, 1758–59." *International Journal of Turkish Studies* 8, nos. 1 & 2 (2002): 73–88.

Anderson, J. N. D. "Homicide in Islamic Law." *Bulletin of the School of Oriental and African Studies* 13 (1951): 811–28.

Atanasov, Shteriu. *Selskite văstaniia v Bălgariia kăm kraia na XVIII i nachaloto na XIX v i săzdavaneto na Bălgarskata zemska voiska.* Sofia: Dărzhavno voenno izdatelstvo, 1958.

Bajraktarević Ast, F. "Paswanoghlu." *Encyclopedia of Islam,* 2d ed., vol. 8, 284–85. Leiden, 1995.

Barkey, Karen. *Bandits and Bureaucrats: The Ottoman Route to State Centralization.* Ithaca, N.Y. and London: Cornell University Press, 1994.

Bartl, Peter. "Albanien im Russisch-Österreichischen Türkenkrieg, 1787–1792." In *Albanien in Vergangenheit und Gegenwart,* ed. Klaus-Detlev Grothusen, 47–70. Munich: Südosteuropa-Studien, 1991.

Beaujour, Louis-Auguste-Félix de. *Tableau du commerce de la Grèce, formé d'après une année moyenne, depuis 1787 jusqu'en 1797,* 2 vols. Paris: Ant.-Aug. Renouard, 1800.

Beldiceanu, Nicoara. "Eflak" *Encyclopedia of Islam* 2d ed. (CD version).

Bennet, John, Jack Davis, and Fariba Zarinebaf-Shahr. "Sir William Gell's Itinerary in the Pylia and Regional Landscapes in the Morea in the Second Ottoman Period." *Hesperia* 69 (2000): 343–80.

Boehm, Christopher. *Blood Revenge: The Enactment and Management of Conflict in Montenegro and Other Tribal Societies.* Philadelphia: University of Pennsylvania Press, 1984.

Botzaris, Notis. *Visions balkaniques dans la préparation de la révolution greque (1789–1821).* Genève-Paris, 1962.

Bracewell, Catherine W. *The Uskoks of Senj: Piracy, Banditry, and Holy War in the Sixteenth-Century Adriatic.* Ithaca, N.Y.: Cornell University Press, 1992.

Çağatay Uluçay, M.. "Sürgünler" [Exiles]. *Belleten* 15 (1951): 507–92.

Ceauşescu, Ilie. "Military Aspects of the National Struggle of the Rumanian Principalities in the Eighteenth Century." In *East Central European Society and War in the Pre-Revolutionary Eighteenth Century,* ed. Gunther E. Rothenberg, Béla A. Király, and Peter F. Sugar, 371–85. Boulder, Colo.: Social Science Monographs; New York: dist. by Columbia University Press, 1982.

Cevad, Ahmed. *Tarih-i Askeri-i Osmani.* Istanbul, 1880.

Cevdet, Ahmed. *Tarih-i Cevdet.* Istanbul, 1303/1886.

Chirot, Daniel. *Social Change in a Peripheral Society: The Creation of a Balkan Colony.* New York: Academic Press, 1976.

Clayer, Nathalie. "Note sur la survivance du système des *timâr* dans la région de Shkodër au début du XXe siècle." *Turcica* 29 (1997): 423–31.

———. "The Myth of Ali Pasha and the Bektashis. The Construction of an 'Albanian Bektashi National History'." In *Albanian Identities: Myth and History,* ed. Stephanie Schwandner-Sievers and Bernd J. Fischer, 127–33. London: Hurst & Company, 2002.

Constantiniu, Florin. "Tradition and Innovation in the Eighteenth-Century Military Structures of the Rumanian Lands." In *East Central European Society and War in the Pre-Revolutionary Eighteenth Century*, ed. Gunther E. Rothenberg, Béla A. Király and Peter F. Sugar, 387–99. Boulder, Colo.: Social Science Monographs; New York: dist. by Columbia University Press, 1982.

Cvetkova, Bistra. "Un document turc inédit concernant un mouvement de résistance en Bulgarie du Nord-Ouest au XVIIIe siècle." *Rocznik Orientaliztyczny* 36 (1976): 93–100.

———. "The Bulgarian Haiduk Movement in the 15th to 18th Centuries." In *East Central European Society in the Pre-Revolutionary Eighteenth Century*, ed. Gunther Rothenberg, Béla Király, and Peter Sugar, 301–38. Boulder, Colo: Social Science Monographs, 1982.

———, ed. *Frenski pătepisi za Balkanite, XV–XVIII v.* Sofia: Nauka i izkustvo, 1975.

Daskalakis, Apostolos. "'Thourios Hymnos' le chant de la liberté de Rhigas Velestinlis." *Balkan Studies* 4, no. 2 (1963): 315–46.

Dávid, Géza. "The *Eyalet* of Temesvár in the Eighteenth Century." *Oriente Moderno* NS 18, no. 1 (1999): 113–28.

de Groot, Alexander. "Protection and Nationality. The Decline of the Drogmans." In *Istanbul et les langues orientales: Actes du colloque organise par l'IFEA et l'INALCO, Istanbul, 29–31 mai 1995*, ed. Frederick Hitzel, 235–55. *Varia Turcica*, 31, Paris-Montreal: l'Harmattan, 1997.

de Tott, Baron. *Memoirs of Baron de Tott*, vol. 1. London: G.G.J. and J. Robinson, 1785.

Decei, Aurel. "Eflak," *İslam Ansiklopedisi*, vol. 4, 178–89. Istanbul, 1964.

Dimitrov, Strashimir. *Văstanieto ot 1850 g. v Bălgariia*. Sofia: BAN, 1972.

Dixon, Simon. *The Modernisation of Russia 1676–1825*. New York: Cambridge University Press, 1999.

Djevad, Ahmed. *L'Etat militaire Ottoman depuis la fondation de l'Empire jusqu'à nos jours*. Constantinople: Imp. Du Journal "La Turquie," 1882.

Djordjević, Dimitrije. "Agrarian Factors in Nineteenth-century Balkan Revolutions." In *War and Society in East Central Europe*, ed. Gunther E. Rothenberg and Béla A. Király, vol. 1, 163–82. New York: Brooklyn College Press, 1979.

Documente privind Istoria Românici. Collectia Eudoxiu Hurmuzaki (seria noua), vol. 4, Rapoarte diplomatiçe Ruse (1797–1806). Bucharest: Ed. Ştinţifica, 1974.

Doumani, Beshara. *Rediscovering Palestine: Merchants and Peasants in Jabal Nablus, 1700–1900*. Berkeley, Los Angeles, and London: University of California Press, 1995.

Duijzings, Ger. *Religion and the Politics of Identity in Kosovo*. New York: Columbia University Press, 2000.

Duka, Ferit. *Berati në Kohën Osmane (shek. XVI–XVIII)*. Tirana: Toena, 2001.

Durǎ, Nicolae. "New Discoveries—on the Basis of Original Documentary Materials—on the Life and Activity of Bishop Sofronij Vračanski (1739–1813) in Wallachia, His Adoptive Country (1802–1813)." *Bulgarian Historical Review*, 19/1 (1991): 29–46.

Durham, Mary Edith. *Some Tribal Origins, Laws, and Customs of the Balkans*. London: George Allen & Unwin Ltd., 1928.

Eren, A. Cevat. "Pazvand-oğlu." *İslam Ansiklopedisi*, vol. 9, 532–35. Istanbul, 1964.

Ergene, Boğaç A. "On Ottoman Justice: Interpretations in Conflict (1600–1800)." *Islamic Law and Society* 8, no. 1 (2001): 52–87.

Fahmy, Khaled. *All the Pasha's Men: Mehmed Ali, His Army and the Making of Modern Egypt*. New York: Cambridge University Press, 1997.

Faroqhi, Suraiya. "Migration into Eighteenth-Century 'Greater Istanbul' as Reflected in the Kadi Registers of Eyüp." *Turcica* 30 (1998): 163–83.

―――. *Approaching Ottoman History: An Introduction to the Sources*. London: Cambridge University Press, 1999.

―――. "The Life and Death of Outlaws in Çorum." In *Armağan-Festschrift für Andreas Tietze*, ed. Ingeborg Baldauf and Suraiya Faroqhi with Rudolf Veselý, 59–76. Prague: Enigma Corporation, 1994.

―――. "Sidjill," *The Encyclopaedia of Islam*, new edition, vol. 9. Leiden: Brill, 1997.

Feuillet, Jacque. *Sofroni Vračanski: Vie et tribulations du pecheur Sofroni*. Sofia: Sofia-Press, 1986.

Fielding, Henry. *An Enquiry into the Causes of Robbers*. London: A. Millar, 1751.

Fleischer, Cornell. *Bureaucrat and Intellectual in the Ottoman Empire: The Historian Mustafa Ali (1541–1600)*. Princeton: Princeton University Press, 1986.

Fleming, Katherine E. *The Muslim Bonaparte: Diplomacy and Orientalism in Ali Pasha's Greece*. Princeton: Princeton University Press, 1999.

Frashëri, Kristo. *The History of Albania (a Brief Survey)*. Tirana, 1964.

Gandev, Hristo. "Zarazhdane na kapitalisticheski otnosheniia v chiflishkoto stopanstvo na Severozapadna Bălgariia prez XVIII vek." In idem, *Problemi na Bălgarskoto Văzrazhdane*, 271–394. Sofia: Nauka i izkustvo, 1976.

Gara, Eleni. "Dolophonoi kai Dikastes sten Othomanike Veroia" [Murderers and Judges in Ottoman Veroia (Kara Ferye)]. *IMEros* 1 (2001): 113–30.

Genç, Mehmet. "L'économie ottomane et la guerre au XVIIIe siècle." *Turcica* 27 (1995): 177–96.

Gerber, Haim. *State, Society, and Law in Islam: Ottoman Law in Comparative Perspective*. Albany: State University of New York Press, 1994.

Gerolymatos, Andre. *The Balkan Wars: Conquest, Revolution, and Retribution from the Ottoman Era to the Twentieth Century and Beyond*. New York: Basic Books, 2002.

Gerov, N., compiler. *Rechnik na bălgarskiia ezik*, ed. T. Panchev. Plovdiv, 1901.

Ginio, Eyal. "The Administration of Criminal Justice in Ottoman Selânik (Salonica) during the Eighteenth Century." *Turcica* 30 (1998): 185–209.

Glenny, Misha. *Balkans, 1804–1999: Nationalism, War and the Great Powers.* London: Granta Books, 2000.

Grachev, Viktor. *Balkanskie vladeniia Osmanskoi imperii na rubezhe XVIII–XIX vv.* Moscow: Nauka, 1990.

Gradeva, Rossitsa. "War and Peace along the Danube: Vidin at the End of the 17th Century." *Oriente Moderno* NS 20, no. 1 (2001): 149–75.

Guboğlu, M. "Doua manuscrise turcesti de Ahmed Resmi Efendi, in Biblioteca 'V. A. Urecchia' din Galaţi privand tarile române." In *100 de ani de la infintarea primei biblioteci publice din judetul,* 15–49. Galaţi, 1974.

Gueorguiev, Yordan. "Grad Vratsa." *Sbornik za narodni umotvoreniia, nauka i knizhnina* 20 (1904).

Hasluck, F. W. *Christianity and Islam under the Sultans.* vol. 2. New York: Octagon Books, 1973.

Hathaway, Jane. *Politics of Households in Ottoman Egypt: The Rise of the Qazdağlıs.* New York: Cambridge University Press, 1997.

Heyd, Uriel. *Studies in Old Ottoman Criminal Law,* ed. V. L. Ménage. Oxford: Oxford University Press, 1973.

Hickok, Michael. *Ottoman Military Administration in Eighteenth-Century Bosnia.* New York: Brill, 1997.

Hobsbawm, Eric. *Bandits.* London: Weidenfeld and Nicolson, 2000.

Hupchick, Dennis. *The Balkans: From Constantinople to Communism.* New York: Palgrave, 2002.

Hurewitz, J. C. "The Europeanization of Ottoman Diplomacy: the Conversion from Unilateralism to Reciprocity in the Nineteenth Century." *Middle East Journal* 23 (1961): 741–52.

Iakichitch, Grégoire. "Notes sur Passvan Oglou par l'adjutant-commandant Mériage." *Revue Slave* 1 (1906): 261–79; 418–29; 2 (1907): 139–44, 436–48; 3 (1907): 138–44, 278–88.

Ianeva, Svetla. "Dimitraki Tsenov HADZHITOSHEV." In *Koi koi e sred bălgarite, XV–XIX v.,* ed. Iliia Todev, 281–83. Sofia: Anubis, 2000.

Ihchiev, Diamandi. "Turski dărzhavni dokumenti za kărdzhaliite." *Sbornik za narodni umotvoreniia, nauka i knizhnina* 22–23 (Sofia, 1906–1907): 1–71

———. "Turski dărzhavni dokumenti za Osman Pazvantoglu Vidinski." *Sbornik za narodni umotvoreniia, nauka i knizhnina* 24, no. 1 (Sofia, 1908): 1–126

İnalcık, Halil. "Arnawutluk." *The Encyclopedia of Islam.* Leiden: Brill, 1960.

———. "Stefan Dušan'dan Osmanlı İmparatorluğuna." In *Fuad Köprülü Armağanı, Mélanges Fuad Köprülü.* Istanbul: Dil ve Tarih-Coğrafya Fakültesi, 1953.

———. "Adâletnâmeler" [Rescripts of Justice]. *Belgeler* 2 (1965): 49–145.

———. "Centralization and Decentralization in Ottoman Administration." In *Studies in Eighteenth-Century Islamic History,* ed. Thomas Naff and Roger Owen, 27–52. Carbondale and Edwardsville–London and Amsterdam: Southern Illinois University Press–Feffer and Simons, 1977.

Irechek, Konstantin. *Istoriia na bălgarite*. Sofia: Nauka i izkustvo, 1978.

Israel, Fred, ed. *Major Peace Treaties of Modern History, 1648–1967*, vol. 2. New York: Chelsea House Publishers, 1980.

Ivanova, Svetlana. "The Sicills of the Ottoman Kadis. Observations on the Sicill Collection of the National Library in Sofia, Bulgaria." In *Pax Ottomana. Studies in Memoriam Prof. Dr. Nejat Göyünç*, ed. Kemal Çiçek, 51–76. Ankara: Yeni Türkiye, 2001.

————. "The 'own' foreigners of the Empire. Armenians and Acem Tüccars, 17th–18th centuries," *Oriente Moderno* (forthcoming).

Jennings, Ronald C. "Limitations of the Judicial Powers of the Kadi in 17th c. Ottoman Kayseri." *Studia Islamica* 50 (1979): 151–84.

Kabrda, Joseph. "Raia." *Izvestiia na Istoricheskoto druzhestvo v Sofiia* 14–15 (1937): 176–85.

Kafadar, Cemal. *Between Two Worlds: The Construction of the Ottoman State*. Berkeley: University of California Press, 1995.

Kenderova, St. and Z. Ivanova, compilers. *From the Collections of Ottoman Libraries in Bulgaria during the 18th–19th centuries: Catalogue of the Exhibition of Manuscripts and Old Printed Books, Sofia, May 1998*. Sofia: NBKM, 1999.

Kennedy, Paul. *The Rise and Fall of the Great Powers: Economic Change and Military Conflict from 1500 to 2000*. New York: Random House, 1988.

Keskioğlu, Osman. *Bulgaristan'da Müslümanlar ve İslam Eserleri*. n. p., n. d.

Kiel, Machiel. *Ottoman Architecture in Albania (1385–1912)*. Istanbul: Research Center for Islamic History, Art and Culture, 1990.

————. "Urban Development in Bulgaria in the Turkish Period." *International Journal of Turkish Studies* 4, no. 2 (1989): 79–158.

Koliopoulos, John. *Brigands with a Cause: Brigandage and Irredentism in Modern Greece, 1821–1912*. New York: Oxford University Press, 1987.

Leake, William Martin. *Travels in Northern Greece*, 4 vols. London: J. Rodwell, 1835.

Leger, Louis. "La Bulgarie sous Pasvan Oglou. Memoires de l'évêque Sofroni." In idem. *La Bulgarie*, 81–141. Paris, 1885.

Lewis, Bernard. "Some Reflections on the Decline of the Ottoman Empire." *Studia Islamica* 9 (1958): 111–27.

Linbaugh, Peter. "The Tyburn Riot Against the Surgeons." In *Albion's Fatal Tree: Crime and Society in Eighteenth-Century England*, ed. Douglas Hay, et. al. New York: Pantheon Books, 1975.

Malcolm, Noel. *Kosovo: A Short History*. New York: New York University Press, 1998.

Maleev, M. L. "Opis na neduhovnite knigi ot vidinskata biblioteka na Pazvantoglu Osman aga." *Sbornik za narodni umotvoreniia, nauka i knizhina* 3 (1890): 405–409.

Manessis, A. J. "L'activité et les projets politiques d'un patriote Grec dans les Balkans vers la fin du XVIIIe siècle." *Balkan Studies* 3, no. 1 (1962): 75–118.

Marcus, Abraham. *The Middle East on the Eve of Modernity: Aleppo in the Eighteenth Century*. New York: Columbia University Press, 1989.

Marinescu, Florin. "The Trade of Wallachia with the Ottoman Empire Between 1791 and 1821." *Balkan Studies* 22 (1981): 292–93.

Matuz, Josef E. "Transmission of Directives from the Center to the Periphery in the Ottoman State from the Beginning until the Seventeenth Century." In *Decision Making and Change in the Ottoman Empire*, ed. Caesar E. Farah, 19–27. Kirksville, Missouri: Thomas Jefferson University Press, 1993.

Mazower, Mark. *The Balkans*. London: Weidenfeld and Nicolson, 2000.

McGowan, Bruce. "The Age of the *Ayan*s, 1699–1812." In *An Economic and Social History of the Ottoman Empire, 1300–1914*, ed. Halil İnalcık with Donald Quataert, 637–758. Cambridge: Cambridge University Press, 1994.

McNeill, William H. *Europe's Steppe Frontier, 1500–1800*. Chicago: Chicago University Press, 1966.

Mile, Ligor. "De l'extension du système des *çiftlig* sur les territoires albanais." In *Deuxieme Conférence des Études Albanologiques*, vol. 2, 101–108. Tirana, 1970.

Mitrany, David. *The Land & the Peasant in Rumania*. London: Oxford University Press, 1930; reprint, New York: Greenwood Press, 1968.

Moreau, Odile. "Bosnian Resistance to Conscription in the Nineteenth Century." In *Arming the State: Military Conscription in the Middle East and Central Asia, 1775–1925*, ed. Erich J. Zürcher, 129–37. New York: I.B. Tauris Publishers, 1999.

Muahedat mecmuası, vol. 3. Istanbul, 1880.

Mundy, Martha. "Village Land and Individual Title: *Musha'* and Ottoman Land Registration in the 'Ajlun District." In *Village, Steppe and State: The Social Origins of Modern Jordan*, ed. Eugene L. Rogan and Tariq Tell, 58–79. London: British Academic Press, 1994.

Murphey, Rhoads. *Ottoman Warfare, 1500–1700*. New Brunswick: Rutgers University Press, 1999.

Mutafchieva, Vera. *Kniga za Sofronii*. Sofia: Voenno Izdatelstvo, 1978.

———. *Kărdzhaliisko vreme*. Sofia: Nauka i izkustvo, 1977.

Nachev, V. and N. Fermandzhiev, eds., *Pisahme da se znae. Pripiski i letopisi*. Sofia: OF, 1984.

Naçi, Stavri. "Le Facteur Albanais dans la Commerce Balkanique au XVIIIe Siecle." *Studia Albanica* 7/2 (1970): 37–42.

———. "Le Pachalik de Shkodër considéré dans son développement économique et social au XVIIIe siècle." *Studia Albanica* 3/1 (1966): 123–44.

———. *Pashallëku i Shkodrës nën sundimin e Bushatllive në gjysmën e dytë të shek. XVIII*. Tirana: University of Tirana, 1964.

Nagata, Yuzo. "The Role of Ayans in Regional Development during the Pre-Tanzimat Period in Turkey: A Case Study of the Karaosmanoğlu Family." In Yuzo Nagata, *Studies on the Social and Economic History of the Ottoman Empire*, 119–33. Izmir: Akademi Kitabevi, 1995.

———. *Muhsin-zâde Mehmed Paşa ve Âyânlık Müessesesi* [Muhsin-zâde Mehmed Pasha and the Institution of *Ayan*ship]. Izmir: Akademi Kitabevi, 1999 (originally published in 1976).

————. *Tarihte Âyânlar. Karaosmanoğulları Üzerinde Bir İnceleme* [The Ayans in History. An Investigation about the Karaosmanoğulları]. Ankara: Türk Tarih Kurumu, 1997.

Novaković, Stojan. *Tursko tsarstvo pred srbski ustanak*. Belgrade, 1906.

Olson, Robert. "Jews, Janissaries, Esnaf and the Revolt of 1740 in Istanbul." *Journal of the Economic and Social History of the Orient* 20/2 (1977): 185–207.

Oreshkov, Pavel. "Niakolko dokumenta za Pazvantoglu i Sofroniia Vrachanski (1800–1812)." *Sbornik na BAN* 3 (Sofia, 1914): 1–54

Orhonlu, Cengiz. "Ahmed Resmi Efendi'nin Eflâk Coğrafyası." *Güney Doğu Avrupa Araştırmaları Dergisi* 4/5 (1975/76): 1–14.

————. "The Geography of Wallachia Written by A Turkish Politician." *Revue des études sud-est européenes* 13 (1975): 447–52.

Ostrowski, Donald. *Muscovy and the Mongols: Cross-Cultural Influences on the Steppe Frontier, 1304–1589*. New York: Cambridge University Press, 1998.

Özkaya, Yücel. "XVIII. Yüzyılın İkinci Yarısına Ait Sosyal Yaşantıyı Ortaya Koyan bir Belge." *OTAM* 2 (1991): 303–34.

————. *Osmanlı İmperatorluğunda Dağlı İsyanları (1791–1808)*. Ankara: Dil ve Tarih-Coğrafya Fakültesi, 1983.

————. "Rumeli'de Âyânlık ile İlgili Bazı Bilgiler" [Some Information Concerning the Ayanship in Rumeli]. In *VIII. Türk Tarih Kongresi (Ankara 11–15 Ekim 1976): Kongreye Sunulan Bildiriler*, vol. 2, 1407–16. Ankara: Türk Tarih Kurumu, 1981.

————. *Osmanlı İmparatorluğu'nda Âyânlık* [The Ayanship in the Ottoman Empire]. Ankara: Türk Tarih Kurumu, 1994 (originally published in 1977).

Pakalın, Mehmet Zeki. *Osmanlı Tarih Deyimleri ve Terimleri Sözlüğü* [Dictionary of Ottoman Historical Expressions and Terms], 3 vols. Istanbul: Milli Eğitim Basımevi, 1946–1956.

Panaite, Viorel. "Power Relationships in the Ottoman Empire: The Sultans and the Tribute-Paying Princes of Wallachia and Moldavia from the Sixteenth to the Eighteenth Century." *International Journal of Turkish Studies* 7 (2001): 26–53.

————. "The Reʿayas of the Tributary-Protected Principalities: The Sixteenth to the Eighteenth Century." *International Journal of Turkish Studies* 9 (2003): 79–117.

————. "The Voivodes of the Danubian Principalities—as *Harâcgüzarlar* of the Ottoman Sultans." *International Journal of Turkish Studies* 9 (2003): 59–78.

————. *The Ottoman Law of War and Peace: The Ottoman Empire and Tribute Payers*. Boulder, Colo: East European Monographs; NewYork: distributed by Columbia University Press, 2000.

Panzac, Daniel. *La Peste dans l'Empire Ottoman, 1700–1850*. Leuven: Editions Peeters, 1985.

Pavlović, Ivan. "Ispisi iz frantsuskih arhiva o Pazvantoglu (od 1795 do 1807 godina)." *Spomenik Srpske kraljevske akademiye*, Pt. 3 (Belgrade, 1890): 105–28.

Popov, L. "Prinos za izuchavane minaloto na bălgarskoto otechestvo." *Sbornik za narodni umotvoreniia, nauka i knizhnina* 24, no. 1 (Sofia, 1908): 1–157.

Peters, Rudolph. "Murder on the Nile: Homicide Trials in 19th Century Egyptian Shari'a Courts." *Die Welt des Islams* XXX (1990): 98–116.

Peyfuss, Max. *Die Druckerei von Moschopolis, 1731–1769: Buchdruck und Heiligenverehrung im Erzbistum Achrida.* Vienna: Böhlau, 1989.

Pouqueville, François C. H. I. *Travels through Morea, Albania, and several other parts of the Ottoman Empire to Constantinople during the years 1798, 1799, 1800, and 1801.* London, 1806.

Racheva, Valentina. "Văprositelni okolo politicheskata deinost na Sofronii Vrachanski." *Istoriia,* no. 1 (Sofia, 1995): 31–40.

Radkova, Rumiana. *Văzrozhdenetsăt Hristo Dupnichanin.* Sofia: BAN, 1997.

Robert, Ciprien. *Les Slaves de Turquie,* vol. 2, Paris: Passard, 1852.

Rothenberg, Gunther. "The Habsburg Military Border System: Some Reconsiderations." In *War and Society in East Central Europe,* ed. Gunther E. Rothenberg and Béla A. Király, vol. 1, 361–92. New York: Columbia University Press, 1979.

———. *The Austrian Military Border in Croatia, 1522–1747.* Urbana: University of Illinois Press, 1960.

Rumiantsev, P. A. [Collected Documents.] Moscow, 1953.

Sadat, Deena R. "Âyân and Ağa: The Transformation of the Bektashi Corps in the 18th Century." *Muslim World* 63 (1973): 206–19.

———. "Rumeli Ayanlari: The Eighteenth Century." *Journal of Modern History* 44 (1972): 346–63.

Salzmann, Ariel. "An Ancien Régime Revisited: 'Privatization' and Political Economy in the Eighteenth-Century Ottoman Empire." *Politics and Society* 21 (1993): 393–423.

Sanad, Nagaty. *The Theory of Crime and Criminal Responsibility in Islamic Law: Shari'a.* Chicago: Office of International Criminal Justice, 1991.

Şaşmazer, Lynne M. "Policing Bread Price and Production in Ottoman Istanbul, 1793–1807." *The Turkish Studies Association Bulletin* 24, no. 1 (2000): 21–40.

Saul, Norman. *Russia and the Mediterranean, 1797–1807.* Chicago: University of Chicago Press, 1970.

Schacht, Joseph. *An Introduction to Islamic Law.* Oxford: Oxford University Press, 1964.

Schroeder, Paul. *The Transformation of European Politics, 1763–1848.* New York: Oxford University Press, 1996.

Şen, Ömer. *Osmanlı Panayırları (18. –19. Yüzyıl).* Istanbul: Eren, 1996.

Sharpe, J. A. *Crime in Early Modern England, 1550–1750.* London: Longman, 1984.

Shaw, Stanford J. *Between Old and New: The Ottoman Empire under Sultan Selim III (1789–1807).* Cambridge, Mass.: Harvard University Press, 1971.

Shinder, Joel. "Early Ottoman Administration in the Wilderness: Some Limits on Comparision." *International Journal of Middle Eastern Studies* 9 (1978): 497–517.

Skiotis, Dennis. "From Bandit to Pasha: First Steps in the Rise to Power of Ali of Tepelen, 1750–1784." *International Journal of Middle Eastern Studies* 2 (1971): 219–44.

Sofronii Vrachanski. *Zhitie i stradanie greshnago Sofroniia.* ed. N. Dyilevskii, Sofia: Nauka i izkustvo, 1989.

Staikos, Konstantinos. *Greek editions from the time of the Neohellenic Enlightenment.* Athens: Europaiko Politiko Kentro-Delfon, 1998.

Stavrianos, Leften S. *The Balkans Since 1453.* New York: New York University Press, 2000.

Staynova, Mihaila. "Ottoman Libraries in Vidin." *Etudes balkaniques*, no. 2 (Sofia, 1979).

———. "Za vakăfskata deinost na Osman Pazvantoglu văv Vidin i Vidinskiia krai." *Vekove*, no. 6 (Sofia, 1982).

———. *Osmanskite biblioteki v bălgarskite zemi, XV–XIX v.* Sofia: NBKM, 1982.

Stoye, John. *Marsigli's Europe, 1680–1730.* New Haven: Yale University Press, 1994.

Sugar, Peter. "Unity and Diversity in the Lands of Southeastern Europe in the Eighteenth Century." In *East Central European Society and War in the Pre-Revolutionary Eighteenth Century*, ed. Gunther E. Rothenberg, Béla A. Király and Peter F. Sugar, 255–70. Boulder, Colo.: Social Science Monographs; New York: dist. by Columbia University Press, 1982.

———. *Southeastern Europe Under Ottoman Rule 1354–1804.* Seattle and London: University of Washington Press, 1977.

Svoronos, Nicolas. *Le commerce de Salonique au XVIIIe siècle.* Paris: Presses Universitaires de France, 1956.

Tarashoeva, V., K. Mircheva, V. Harizanov, and N. Doynov, eds., *Semeen arhiv na Hadzhitoshevi*, vol. 2 (1827–1878). Sofia: BG Print, 2002.

Theophilowa, Maria. *Die Rebellion des Paschas Paswan-Ogllou und ihre Bedeutung für die bulgarische Befreiungsbewegung im XIX Jahrhundert.* Zürich: Gebr. Leeman, 1914 (Bulgarian translation, Teofilova, Maria. *Buntăt na Pazvanoglu i negovoto znachenie za Bălgarskoto osvoboditelno dvizhenie v XIX vek. Prinos kăm predistoriiata na bălgarskoto osvoboditelno dvizhenie.* Sofia: Hemus, 1932).

Thorton, Thomas. *The Present State of Turkey; or A Description of the Political, Civil, and Religious, Constitution, Government, and Laws of the Ottoman Empire*, vol. 1. London: Joseph Mawan, 1809.

Todorov, Vărban. "Malko izvestno izdanie za Osman Pazvantoglu." *Istoricheski pregled*, no. 3 (Sofia, 1990): 84–91.

Todorova, Maria. ed., *Angliiski pătepisi za Balkanite, kraia na XVI v.–30te godini na XIX v.* Sofia: Nauka i izkustvo, 1987.

———. "Bulgarian Historical Writing, on the Ottoman Empire." *New Perspectives on Turkey* 12 (1995): 97–118.

———. *Imagining the Balkans.* New York: Oxford University Press, 1997.

Toledano, Ehud. "The Emergence of Ottoman-Local Elites (1700–1900): A Framework for Research." In *Middle Eastern Politics and Ideas: A History from Within*, ed. Ilan Pappé and Moshe Ma'oz, 145–62. London; New York: Tauris Academic Studies; dist. in the U. S. and Canada by St. Martin's Press, 1997.

Tsvetkov, Andrei. . "Politichesko dvizhenie văv Vratsa ot kraia na XVIII i nachaloto na XIX vek." In *Istoriia na grad Vratsa*, vol. 1, *Ot drevnostta do Osvobozhdenieto*. Sofia: OF, 1976.

Tsvetkova, Bistra (see: Cvetkova, Bistra).

Uzunçarşılı, İsmail H. *Osmanlı Tarihi*, vol. 4/2. Ankara: Türk Tarih Kurumu 1983.

Vankov, Simeon. *Osman Paspanoglu, Vidinski pasha. Stranitsi ot istoriiata na Iztochniia văpros*. *Voennoistoricheski sbornik* 62, Sofia, 1947.

Vasdravelles, Ioannes K., ed. *Historika Archeia Makedonias. B'. Archeion Veroias–Naouses 1598–1886* [Historical Archives of Macedonia. II. Archive of Veroia–Naoussa 1598–1886]. Thessaloniki: Hetaireia Makedonikon Spoudon, 1954.

Vasıf Efendi, Ahmed. *Précis historique de la guerre des turcs contres les russes*. Paris, 1872.

Văzvăzova-Teodorova, K., Z. Markova, E. Pavlova-Teodorova and V. Harizanov, eds., *Semeen arhiv na Hadzhitoshevi (1754–1827)*. vol. 1, Sofia: BAN, 1984.

Veinstein, Gilles. "Les Provinces Balkaniques (1606–1774)." In *Histoire de l'Empire Ottoman*, ed. Robert Mantran, 287–340. Paris: Fayard, 1989.

———. "'Âyân' de la région d'Izmir et commerce du Levant (deuxième moitié du XVIIIe siècle)." *Revue de l'Occident Musulman et de la Méditerranée* 20 (1975): 131–47.

Velestinlis, Rigas. *Revolyutsionno*. Sofia: Izdatelska kăshta Ivan Vazov, 1998.

Vranousis, L. *Rhigas Velestinlis*. Athens, 1954.

Vukičević, M. *Karadjordje*. vols. 1–2, Belgrade, 1907–1912.

Vutova, Nina, ed., *Sofronii Vrachanski, 1739–1813: Bio-bibliografski ukazatel*. Sofia: NBKM, 1989.

Wachtel, Andrew. *Making a Nation, Breaking a Nation*. Stanford: Stanford University Press, 2000.

Wilkinson, William. *An Account of the Principalities of Wallachia and Moldavia*. London: Longman, 1820; reprint New York: Arno Press, 1971.

Wolff, Larry. *Inventing Eastern Europe: The Map of Civilization on the Mind of the Enlightenment*. Stanford: Stanford University Press, 1994.

Yotsov, Dimităr. "Materiali za Pazvant-oglu, izvlecheni iz ruskite arhivi," *Periodichesko spisanie na BKD v Sofiia* 68 (Sofia, 1908): 749–55.

Zens, Robert. "Pasvanoğlu Osman Paşa and the Paşalık of Belgrade, 1791–1807." *International Journal of Turkish Studies* 8, nos. 1 & 2 (2002): 89–104.

Zlatev, Todor. *Bălgarskite gradove po r. Dunav prez epohata na Văzrazhdaneto*. Sofia: Nauka i Izkustvo, 1962.

Zoidis, Georgios. *Rigas Velestinlis*. Sofia: OF, 1973.

About the Editor and Contributors

ANTONIS ANASTASOPOULOS is Lecturer in Turkish Studies in the Department of History and Archaeology of the University of Crete. He has published on the social and political history of the Ottoman Balkans in the eighteenth century,

MICHAEL R. HICKOK, Special Agent, Federal Bureau of Investigation, is the author of *Ottoman Military Administration in Eighteenth-century Bosnia.*

VIRGINIA H. AKSAN is Associate Professor and Chair of the Department of History, McMaster University. Her publications include the forthcoming *An Empire Besieged: Ottoman Warfare 1700–1870.*

FREDERICK F. ANSCOMBE is Lecturer in Contemporary History and Head Tutor, MA Program in Contemporary History and Politics, Birkbeck College, University of London. He is the author of *The Ottoman Gulf: The Creation of Kuwait, Saudi Arabia, and Qatar.*

ROSSITSA GRADEVA is Associate Professor of History, American University in Bulgaria. Her publications include *Rumeli under the Ottomans, 15th–18th centuries: Institutions and Communities.*